Return of the Indian

From Dee Brown, author of *Bury My Heart at Wounded Knee*

Return of the Indian brings together for the first time the present condition of 40,000,000 indigenous peoples of North, Central and South America. It is a long-needed work that shows the cultural diversity of the two continents as well as significant parallel historical courses.

Throughout the narrative, Phillip Wearne demonstrates the importance of land in the struggle for indigenous rights, a struggle that began with the arrival of Columbus and continues to this day.

I wish him success with this truly deserving book.

From Matthew Coon Come, Grand Chief, Grand Council of the Crees (of Quebec)

A great book, educational and informative. It's a must reading for those who are interested in indigenous peoples issues.

From Robin Hanbury-Tenison, Survival International

A timely study of Latin America's indigenous peoples and the appalling problems of racism and land theft they still face, but which they are heroically resisting. Wearne's book has that increasingly rare blend of scholarship and accessibility: a fine achievement.

From Norman Lewis, author of *The Missionaries*

All that is of real importance in the history of the Indian races of America is contained in Phillip Wearne's book, which has spread a vast net to gather so many extraordinary facts. His conclusion is the optimistic one that after the 500 years' holocaust following Columbus's voyage of discovery, the worst is almost at an end. Despite the centuries of near-extermination we are astonished to learn that 1,172 ethno-linguistic groups have somehow managed to survive throughout the Americas, and now, as he sees them, are firmly on the march towards a new future. A most impressive account.

From Rodolfo Stavenhagen, anthropologist and Chair, Fund for the Development of Indigenous Peoples of Latin America and the Caribbean

This is a great introduction to the manifold experiences and problems of the native peoples of the Americas. It provides an excellent summary of the background and the historical development of the colonization, incorporation and exploitation of Indians in colonial and post-colonial times. The discussion of their present predicament, centring on the issues of human rights, land and environment is a model of clarity, based on the excellent use the author makes of a large array of source material, which is not always easy to get hold of, and is certainly not usually available to the general public. The book also takes a critical but balanced look at the various current government policies regarding Indian peoples, and ends on an optimistic note, signalling the revival and emergent organizations of indigenous peoples all over the continent. Phillip Wearne is to be congratulated on a most useful, exciting, carefully researched and well-written overview of the indigenous peoples of the American continent, from Alaska to Argentina; a text that will be a 'must' reading for anyone interested in contemporary Latin and North America, and that should certainly find its way into reading lists at academic institutions.

From Julian Burger, author of *The Gaia Atlas of First Peoples* and Secretary of the UN Working Group on Indigenous Populations

Phillip Wearne's well-researched and readable book recounts the tragic story of colonialism, the vigorous efforts to maintain indigenous cultures in the face of aggressive policies of assimilation and, most importantly, the new movement uniting indigenous peoples across the continent.

From Canada to Chile, this book draws together for the first time the experiences and struggles of the indigenous peoples of all the Americas, North and South.

It is an excellent introduction to this important political development. Phillip Wearne writes with passion and sensitivity and his book is especially welcome as the United Nations launches the International Decade of the World's Indigenous People.

From George Monbiot, author of *Poisoned Arrows* and *Amazon Watershed*

Phillip Wearne's depth of understanding, thorough and meticulous scholarship and powerful prose make this an indispensable book. Anyone who wishes to understand the story of the indigenous people of the Americas, their suppression and resistance, should start here.

From Marcus Colchester, World Rainforest Movement

The rise of the Indian movement in the Americas is among the most inspiring renaissances of this century. That isolated Amazonian tribes have been at the forefront of this resurgence of ethnic identity makes it truly remarkable. Confounding white predictions that these were 'disappearing worlds', the Indian peoples of the continent are reclaiming both their history and their future.

In this perceptive and readable account, Phillip Wearne neatly sketches in the scale and scope of this social transformation, tracing the Indians' history through conquest and colonization to the present struggles for territory and self-determination.

From Andrew Gray, anthropologist

The book provides a comprehensive panorama of the indigenous peoples' struggle in the Americas from the tragic history of genocide to the horrific threats which they currently face, yet the author never loses sight of the powerful way in which indigenous peoples are defending their rights to their territories, cultures and, above all, to self-determination.

From Richard Chase Smith, anthropologist, Oxfam America

Phillip Wearne has carefully sifted through a turbulent, complex and even contradictory past to present us with a very comprehensive, even profound view of indigenous America today. Not only does he handle a wealth of detailed information, but he also clearly understands many of the subtleties and complexities of indigenous Amazonians and Andeans, more so in fact than many colleagues who have worked for many years in the region. He touches on, in some cases with surprising depth, all of the important themes and issues facing these peoples today.

Return of the Indian

Conquest and Revival in the Americas

Phillip Wearne

Temple University Press
Philadelphia

Temple University Press, Philadelphia 19122

First published in Great Britain by Cassell
© Phillip Wearne 1996

First published 1996

This book is printed on acid-free paper
for greater longevity

Library of Congress Cataloging-in-Publication Data
A catalogue record for this book is available from the Library of Congress.

ISBN (hardback) 1–56639–500–3
ISBN (paperback) 1–56639–501–1

Typeset by Falcon Oast Graphic Art
Printed and bound in Great Britain
by Cambridge University Press.

Contents

List of Illustrations

Colour Plates

Books from the
Latin America Bureau

The Latin America Bureau (LAB) publishes books on contemporary issues in Latin America and the Caribbean. Current titles include:

- Introductions to Latin American and Caribbean society and culture, economics and politics
- Country guides – Bolivia, Venezuela, Jamaica, Cuba, Colombia, Mexico, Argentina, Brazil, Ecuador and the Eastern Caribbean
- A series on Latin American women's lives and experiences
- Latin American authors in translation: from street children to salsa, from rubber tappers to guerrilla radio stations

Also published by LAB:

Green Guerrillas: Environmental Conflicts and Initiatives in Latin America and the Caribbean

A Reader, edited by Helen Collinson, which brings together the work of top environmental writers on both sides of the Atlantic.

'Provides an enlightening and highly disturbing insight . . . It reminds us just how far we will have to go before the twin goals of environmental sustainability and social justice can begin to be achieved.'

Jonathon Porritt, writer and broadcaster

'This remarkable collection is just what we needed. Its diverse viewpoints share a commitment to justice, a respect for the rich complexity of the social/natural environment and a willingness to challenge received wisdom.'

Richard Levins, Professor of Population Sciences,
Harvard School of Public Health

For a free 20-page LAB Books catalogue, write to LAB, Dept RI, 1 Amwell Street, London EC1R 1UL, or call 0171-278 2829.

LAB Books are distributed in North America by Monthly Review Press, 122 West 27 Street, New York, NY 10001 (Tel: 212-691 2555).

For Catarina and the millions of
indigenous people who
have died defending
their homeland

Foreword by
Rigoberta Menchú Tum

Today, throughout the Americas, people are reflecting deeply about the identity of the indigenous peoples and are starting to take seriously the arguments in favour of pluri-ethnic and multicultural societies. From our diversity will come the true wealth of the Americas.

Even though another millennium is coming to an end without an end to the grave and systematic violations of the rights of indigenous peoples, we have not given up hope or our struggle to establish a new basis for social relations, based on justice, equality and mutual respect between our peoples and cultures.

We should recognize that in some countries, indigenous peoples make up the majority of the local population and, despite their daily experience of marginalization, racism and persistent armed conflicts, they are pursuing their ancestral aspirations for societies based on human dignity, demanding their political, economic, social and cultural rights.

Despite the enormous difficulties and the long and painful road which lies ahead before we can make the world aware of the rights and values of indigenous peoples, we have had some successes. In a significant number of countries, there have been constitutional advances which recognize the cultural and linguistic diversity of their peoples. Mutual respect between indigenous and non-indigenous peoples is increasingly being encouraged, turning the technical and scientific wisdom of indigenous peoples to the benefit of the whole of society. These hopeful trends show that diversity need not be synonymous with conflict, but rather can be a source of wealth in terms of national identity and a source of integral development for all humanity.

For over a decade, the UN Working Group on Indigenous Peoples has been drawing up the draft Declaration of the Rights of the World's Indigenous Peoples. This draft lays out the minimum norms for the protection of the rights of indigenous peoples, who live in harmony with nature and the universe. To achieve peace, development must harmonize economic growth with social, political and cultural progress and the rights to self-determination, justice and freedom. There can be no 'growth' while a people is illiterate, malnourished and still dies of hunger. There can be no 'peace' when racism continues and is even spreading.

The Declaration is a challenge to our consciences as we end this millennium. As we enter the International Decade for the World's Indigenous Peoples, we have the chance to achieve our hopes for peace, justice and equality, rooted in our diversity.

Guatemala, my country, has lived through 34 years of war, with the spilling of our blood, the pain of mothers, widows, children – of a whole people. Nevertheless, today there is dialogue and negotiation to try to achieve a political solution, with the firm belief that there is no problem that can be solved only by brother killing brother. As the Maya people, we maintain the hope that the peace process will one day end in full respect for our rights and identity.

In Guatemala, pain and blood have made it possible for many women to become leading players in developing our organizations, in this struggle to achieve our dreams of peace. They have accumulated great experience on this arduous road, without which, perhaps, they would still be unaware of their basic rights. This rich knowledge gives us confidence and it is the women, the widows and mothers who lost their children in the war, who with their patience are pushing for changes in Guatemala and who are passing on that patience to future generations, just as they have done with the customs and values inherited from our ancestors.

What is fundamental is that new forms of self-defence always emerge. Our people live in permanent resistance. Resistance has not come only from the most recent conflicts; we have always defended our traditional values. But we are also thinking about the future, contributing the best of our culture to solve the world crisis, a consequence of so-called modernity.

Today the theme of human rights is on the agenda of every group in Guatemala. Awareness of human rights is not just about victims, repression and massacres. There is a broader vision of human rights: development, progress, the need for a real democracy, and education.

Little by little, we are moving forward. We have carried on a broad struggle for many years, and many people, many stalwart hearts in many parts of the world, have accompanied us. We have always said that solidarity is a product of consciousness, a product of love, of love for life and for other people.

After so many years of struggle, this period seems to be the end of five hundred years of injustice, five hundred years of night. We are moving into the light of a new era for our peoples. After so many years of waiting for a new dawn, we believe that our voices will make themselves heard, that you will listen to us, and support our legitimate aspirations.

Rigoberta Menchú
Winner of the 1992 Nobel Peace Prize

© PADDY DONNELLY

Acknowledgements

The Sioux people of the North American plains always offered special thanks to their story catcher: the recorder of their history. Inasmuch as I have managed to catch the story of the indigenous peoples of the Americas at all, I have many individuals and institutions to thank.

A number of funders made the research for this project possible. Norwegian Church Aid, the Swedish NGO Foundation for Human Rights, ICCO, the Calpe Trust and the Honduran Committee for Human Rights all had sufficient faith to back this book when it was nothing more than a three-page proposal.

I would also like to thank Survival International and Cultural Survival, both of which put their libraries and expertise at my disposal during the research for this book.

At the other end of the production cycle, many individuals were extremely generous with their time, reading and commenting on the manuscript. Thanks to Julian Burger, Secretary of the United Nations Working Group on Indigenous Populations, Richard Wilson of the anthropology department at the University of Sussex, Terry Janis of the Indian Law Resource Centre and Tracy Ulltveit-Moe of Amnesty International. Particular thanks are due to Andrew Gray, formerly of the International Work Group for Indigenous Affairs, who read, then reread, the manuscript and spent hours dealing with my questions.

Claire Diamond, the Librarian at Canning House in London, searched for books and showed incredible patience with my borrowing requirements. Liz Morrell of Latin America Bureau worked wonders with the photo research. Duncan Green, my editor at Latin America Bureau, coped manfully with delays, inconsistent Quechua spelling and *non sequiturs*, all while writing his own books. My thanks too to Emma Pearce for a first-rate chronology and appendix on population.

Last, but my no means least, thanks to all the indigenous people, some well known, some totally unknown, who have given me their time and views over 15 years of journalism and travel in the Americas. This book is, as far as is possible, their view – in all its splendid diversity. Some are quoted; their organizations named. Others remain anonymous; still others are dead. All are fondly remembered.

Phillip Wearne
December 1995

1
Definitions and Diversity

- In Ecuador, tens of thousands of indigenous people block roads and refuse to supply city markets, shutting down the country for a week in what becomes known as 'The Uprising'.
- In Bolivia, Víctor Hugo Cárdenas, an Aymara activist, is inaugurated as vice-president, donning the vice-presidential sash over a vicuña scarf, a traditional badge of authority. He announces a 'new era' in a speech in Aymara, Guaraní and Quechua, the country's three main indigenous languages.
- In Mexico, a well-drilled Maya army takes over four towns and forces Latin America's longest-ruling party into protracted negotiations on indigenous rights and democratic principles.
- In Canada, Elijah Harper, a Cree-Ojibwa politician, blocks a constitutional agreement with Quebec, opening the way for a new deal for the country's indigenous people, including a constitution recognizing native peoples' 'inherent right to self-rule'.
- In Oslo, Rigoberta Menchú Tum, a 33-year-old K'iche' Maya woman, a one-time domestic servant and illiterate coffee-picker, becomes the youngest-ever winner of the Nobel Peace Prize.

Something is happening in the Americas. A tenacious resistance to the cultural onslaught that began in 1492 with the arrival of a lost Genoese sailor by the name of Christopher Columbus has begun to make sporadic appearances in international headlines. As it does, a myth has been exposed – the myth that the native peoples of the Americas were ever conquered, assimilated, wiped out, or that they never even existed. 'As I go round the world many people I meet are surprised we indigenous peoples of the Americas still exist. They seem to think we died out years ago,' observes Rigoberta Menchú.

The events listed above are as amorphous and diverse as indigenous culture itself, generic 'Indianness' being as much a European imposition as the 'discovery' and 'conquest' of the Americas was a European invention. What seems to be a revival in ethnic consciousness in the Americas defies the categorization or empirical analysis scholars so relish. Moreover, it is ubiquitous, appearing anywhere and everywhere from Alaska and northern Canada to Chile and Argentina.

Although such events may represent nothing as cohesive as a movement across the two continents of the Americas, they do represent a growing clamour for justice. Ask those leading what one scholar, Javier Albó, has labelled the 'return of the Indian' what they are doing and you receive only slight variations on a theme: 'reclaiming our identity', 'demanding our rights', 'regaining our pride and self-worth', 'recovering our spirit'.

The greater prominence given to such events is at least partially a response to another set of stories appearing in the world's media in recent years, illustrating a darker side to the current fate of indigenous people:

- In Brazil, thousands of Yanomami have died as gold prospectors spread diseases and mercury poisoning throughout their Amazon territory. The Yanomami often have no resistance to diseases such as measles, chicken-pox or even the common cold.
- In Guatemala, entire villages of Maya were massacred or displaced during the 1980s as the army unleashed a brutal counter-insurgency campaign in the highland mountain zones of the northwestern *altiplano*.
- In Canada, Hydro-Quebec is defying bitter opposition with its plans to flood tens of thousands of square miles of Cree lands as part of the US$12 billion Great Whale hydroelectric dam scheme, designed to produce cheap energy for export.
- In Paraguay, the New Tribes Mission seeks out uncontacted forest peoples, converts them to Christianity in mission bases, while 'civilizing' them to adhere to its own narrow evangelical norms.

Disease, military conquest, multinational capitalism, religious conversion ... the indigenous peoples of the Americas are today losing life and land to the same forces that have devastated their numbers and culture for more than five hundred years. For many indigenous peoples the threat has intensified markedly in recent years. 'We have been pushed to the edge of the cliff ... now they want to push us over,' explains one Innu from Canada.

Growing land shortages have forced waves of settlers on to what were once marginal, indigenous lands. Free-market economics and state budget cuts have undermined subsistence economies and what little social provision indigenous communities enjoy. Civil wars have seen whole villages massacred, put to flight, caught in the cross-fire or forced to take sides. As an editorial in one indigenous publication, *Pueblo Indio*, puts it, 'Only our patience has saved us from extermination, but even the patience of the Indian has its limit.'

Yet stories about the renewed threats to indigenous peoples have at least served to expose other myths: that the conquest of the Americas, North, South and Centre, was all over within a few decades of the arrival of Europeans; that it was carried out by a few brutal brigands with a bloodlust and greed exceptional even by the standards of their own age; that there is no connection between what is happening today and what happened yesterday. The conquest is five hundred years old and continues today, but so is indigenous resistance. 'There comes a point where you can't take any more. This is the message we're passing on to our children,' says Sirionó leader Juana Irubi, whose tenth child, Anahi Dignidad, was born on a three-hundred-mile protest march by indigenous people to the Bolivian capital La Paz in 1990.

Numbers and Types: Indigenous Peoples Today

That both conquest and resistance are still going on comes as a shock to those who have always assumed that the indigenous peoples of the Americas are on their way out, set to disappear through assimilation as 'modernity' and 'progress' radiate out from the continents' cities. Vivid costumes in Mexican museums or pyramids in 'lost' jungle cities in Peru are fine; the real thing in the form of protesting peasants, guerrilla fighters or slum dwellers' organizers is less palatable.

'Mexicans make no connection between their Aztec ancestors and the poor Indian selling vegetables on the pavement,' notes one official in Mexico's National Indigenous Institute. 'For most Mexicans one represents historic pride; the other contemporary shame.' Ariel Araujo, a Mocoví leader from northern Argentina agrees. 'According to Argentina's official history, we were exterminated at the beginning of the century. So why are there more than 1½ million of us today?'

In fact there are an estimated 40 million indigenous people in the Americas today, about 6 per cent of the total population, and their numbers are growing faster than the rest of the population. They are the surviving descendants of what can only be called a holocaust: the events that followed the arrival of Europeans in the Americas at the end of the fifteenth century. The greatest killing, followed by the greatest plunder, following arguably the most important 'discovery' in world history (Plate 2).

Estimates of the number of people living in the Americas in 1492 range as high as 112 million, about one-fifth of the world's entire population at the time. Estimates of how low their numbers fell as a result of disease, starvation, slave labour and post-conquest conflict go as low as 2 million. The continued existence and recovery of the indigenous peoples of the Americas in the face of

3

2. *Guyana: an Arawak family, some of the few remaining descendants of the people who first greeted Columbus, and were subsequently almost wiped out.*
© LUKE HOLLAND

what they and their ancestors have suffered is the best testimony to the tenacity of their resistance.

The indigenous peoples of today are concentrated in the same places as their distant ancestors, the sites of the Aztec, Inka and Maya civilizations. Guatemala (5.4 million) and Bolivia (about 5 million) have majority indigenous populations, with Peru counting more than 8 million, Mexico at least 10.5 million and Ecuador about 3.8 million. The three largest countries have relatively small indigenous populations: Canada has an estimated 892,000 or 3.4 per cent of its total, the United States just under 2 million or 0.8 per cent and Brazil about 325,000 or 0.2 per cent of its 165 million people.

Traditionally, the continents' indigenous peoples can be divided into two distinct cultural groups. Highland peoples (Plate 3) tend to grow staples such as maize, beans and potatoes on largely inadequate strips of land in the most mountainous, least fertile regions – the marginal 'regions of refuge' into which they have been pushed over the centuries. They tend to live in villages or hamlets where there is little, if any, non-indigenous population. They predominate in the Andean countries and farther north in Guatemala and Mexico. Many highland people survive by supplementary seasonal work on export-crop plantations or paid work in the cities to which increasing numbers are being forced to migrate as they face the double squeeze of a contracting land base and growing numbers.

Lowland peoples (Plate 4) account for less than 5 per cent of the continents' total indigenous population, but perhaps 80 per cent of the different ethno-linguistic groups. They too are confined to the remotest parts of the continent. They fish, hunt and practise slash-and-burn farming or horticulture. They live in the Amazon basin, the remains of the forests of Central America and to a lesser extent on the plains and sub-Arctic tundra of Canada and the United States.

In some areas the lifestyles of highland and lowland peoples overlap, but in any case another yardstick may be more useful: the level of contact with the dominant Hispanic, Anglophone or Francophone cultures. Through their contact with representatives of the state, their dress, migration patterns and proficiency in European languages, highland peoples tend to show a greater degree of association with the dominant groups. Governments, political parties and trade unions have at times made concerted efforts to 'incorporate' them into national institutions, often by redefining them as 'peasants' rather than indigenous peoples.

Lowland peoples, on the other hand, tend, at least until relatively recently, to have had less, if any, contact with the outside world. Tribal, aboriginal and fiercely independent, lowland peoples have led much of the recent growth in indigenous resistance and organization, attracting attention out of all proportion

5

3. *Colombia – an Arhuaco man*
© ERIC LAWRIE/HUTCHISON

4. *Brazil: the Yanomami people have been devastated in recent years by Western diseases and cultural disruption, both introduced by invading gold prospectors.*
© VICTOR ENGELBERT 1980/SURVIVAL INTERNATIONAL

to their numbers. 'Five centuries of contact has produced only marginalization, exploitation and misery for our highland colleagues. We're not volunteering for the same,' says Evaristo Nugkuag, an Aguaruna leader from lowland Peru.

Such differences stem from pre-Columbian times. When Columbus first reached the Americas, highland peoples of the Andes, Mexico and Central America had already experienced thousands of years of assimilation into urban-based indigenous civilizations, empires and kingdoms, whose influence had been spread by conquest and trade. Adapting to life under the rule of outsiders was already part of their cultural baggage.

Most lowland peoples, on the other hand, had never been assimilated into broader political structures and had a profound sense of personal autonomy. Such differences helped determine their reaction to colonial rule, and to state power today.

7

Languages: Speaking in Many Tongues

There are roughly 800 known ethno-linguistic groups in the Americas today, down from a total believed to have been more than 2,000 at the end of the fifteenth century. The largest single group today are those speaking Quechua, numbering about 11 million. They speak the language of the Inkas, *runasimi*, literally 'mouth of the people' or 'human speech' in Quechua, and live in the lands of their former empire, the *Tawantinsuyu*, comprising modern-day Peru, Bolivia, Ecuador, southern Colombia and northern fractions of Chile and Argentina.

They are followed by the Maya, scattered throughout southern Mexico, Guatemala, Belize and Honduras, numbering about 9 million but speaking more than 30 different, but related, languages in both highland and lowland areas. Aymara, spoken by about 2 million people centred around Lakes Titicaca and Poopo in Peru and Bolivia, as well as in Bolivia's capital La Paz, is the third most widely spoken language. Nahuatl, the language of the Aztecs, spoken by about 1 million people today in Mexico City and central Mexico, is also significant. In North America, Cree, with an estimated 64,000 speakers mainly in Canada, along with Navaho, with about 130,000 speakers in the USA, are numerically the most important indigenous languages.

None of these languages or any others are recognized as official languages in the countries concerned, although Quechua assumed that status in Peru under a reformist government from 1969 before being downgraded later. The most curious exception is Guaraní, the native language of about 35,000 Guaraní Indians in Paraguay and tens of thousands more in Bolivia, Brazil and Argentina. Guaraní became an official language in Paraguay in 1992 but has for centuries been a lingua franca, especially outside the capital, Asunción. Perhaps 90 per cent of Paraguay's 4.2 million people speak it as their own language, reserving Spanish for public speech. This makes Guaraní the second most widely spoken indigenous language in the Americas, although most of its speakers would be horrified to be described as indigenous. The case illustrates the complexity of definition discussed in the following section.

History shows that the smallest language groups are those most in danger of extinction. Some 66 per cent of the ethno-linguistic groups in the Americas have fewer than 5,000 speakers; some have just a handful. In North America, 80 per cent of indigenous languages are no longer taught to children, according to University of Alaska linguist Michael Krauss. Unless something changes fast, he believes, such languages are doomed.

Brazil is the most ethno-linguistically diverse country in the region, although figures for the number of groups vary from 200 to 300. The most complete survey to date, *Indigenous Peoples of Brazil* by the Ecumenical Documentation and Information Centre (CEDI), puts the figure at just over 200. Of these, 84

8

groups (40 per cent of the total) have populations of less than 200, 45 groups have populations of between 200 and 500 people, and 30 groups have between 500 and 1,000 members. This means that a staggering 77 per cent of the Indian peoples of Brazil have populations of less than 1,000. Only four groups (the Guajajára, Potiguára, Xavánte and Yanomami) have populations of between 5,000 and 10,000; another four (the Terêna, Makuxí, Ticuna and Kaingang) have populations between 10,000 and 20,000. The Guaraní are the only people above this number. The numerical vulnerability explains why Latin America's largest country has 'lost' an average of one indigenous group per year since 1900, amounting to one-third of its cultures.

However, the United States and Canada are not far behind in either diversity or vulnerability. According to *Ethnologue: Languages of the World*, the United States has more than 170 known language groups, more than two-thirds of which have fewer than 5,000 speakers. In Canada, 56 of the more than 70 indigenous languages fall into the same category. Unsurprisingly, 90 per cent of Canada's indigenous languages are considered declining or endangered, nearly 30 per cent of them on the brink of extinction.

Despite phenomenal variety, Indian languages throughout the Americas show common features that distinguish them markedly from European tongues. These include glottal stops – as in kʼicheʼ, for example – an interruption of breath caused by suddenly closing the vocal cords; reduplication, the doubling or trebling of part or all of a word in order to change meaning; and polysynthesis, the conglomeration of many words into a single word to carry the meaning of what might be a whole sentence in a European language.

The complexity and flexibility of indigenous languages was complemented by the way in which they universally mirrored the speakers' view of the universe and their immediate world. Cultural norms were reflected in many languages' distinction between inalienable relationships like those with relatives or even animals and less fundamental possessions such as tools or other objects. Both major Inuit languages, Yupik and Inupik, have dozens of words for snow and ice; Amazonian Indians have words that make subtle distinctions between the age and size of important rain forest plants.

Today, the indigenous languages of the Americas are written in a variety of forms. Cree, for instance, is still written in a system of syllabic symbols produced by a Protestant missionary in 1840. Cherokee is today written in an unchanged 86-character syllabary completed by Sequoyah (George Guess) in 1821. Convinced that the white man's power sprang from his mastery of the written word, Sequoyah, an untrained craftsman, laboured for 12 years at a task normally restricted to highly trained linguists. But most indigenous languages are written in the Roman alphabet, with their clusters of consonants and glottal stop marks (ʼ) being the most distinguishing features to those speaking only European languages.

9

Names and Identities: Culture and Language First

Who are these people? Natives, tribals, First Peoples, Amerindians, Indians, Native Americans, indigenous peoples? How should we define or identify them? How do they identify themselves? Columbus called them 'Indians', dying convinced that he had sailed around the world to reach Asia. Ironically, a label that stuck and became a term of contempt throughout the Americas was probably not so far from the truth. Genetics and archaeology suggest that 30,000 years before the arrival of Europeans, the ancestors of today's indigenous peoples crossed the neck of land that linked Asia to the Americas across the Bering Straits, although the origin myths of many native Americans tell a variety of different tales.

The first peoples who set foot in the Americas spread throughout the continents, surviving in every environment from desert to jungle in one of history's most successful tales of adaptation and evolution. Initially they were hunter-gatherers, but many settled, raised livestock and crops and, in the case of empires such as those of the Inkas, Aztecs and Mayas, founded civilizations that rivalled ancient Greece and Egypt in architecture, agriculture, mathematics and astronomy. The main objection to the term 'Indian' today is its colonial, external imposition. As a Eurocentric error, it perpetuates the myth that there was or is such a thing as generic 'Indianness'. Indigenous American societies in the sixteenth century were more varied than the European nationalities invading their continent. They remain so today.

A universal term denies indigenous peoples the chance to identify themselves by their own names in their own languages. As such it can be a barrier. 'How I loathe the term "Indian" ... "Indian" is used to sell things – souvenirs, cigars, cigarettes, gasoline, cars ... "Indian" is a figment of the white man's imagination,' says Lenore Keeshig-Tobias, an Ojibwa from Canada.

Stripping someone of their name and identity, then redefining them in your own terms, is the first step towards dehumanizing people, an essential part of the conquest and colonization of the Americas. It happened throughout the Americas on both a collective and individual basis, as many indigenous people were given European names as part of their conversion to Christianity.

This book identifies peoples or individuals by their own names wherever possible. However, this is a general book and both author and reader need a collective noun to describe the indigenous peoples of the Americas. This writer uses the word 'Indian' at times because it is convenient and universally recognized; 'indigene' the English equivalent of the universal Spanish term *indígena*, is neither. However, the term carries a health warning. All generalizations are dangerous and none more so than those referring to the indigenous peoples of the Americas. In parts of North America in particular indigenous peoples are

10

reclaiming the word 'Indian'. They wear it as a badge of pride, as do individual groups who call themselves by the names colonists gave them, such as the Seminoles ('runaways') of the Florida Everglades or the Xicaques ('untamed rebels') of Yoro province in north-central Honduras. In many parts of South and Central America, however, the Spanish and Portuguese equivalent, *indio*, remains a racist insult. The reader should bear in mind the pitfalls of both language and its inevitable generalizations. In a balancing effort, this book uses many other terms, in particular 'indigenous peoples', the plural being essential to underline their distinctiveness.

Although there is no universally accepted definition of indigenous peoples, it is worth remembering that, like the term 'Indian', it is an externally imposed and relative term. The indigenous peoples of the Americas are only indigenous because they and their territories were colonized by others. Most of their own terms for themselves mean simply 'people' – Runa in Quechua, Shuar in Shuar, Eenou in Cree.

Historically, it is clear that the continents' indigenous peoples are the pure-blooded descendants of its original inhabitants. In that, they are different from the white European invaders and the *mestizos*, *ladinos*, *mistis* or mixed-bloods who were the product of conquest and who now predominate in Peru, Mexico, Ecuador and elsewhere. Yet many people defined today as *ladinos* or *mestizos* are in fact racially indigenous. Racially at least, they are 'de-ethnicized' indigenous people.

Although social classification has hinged on different criteria over the centuries, today culture remains the best means of defining status. Anyone who is considered culturally Hispanic, Anglo or French is non-indigenous, whatever their ancestry. Yet throughout the Americas, culture has become intertwined with race and class, so that classifications are often considered interchangeable. Indians tend to be poor, rural, peasants or hunters, under- or unemployed; 'whites' (in Latin America at least) tend to be rich, urban, professional or in business.

Knowing what we mean by culture is one thing; defining it is another. A common set of values, beliefs and practices that bind a group of people together in a common perception or understanding of life might be one theoretical definition. A lifestyle or common way of life might be a more practical definition. Culture as a means of making sense of life, giving it meaning, might be a more spiritual interpretation (Plate 5).

Although cultural diversity is the norm in the Americas, there are common threads. Traditionally, indigenous culture has been based on peasant farming or hunting in an often marginal rural area in a monolingual community with a collective identity. Such a community is governed by a strong ceremonial understanding of life based on ancestors, traditions and deities embedded within

11

5. *Chile: a Mapuche woman shaman next to a sacred rewe tree.*
© SARAH WHEELER/SURVIVAL INTERNATIONAL

the immediate environment of mountains, rivers, forests and the earth. Its culture is rooted in the traditions of co-operation, community, consensus and above all continuity, the ground rules that have ensured the survival of individual peoples. 'Listen to your mother and you will live long,' as one Dene adage puts it.

But culture is intangible. Europeans and *mestizos* have found it easier to define indigenous peoples by externals such as racial features, dress and language. Although none of these is definitive, language or first language remains arguably the most important tangible indicator (Plate 6).

An indigenous language is nearly always unique to the people that speak it, although some distinct groups share a language. Yet some individuals who are clearly culturally indigenous do not speak an indigenous language and in some cases whole peoples have adopted another language (European or indigenous) as their own.

Despite such caveats, language is the main means of conveying culture and values – what one indigenous leader described as 'accessing self'. It is the essential means of transmitting myth, history and song in cultures that remain largely oral. 'It captures the ideas of a people and the feelings and values of their existence,' says Robert St. Clair in his study *Language Renewal among American Indian Tribes*. 'To deny one his or her native language is comparable to more blatant forms of genocide. When the language goes so does the culture.'

One good example of both points comes from the Odawa language, whose speakers live in northern Michigan in the United States. There are five hundred ways to say 'love' in the Odawa language yet by 1992 there was only one person, Kenny Pheasant, who could say them all. For Odawa, read any one of scores of other threatened or extinct indigenous tongues in the Americas today.

Eli Taylor, a Sioux, has captured what indigenous linguistic expression and the threat to it can mean culturally. 'Our native language gives a name to relations among kin, to roles and responsibilities among family members, to ties within the broader clan group ... There are no English words for these relationships ... if you destroy our languages you break down not only those relationships but those that describe man's connection with nature, the Great Spirit and the order of things. Without languages we will cease to exist as separate people.'

Name Calling: The Right to Define

If culture, in particular values and perception, is the only real test of ethnicity, then it follows that only indigenous people of a specific ethno-linguistic group can identify members of the same group. 'An Indian is someone who thinks of themselves as an Indian,' N. Scott Momaday, a Kiowa-Cherokee Pulitzer-prize-

6. *Ecuador: school lessons in Quichua. The right to be educated in their own language has been a central demand of indigenous organizations.*
© PAUL SMITH

winning novelist wrote in his novel *House Made of Dawn* (New York: Harper and Row, 1969). 'But that is not so easy to do ... You have to have a certain experience of the world in order to formulate this idea. I know how my father saw the world and his father before him. That's how I see the world.'

This vision of the world and an awareness of it is for many indigenous leaders the foundation of the current surge in ethnic consciousness. 'We need to recover not only our identity but the right to define that identity ourselves. It should not be left to some European or North American academic,' claims Alberto Esquit, a Maya archivist in Guatemala City.

'The definition of the Dene is the right of the Dene. The Dene know who they are,' noted what became known as the Dene Declaration, a land claim submitted to the Canadian government in 1974. Indigenous people in the Americas are clear that you do not have to wear feathers or body paint to be one of them. Those who see indigenous culture as nothing more than externals will never see the whole, they point out. 'I spend most of my life trying to reaffirm that I am

Indian, then I hear people say, "But you wear jeans, a watch, sneakers and speak Portuguese!",' says Eliane Potiguára, a Potiguára Indian and founder of the Indigenous Woman's Education Group (GRUMIN) in Brazil. 'This society only understands Indians naked in the forest or poor in the slums of big cities.'

The issue of definition has been tested in court. When Hydro-Quebec tried to defend itself against a Cree lawsuit by claiming that Canada's Cree people could no longer be considered a distinct culture because they used snowmobiles, ate hamburgers and hunted with rifles, Cree lawyers turned the tables on them. They turned the courtroom into a cultural festival, calling elders, hunters and mothers to testify to their intimate connection to the land through story-telling, oral history and song, all in their own language. The court found in favour of the Cree.

Yet any such definition, even by members of the same ethno-linguistic group, is subjective. Indigenous self-identification often involves cutting through five hundred years of colonization and imposed identity. If you ask indigenous people today who they are you will get answers which reflect this.

In the mines of Potosí, monolingual Quechua miners scraping a living from shafts first bored by the Spaniards identify themselves as unionized miners rather than Inka-descended Runa. Aymara subsistence farmers coming into Puno market in southern Peru to sell vegetables identify themselves as communal-farmers rather than descendants of the vibrant Lake Titicaca cultures. Mohawks building New York skyscrapers are more likely to see themselves as specialist construction workers than as the heirs to the Six Nations Confederacy, the greatest native polity in North America.

Such responses are not just a reflection of hundreds of years of imposed identity or even the diversity of peoples referred to collectively as 'Indians'. They are part of a basic indigenous survival technique of denying identity by telling the *patrón* or boss what he wants to hear. 'When we interact, even when we make our demands, we have to do so in a way the rest of society will understand,' one Maya activist explains. 'That in itself can involve compromises.'

Self-definition in terms of external identities imposed at different times by governments or political parties keen to mobilize or control indigenous peoples has become a key part of an adapted (Plate 7), but still indigenous, way of life. The apparent submissiveness is often superficial; the real Indian lies just below the surface. Consciously or not, many have followed the century-old advice of Cree Chief Pound Maker. 'Our old way of life is gone but that does not mean we should sit back and become imitation white men,' he warned in 1886. 'Our beliefs are good. The spirits served us well. No white man has shown me anything that is better. We at least lived by what we believed.'

Most indigenous people are only too aware of who they are, their ethnic consciousness sharpened rather than blunted by years of racism and oppression. It does not follow that a 'white' questioner is going to be privy to

15

7. *Canada: Cree skidoo driver at Hudson Bay. The Cree have been quick to take advantage of the benefits of modern technology in the harsh Arctic conditions.*
© BRIAN MOSER/HUTCHISON

that vision or definition. Dishonour, exploitation, betrayal and 'forked tongues' – the well-known North American expression for being two-faced – are synonymous with those of European descent in the Americas. After years of treaty violations, massacres and land seizures, it is hardly surprising that indigenous literature, legend and oral tradition are full of tales of the white man's or *mestizo*'s shameless nature. In popular mythology, he is often the coyote, raven or fox, the most cunning and shameless members of the animal kingdom. In the words of Nahuatl poet Joel Martínez Hernández:

Se tsontlixiuitl in techmachte Four hundred years have taught us
tlen kineki koyotl what coyote wants

Yet today, pride in identifying oneself as a member of an ethnic group is a growing phenomenon in the Americas. What indigenous leaders describe as 'reclaiming identity' often amounts to reasserting a historic ethnic pride and sense of self-worth in the face of intensified threats to indigenous culture.

16

People who for hundreds of years have been too ashamed, too afraid, too uncertain or simply too unaware of their own identity and heritage to admit to, let alone proclaim, it are 'coming out'. 'Recovering reality is the challenge,' insists Uruguayan author Eduardo Galeano. 'The lies, the hidden, betrayed reality of the history of the Americas must be recovered to change our current reality.'

The lifting of what Galeano has termed 'collective amnesia' has been encouraged by means of oral history workshops, indigenous-language radio stations, Indian-language newspapers and literature and a surge in interest in traditional religions and medicine. As one Mam refugee living in exile in Mexico explains, this consciousness-raising process fuels itself. 'The more you learn about yourself and your people, the more you realize that it wasn't just our mineral wealth, land or even our lives that the invaders stole, it was our history, our nationality, our memory, even our soul.'

Reclaiming identity has involved reclaiming names: personal names, collective names, place names. While hundreds of Indian words mark places on the maps of the Americas today or are used in everyday speech in English, Spanish or French, thousands of others have been lost, misinterpreted or misspelt in an alien alphabet or language that was never designed to accommodate them. Today, many indigenous people in the Americas are reclaiming their ancestral names while Indian linguists are redefining indigenous sounds. Many names in this book take account of this process and will thus be less immediately recognizable to some readers. For instance, Cuzco, the Peruvian city that was the capital of the Inka empire, is written Qosqo; Carib, Kwaib, and Quiché, Kʼicheˡ.

Nations and Peoples: Self-Identification, Self-Determination

In the offices of umbrella organizations such as ONIC, the National Organization of Colombian Indigenous Peoples in Bogotá, indigenous activists define themselves today as 'peoples' in terms of their 'nationality', be it Páez, Guambiano, or Guajiro. It sounds revolutionary and it is. First, it challenges the image of the centralized, dominant nation-state that found one of its most brutal forms of expression in the Americas, with indigenous peoples its major victim. Secondly, it recognizes that the term 'nation' has traditionally been defined by ethnicity and territory. Today, hundreds of different ethnic groups in the Americas can claim separate nationhood on both grounds.

Until independence came to the Americas in the late eighteenth and early nineteenth centuries, the word 'nation' had always referred to the continents' native peoples. The indigenous nations of the Americas first gave meaning to nationality in the continents, a meaning later expropriated by the 'patriots' who fought for independence from Spain, Portugal and Britain. Today, indigenous organizations are defining the term 'nation' by reclaiming such history, just as they are reclaiming their identity, their 'ethnicity'. The key to both is territory: control of and access to the soil, subsoil, air, waters, sea ice and other natural assets that compose indigenous peoples' resource base from Antarctica to the North Pole.

The right to a territory implies the right to a way of life: the right to hunt, fish and practise slash-and-burn agriculture in the case of lowland peoples and, in embracing the right to land, the concept of territory also implies the right to practise communal agriculture in the case of highland peoples. But it implies more: in particular, the right of indigenous peoples to exercise their own legal jurisdiction, including the observance of customary law.

Controlling territory thus gives indigenous peoples the chance of 'self-determination' – the right to determine their own future development and thus the right to nationhood. This issue lies at the heart of the recent rise in indigenous consciousness in the Americas. It is also the root of the hostility of governments in the Americas to the terms 'territory', 'self-determination', 'peoples' and 'nations'. Such terms challenge governments' definition of sovereignty and the nation-state. This challenge is what has become known as the 'national question' in the Americas and beyond. If Chile is a state, can the Mapuche call themselves a nation? Can the Navaho in the United States, the Cree in Canada, or the K'iche' in Guatemala?

While colonial domination shared many characteristics across the Americas, there were marked differences between the indigenous experience under the British, Spanish and Portuguese. One of the most important was the British practice of recognizing indigenous peoples as sovereign nations capable of entering into treaties with the English authorities as equals. Whether the treaties were then respected or not is another matter; the important point was the recognition of indigenous sovereignty, a practice continued by both Canada and the USA until the second half of the nineteenth century.

Neither the Spanish nor the Portuguese recognized such sovereignty for the indigenous Americans they faced, and as a result few treaties were ever signed. Both the different nature of the conquest, and their hierarchical mentality, led the conquerors to see all Indians as vanquished and therefore subjects of a new crown and sword.

As a result, Indian peoples coming out of the English colonial experience have fought for treaty rights and sovereignty as a priority, whereas indigenous groups in Latin America have more traditionally demanded their rights as subjects of Latin American nation states. Such historical differences can produce chasms of misunderstanding when indigenous peoples from north and south America meet.

Ironically, indigenous peoples' claims to territory have come to be based on the concept of eminent domain, the legal provision under which states have

18

traditionally argued in favour of the inalienable nature of national territory and their right to occupy such territory in the national interest. Indigenous nations have reinterpreted the concept, arguing that it applies more appropriately to them as they occupied the land before colonization. Their rights, they argue, pre-date and take precedence over laws subsequently passed by nation-states.

The issue is how 'nations' can share sovereignty within a single territory, or even more contentiously across existing frontiers, as in the case of the Yanomami in Brazil and Venezuela. Many indigenous peoples remain mystified as to why this should be a problem. 'In the Amazon, in a province created in 1964, we are being told we must have land titles ... we who have been the owners of these lands for thousands of years!' complains Ampam Karakras of CONAIE, Ecuador's indigenous confederation. 'We have become exiles in our own lands. This is why we say we must have more authority.'

Some indigenous leaders have distinguished between what might be termed internal self-determination – the right to control education, social affairs, health care, religion and cultural activities – and external self-determination, covering areas such as defence, foreign relations and external trade, which should be left in the hands of a larger political entity, such as a federal state. But for many this is nothing less than the distinction between autonomy and genuine self-determination. For them, internal self-determination can become a stepping-stone to external self-determination if the nation in question so chooses. Some have already made that choice and are in the process of implementing it. Shoshone people from the southwest of the United States already carry their own passports, and the Mohawk nation boasts an embassy in the Dutch capital, The Hague.

Almost without exception, indigenous peoples and organizations in the Americas are striving for a plural 'multinational' society that rejects assimilation and integration but for the most part rejects complete separation as well. Their aim, in the words of the Aymara vice-president of Bolivia, Víctor Hugo Cárdenas, is 'to construct a pluricultural, pluriethnic and plurinational society'. As one Maya activist puts it, 'We want a role in the states from which we have been so long excluded, rather than their overthrow or break-up.'

'Multinational' describes the Americas before the arrival of the Europeans. Ever since the conquest, indigenous peoples have been baffled by the colonists' need to superimpose an alien identity on them. To them it demonstrated a lack of respect, and statement after statement from indigenous leaders has called for the mutual tolerance and acceptance that would allow all to live together. 'We only ask an even chance to live as other men live. We ask to be recognized as men,' Chief Joseph of the Nez Percé pleaded to US congressmen in 1879.

'You say, "Why do not the Indians till the ground and live as we do?" May we,

19

with equal propriety, ask why the white people do not hunt and live as we do?', Corn Tassel, a Cherokee statesman asked US commissioners in 1785. 'We are a separate people!' Plural, multiethnic diversity was not only possible but natural to indigenous people, a reflection of the natural world around them. As Tatanka Yotanka (Sitting Bull), the great nineteenth-century Sioux chief, said, 'It is not necessary that eagles should be crows.'

It is vital for indigenous peoples to be seen as 'nations' and 'peoples' rather than simply 'ethnic groups' and 'people'. The terminology has a specific connotation in international law associated with collective rights and self-determination. 'Peoples' have a right to self-determination; ethnic groups merely the right to minority rights.

There is one more serious problem for any outsider trying to define indigenous identity: it is a moving target. From the Inuit of the Canadian Arctic to the Mapuche of southern Chile, indigenous people in the Americas are constantly redefining their identity. In the past, they were almost universally subsistence farmers, day labourers or hunters – monolingual, illiterate, rural and marginalized. Today millions of indigenous people live in towns and cities; hundreds of thousands work in commerce or factories; tens of thousands are completely bilingual or even trilingual and thousands have university degrees and professional jobs. They are exhibiting one of the most outstanding qualities of their ancestors, the ability to find ways to live in new, often hostile environments without losing their identities or values.

In their offices, at their newspapers or radio stations, in their government departments, many of the new 'urban Indians' are at the forefront of the struggle for indigenous rights. So are they any less indigenous? Many would argue exactly the opposite, on the grounds that experience of the wider world has made them more culturally aware and more political, even if outsiders have yet to recognize this. 'Only Western anthropologists would want to freeze us in some noble-savage state,' complains Valerio Grefa in his office in downtown Quito, Ecuador. 'Who says I can't be Quichua running COICA, the largest multinational indigenous organization in the Americas, in a big city like Quito? Who best defines me – them or me?'

Culture has never been static; to survive, it must evolve. Many of the designs woven into indigenous textiles or clothes by women today would not be recognized by their great-grandparents as being Maya, Mixtec, Mapuche or Mohawk, but they are just as much a part of indigenous culture.

The mobile phones, short-wave radios, computers, modems, faxes and videos you see and hear in indigenous organizations' offices throughout the region are part of the solution, not the problem, a means of defending and campaigning rather than subverting and destroying. 'Culture is how we survive. And adjusting and changing is part of survival,' explains Mohawk leader Kenneth Deer.

Recovering Identity: A Moving Target

Identity is a moving target in another sense: it can be different things at different times. It is quite possible for an indigenous person to take on different identities simultaneously or at different times, to move in and out of different cultures at will. 'Indigenous people have begun to use their ethnic identity strategically and opportunistically,' notes Tomás Huanca, an Aymara ethnohistorian. 'But no one is less Aymara, Quechua or anything else for using his or her ethnicity in an intelligent way.'

Circumstances, interests and motives can all be crucial in determining what identity someone might choose to take at any one time. 'It's quite common to hear a Peruvian lowland Indian declaim, "We Peruvians must all stick together" when claiming some right of citizenship, then hear the same person curse "those damned Peruvians!" when their jungle river valley is being invaded by settlers,' observes one anthropologist.

The Americas are full of examples like that of the Cree, who hunt occasionally on the frozen plains of Quebec not because they need to hunt for food but because they consider it part of themselves and their cultural heritage; of Maya who wear nylon trousers and shirts in Guatemala City but homespun indigenous dress when they return to their highland village; of Aymara who leave jobs in La Paz at planting or harvest time to tend the family plot they retain in their native village.

The difficulties involved in identification are perfectly illustrated in El Salvador, the most densely populated country in the Americas, sandwiched between Guatemala and Honduras in Central America. Anthropologists have concluded that the country has about 500,000 people, just under 10 per cent of the total population, who call themselves and are identified by others as *indios* or *naturales*. Yet these people have lost virtually all the hallmarks of their identity, including their language, dress and most of their culture and customs. They are in anthropological terms almost completely 'acculturated'.

How then are they identified as *indios*? How do they identify themselves? Poorer Spanish, poverty, low self-worth and being 'closer to God' than their *mestizo* counterparts, believes anthropologist Mac Chapin, on the basis of extensive fieldwork in El Salvador. Chapin concludes that 'It may be argued that the Salvadorean Indians' collective identity as victims of injustice and crushing exploitation is the main ingredient that holds them together as an ethnic group.' History within what might be called 'a culture of poverty' or a 'culture of oppression' is perhaps all they have in common, a cultural feature by no means unique to El Salvador, whatever indigenous traits other groups may retain.

The work on El Salvador illustrates the perils of terms like 'acculturation' or 'assimilation' as well as those of identification. Defining peoples as acculturated or assimilated precludes defining them as indigenous, which they often remain.

Mestizaje, the Spanish term for the mixing of races which is often taken to mean cultural mixing, is used quite generally, often politically. The phenomenon produces *mestizos*, *mistis*, *ladinos* or *cholos*, according to country, who may have a number of indigenous traits or none at all and may in any case define themselves very differently from any anthropologist.

A more accurate description is 'syncretism', the blending together of cultures as they absorb and reinterpret elements drawn from each other. It is a term usually applied to religious beliefs, nowhere more pertinently than in the blending of Christian and traditional beliefs that has taken place in the Americas. After the arrival of the Europeans, cultures in the Americas interacted with each other to a much greater extent than is often acknowledged. No cultural conquest ever completed the conquistadores' military victory. Instead, cultural cross-fertilization became a fact of life. It took place in varying degrees in different places, but it was always a two-way process. The concept of 'syncretism' helps correct some of the bias of history. It recognizes the words, place-names, foodstuffs, medicines, traditions, environmental knowledge, biochemical expertise and philosophy that the indigenous peoples of the Americas retain and continue to give to the world beyond their shores.

With so many different cultures in the Americas, it is hardly surprising that recovering identity means different things to different ethno-linguistic groups or individuals. For some it is simply rediscovering history, traditions, names and languages that seemed lost; for others it means adapting technology that once seemed alien; others want control of economic development within their communities. For still others, such objectives can only stem from a deeper recovery of self-esteem. 'We need to concentrate on internal healing: to cure ourselves of prejudices, feelings of inferiority, self-marginalization,' says Quechua leader Tarcila Rivera Zea. 'We must regain our dignity. Without it we cannot help ourselves, let alone others.'

All these efforts are part of the same cultural struggle for economic and political self-determination. The battle is as much practical as spiritual. In many communities traditional forms of communal landholding, working and farming have become the basis for renewed economic development. 'Cultural rescue is impossible without development at the community level, and the converse is also true,' notes Ecuadorean Quichua activist Juan García.

Although culture is the obvious vehicle, self-identification, followed by self-determination, is clearly the aim. What these two terms mean in theory has been set out respectively by two agencies of the United Nations: self-identification by the International Labour Organization (ILO), self-determination by the UN Working Group on Indigenous Populations in its proposed Universal Declaration on Indigenous Rights. In practice both principles are being interpreted in different ways by different peoples in different regions of the Americas. In some cases, vociferous, well-organized indigenous nations are securing considerable autonomy. In an age when the concept of the nation-state seems increasingly outdated, they may go on to secede in name or practice. At the other end of the scale, many indigenous communities would be content just to be listened to or be able to prevent outside authorities blocking the democratic decisions of their traditional councils or elders.

The struggle of indigenous people is evolving all the time with a dynamism and momentum of its own. Securing some rights often gives people the weapons and confidence with which to fight for more. 'At the moment it's about forcing governments to recognize that they are plurinational, pluriethnic states,' says Evaristo Nugkuag, a leading Aguaruna activist from Peru. 'In the future who knows? This is uncharted territory.'

Mother Earth: The Fight for Land

However diverse the struggles waged by indigenous peoples, all have in common the fight for land. The struggle for possession, legal recognition and demarcation of land and territory may involve demanding the recognition of hundreds of square miles of forest territory in the case of lowland peoples; the fight for a legal title to a few square yards of steep, eroded mountainside in the case of highland peoples; or a concerted effort to get state, provincial or federal governments to recognize communal rights to land enshrined in treaties signed more than a century ago.

The continents' indigenous peoples define themselves primarily through their relationship to the land. Whereas the names they give themselves – Inuit, Kayapó, Runa (Quechua) – often mean simply 'people', the names they give their territories usually translate simply as 'land'. The two are inseparable. As the World Council of Indigenous Peoples, a global federation based in Canada, noted in 1985, 'Next to shooting indigenous peoples, the surest way to kill us is to separate us from our part of the earth.'

For most indigenous peoples land is 'Mother Earth'; the Pacha Mama of the Andes. It feeds, supports and teaches; it is a sentient being that has to be apologized to before being tilled, thanked for its harvests and nourished with sacrificial offerings. Many ethnic groups believe it or its fruit gave them birth. The *Popul Vuh* (Book from the Seat of Authority or Book of Counsel) is a sacred K'iche' Maya text whose lengthy tale of genesis tells how the first people were created out of maize flour, the clay of Adam having proved unsuitable (Plate 8).

Something of that genesis survives today in Latin America in the traditional belief amongst some indigenous peoples that if they do not eat the potatoes,

23

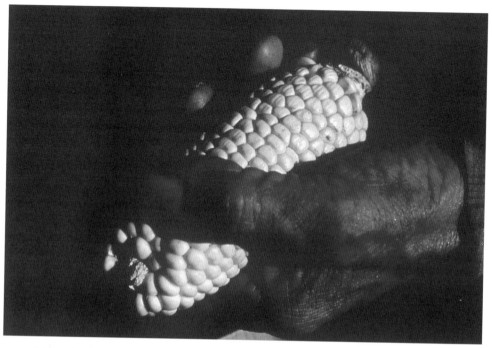

8. *Men of maize: Indian creation myths in various parts of the Americas say the gods made the first men from maize, which remains a staple food.*
© JOHN RUNNING/SURVIVAL INTERNATIONAL

maize or game that form their staples, they will somehow lose their identity. The literal belief that you are what you eat and that what you eat should come from the land nurtured by previous generations, prevails throughout the Americas. 'A person is born with animals. He has to eat animals. That is why animals and people are as one,' observes one Inuit hunter.

Land is identity – past, present and future. The earth is literally and figuratively the home of the ancestors, the people who gave the current generations life and who demand veneration in traditional rituals and custom. Land represents, in one indigenous activist's words, 'the living pages of our unwritten history'. Such history is more important than legal ownership. 'The bones of our grandparents' grandparents, resting in the ground, are our titles to the ownership of the land,' explains one Guajiro elder from Colombia.

Land on which to raise crops or hunt both is essential to provide for immediate material needs and represents the future, the inheritance held in trust for children and grandchildren. More than any other facet of indigenous life, culture revolves around land and land around culture. 'Culture is like a tree. If the green branches – language, legends and customs – are carelessly lopped off, then the roots that bind people to their place on the earth and to each other begin to wither. The wind and the rain carry the topsoil away; the land becomes desert,' says Mariano López, a Tzotzil leader from Chiapas, Mexico.

This sense of place and connection to the land extends to all living things. Plants, animals and human beings are all mutually dependent on the earth, rivers, mountains and forest. What outsiders call environmental awareness is for indigenous people simply the logic of observation and interdependence. The material and spiritual worlds are interwoven. 'The land is a part of our body and we are part of the land,' says Buffalo Tiger, a Miccosukee.

In most indigenous societies, land traditionally could not be privately owned, but was held communally for use by each village or family group according to need. The seizure of such land was the basis of the conquest and the key to the fundamental clash of two irreconcilable philosophies. Indigenous land contained the mineral wealth, gold, silver and more recently oil, plus the forest resources, timber and now biotechnology, that the conquistadores and their descendants coveted.

From the prairies to the pampas, indigenous land has grown the cash crops such as sugar-cane, coffee, bananas, wheat and soya beans that have made the Americas a massively profitable enterprise for a few and a place of malnutrition and hunger for many. The expansion of commercial crops has meant less or no land for hunting game or planting staples for people who knew no other way of life.

Ultimately, nothing has undermined indigenous cultures like the loss of their lands (Plate 9). Expropriation, enclosure, expulsion – land grabs have happened in different ways in different areas at different times, but they remain the most important aspect of the continuing conquest. From mass marches to land occupations, most indigenous mobilization has centred on securing title, demarcation and protection of land. Seminal protests such as the 1990 uprising in Ecuador and the 'March for Land and Dignity' in Bolivia the same year have won presidential decrees guaranteeing large tracts and have forced the international community to acknowledge the importance of land rights to the maintenance of indigenous culture.

As the struggle for land has evolved, so has an indigenous strategy to protect it or secure it. Armed struggle has always been an option for some. Comando Quintín Lame in Colombia was an armed indigenous movement designed to protect farmers and their lands, while guerrilla armies in Mexico, Guatemala and Peru have recruited large numbers of indigenous fighters to their ranks.

Favourable national and international circumstances have been vital to the progress indigenous peoples have made in winning land rights in recent years. In Latin America, the eclipse of military dictatorships has created at least a

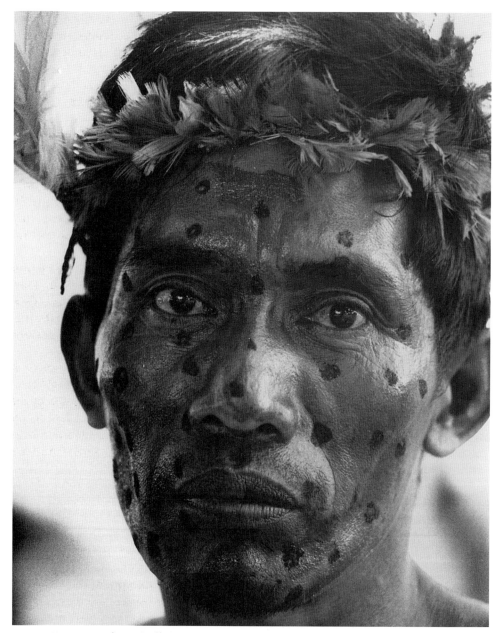

9. *Paraguay: forced off their land by cattle ranchers, farmers and loggers, the Chamacoco Indians are struggling to rebuild their communities in several small settlements on the upper river Paraguay.*
© LUKE HOLLAND

limited level of democratic space in which to organize. The worldwide growth in the environmental and development lobbies has allowed indigenous grass-roots organizations on the ground to forge powerful international alliances.

The first step has been legal registration to replace the oral tradition and historic claims that have been the basis of indigenous land tenure to date. 'In the past, indigenous peoples have lost their land simply because they couldn't prove they owned it,' says Mac Chapin, an anthropologist who heads Native Lands, a Washington-based organization that helps indigenous communities to map their territory.

In many areas, legal titles to both swathes of lowland forest and tiny highland plots have been successfully established, but that simply raises another problem: enforcement. 'Many of the rights we have on paper now are excellent. It's the impunity with which they are violated that's our principal problem,' says Antonio Jacanamijoy, deputy president of ONIC in his office in downtown Bogotá, Colombia.

Throughout the Amazon basin and expanses of North America, indigenous guards now patrol the frontiers of huge tracts of land on foot, by canoe, snow-mobile or four-wheel-drive jeep. In some places, short-wave radios link these foot soldiers to the nearest community centres from which faxes, computer networks and telephones can alert national security forces and international support networks.

In many areas these front-line activists continue to pay the same price as their warrior ancestors did years ago. Since 1974, more than 400 indigenous leaders have been killed in Colombia. Up to 3,500 Ashaninka have died or disappeared during 15 years of violence in Peru; another 10,000 have had to flee their homes. Thousands of Maya community activists, lay preachers and organizers – anyone showing leadership ability or potential – have been murdered or 'disappeared' in Guatemala over the same period.

Poverty and Resistance: The Weapons of the Weak

The loss of indigenous peoples' lands combines with lack of access to social services such as health and education to ensure that throughout the continent they are the most marginalized segment of the population. Without exception, they have the lowest incomes, the highest rates of infant mortality, the lowest life expectancies, the highest malnutrition rates and the lowest rates of literacy and secondary school education. Indeed, as the evidence from El Salvador cited above illustrates, being poor, marginalized and overworked is frequently part of the definition of being indigenous in the eyes of both indigenous and non-indigenous peoples.

The statistics are so stark that they glare through imponderables such as the problems of determining ethnicity or making cultural allowances for attitudes to paid employment or social services. According to a study by George Psacharopoulos and Harry A. Patrinos, *Indigenous People and Poverty in Latin America: An Empirical Analysis*, 48.1 per cent of the non-indigenous population in Bolivia in 1989 was classified as poor but the figure rose to 63.7 per cent of the bilingual indigenous population and 73.5 per cent of those speaking only an indigenous language.

In Mexico, municipal districts which are less than 10 per cent indigenous have a poverty headcount index of 18 per cent; in districts 10–40 per cent indigenous, 46 per cent of the population is poor, and in those over 70 per cent indigenous, more than 80 per cent of the population is poor. In the United States, seven of the ten poorest counties in the country contain Indian reservations.

But caution is advisable. Poverty, illiteracy and mortality are Western indices. There are no equivalents to measure cultural vitality, spiritual well-being or ethnic consciousness. After five hundred years of supposed domination, the weakness and dependence of most nation-states in the Americas contrasts starkly with the strength and self-sufficiency of indigenous culture. Five hundred years after Europeans set out to conquer, assimilate and convert the continent, indigenous peoples remain distinct. They speak their own languages, follow their own traditions, farm and hunt much as their ancestors did. Moreover, they are increasing in number and becoming steadily more vociferous in demanding their rights.

Sheer survival is the best evidence of the scale and success of ethnic resistance. It is not just the noted resistance of some relatively well-known indigenous leaders over the past five hundred years, although the rebellions they led are often at best footnotes in Western history, but the ordinary, everyday resistance of ordinary, everyday peasants. Foot-dragging, false compliance, dissimulation, feigned ignorance, even sabotage and isolated acts of violence – these are what James Scott, the Eugene Meyer Professor of Political Science at Yale University, has termed 'the weapons of the weak' in his book of the same name. These are the tactics of the ruled in their low-key, daily struggle against their rulers. As an Ethiopian, but universally applicable proverb quoted by Scott runs, 'When the great lord passes, the wise peasant bows deeply and farts silently.'

Indigenizing useful Western imports, ejecting the assimilated from their communities, diversifying economically wherever possible – indigenous peoples in the Americas have rarely sought direct confrontation with the state. That, they know from bitter experience, is likely to be met with genocidal repression and the occupation of their communities. This has not prevented them testing the limits of the possible at every available opportunity and constantly developing

28

new ideas to dilute and divert whatever power the state may exercise over their lives. Amorphous, unseen and rooted in the smallest mountain village or remotest river valley, indigenous resistance acts like a gas released into the atmosphere: it fills every space available. Today, such resistance shows itself best in the cultural redoubts that are indigenous villages, reservations or protected areas (Plate 10), ironically the areas indigenous people were confined to as transit camps on their road to 'disappearance'. These areas have now become centres of cultural revival: primary health care promoters have been trained to combat preventable disease, bilingual community teachers to reduce illiteracy, young shamans to revive traditional medicine and oral tradition.

The recent surge in such community development is as diverse as indigenous culture itself, ranging from pig- or chicken-breeding co-operatives designed to offset the worst effects of inflation and government budget cuts, to literacy classes designed to help migrants find work in the cities. Once the generic 'Indian' myth is rejected, indigenous society in the Americas emerges as plural and localized rather than uniform and homogeneous and the state as weak and dysfunctional rather than omnipotent and hegemonic. Just like the conquest itself, nation-states in the Americas have never been all they were made out to be.

In the 'New World', the nation-state, a European import, has never been the integrated, centralized model it became in the Old World. The continents' indigenous peoples, their communities and culture, have played a leading role in keeping these 'nation'-states weak through the skill and effectiveness of their resistance. 'I will die, but I will rise again and I will be millions,' said Tupaq Katari, the Aymara chief, moments before his execution for rebellion against colonial rule in 1781. His words must seem prophetic to many governments in the Americas today, besieged by indigenous demands from all sides.

To the many indigenous peoples of the Americas who share a cyclical or oscillating sense of the flow of time, everything that happens is balanced or redressed by an opposite at some point in the future. The only surprise to them is that non-indigenous peoples are taken aback by the upsurge in indigenous consciousness. 'What did you expect?', asks Valerio Grefa, the head of COICA in Ecuador. 'Our people have always expected nothing less.' Indian legends throughout the Americas reveal a belief in change, role reversal, a renewal which will turn the tables. 'When the new world comes, the white people will be Indians and the Indians will be white people,' says one Apache fable.

Action breeding reaction, conquest leading to reconquest, ups causing downs; such cycles are part of the everyday indigenous world. Many in the Andes are convinced that the *pachakutʼi*, literally the 'balance upheaval' that legends and oral history have prophesied for centuries, has finally arrived.

10. *USA: Navaho woman weaving a rug on a reservation in New Mexico.*
© HULTON DEUTSCH

Bibliography

Albó, Javier, 'El retorno del indio'. *Revista Andina* (Cuzco: Centro de Estudios Rurales Andinos Bartolomé de las Casas), year 9, no. 2 (Dec. 1991).

Chapin, Mac, 'The 500,000 invisible Indians of El Salvador'. *Cultural Survival Quarterly*, vol. 13, no. 3 (1989).

Ethnologue: Languages of the World, ed. Barbara F. Grimes (Dallas: Summer Institute of Linguistics, 1992).

The First Nations 1492–1992. NACLA Report on the Americas (New York: North American Congress on Latin America) vol. 25, no. 3 (Dec. 1991).

The Gaia Atlas of First Peoples, ed. Julian Burger with campaigning groups and native peoples worldwide (London: Gaia Books, 1990).

Katzner, Kenneth, *The Languages of the World* (London and New York: Routledge, 1995).

Materne, Yves (ed.), *The Indian Awakening in Latin America* (New York: Friendship Press, 1980).

Moody, Roger (ed.), *The Indigenous Voice: Visions and Realities* (Utrecht: International Books, 1993).

Psacharopoulos, George, and Patrinos, Harry A. (eds), *Indigenous People and Poverty in Latin America: An Empirical Analysis* (Washington, DC: World Bank Regional and Sectoral Studies Program, 1994).

Scott, James C., *Weapons of the Weak: Everyday Forms of Peasant Resistance* (New Haven, CT: Yale University Press, 1985).

Scott, James C., *Domination and the Arts of Resistance: Hidden Transcripts* (New Haven, CT: Yale University Press, 1990).

Wearne, Phillip, 'The Return of the Indian'. *New Internationalist* (Oxford), no. 256 (June 1994).

Wright, Ronald, *Stolen Continents: The Indian Story* (London: Pimlico Books, 1992).

2
Before Columbus

> For thousands of centuries, centuries in which human races were evolving, forming communities and building the beginnings of national civilizations in Africa, Asia and Europe, the continents we know as the Americas stood empty of mankind and its works ... The story of this new world ... is the story of the creation of a civilization where none existed.

Such a statement might have come from the journal of one of the more reflective conquistadores, the Hispanic adventurers who began conquering the Americas for Spain and Portugal from the late fifteenth century. In fact, it comes from the 1987 edition of *American History: A Survey* (New York: Harper and Row) by three eminent US historians. Its words expose an ethnocentrism as extreme as that of Christopher Columbus himself. They also demonstrate the extent to which the continents' indigenous peoples have been ignored by historians. In many Western textbooks they remain peoples without history, or peoples who existed in a timeless vacuum and did not experience history until Europeans arrived.

All this is hardly surprising. 'History', as a famous US Secretary of State, Henry Kissinger, remarked nearly five hundred years after the arrival of Columbus, 'is the memory of states.' Native Americans had no states in the eyes of the Europeans who arrived on their shores. History, it might also be added, is recorded by the victors, and the extent of the slaughter and destruction by the Europeans means that there have been few, if any, more one-sided confrontations in human experience. Nowhere more than in the Americas has history lived up to Napoleon Bonaparte's definition as 'a set of lies agreed upon'.

It is estimated that between 57 and 112 million people were living in the Americas when Columbus landed in what is now the Bahamas in October 1492 and his Genoese compatriot, Giovanni Caboto (John Cabot), landed in today's Newfoundland, Canada, five years later. The inhabitants of this 'new' world spoke perhaps 2,000 mutually unintelligible languages, lived in a range of environments and societies more varied than anything in Europe, and in the two main centres of population, the Andes and the Valley of Mexico, had developed a knowledge of art, architecture, astronomy and agriculture that rivalled anything in Europe.

The numbers and diversity of the people were the best proof of their success. Their dispersal and adaptation to terrain which varied from the tundra of the Arctic to the rain forest of the Amazon Basin is one of the most remarkable chapters in the story of mankind. By the time Europeans made contact, these peoples had observatories and solar calendars, centuries of highly developed oral traditions and customs, a refined knowledge of their environment and natural medicine, and an ordered spiritual comprehension of their universe.

The larger Caribbean islands which Columbus first explored, such as Hispaniola (Haiti and the Dominican Republic), Cuba and Puerto Rico, were inhabited by Arawak and Kwaib (Carib) peoples. They were sedentary peoples with a relatively complex social structure, living in sturdy houses of wood and thatch, making clothes and hammocks out of cotton and speaking their own language.

The Arawaks and Kwaibs had originally come from the mainland (Plate 11), or *terra firma* (as Columbus christened the coastline of present-day Colombia, Venezuela and the Guianas). They were part of a vast network of lowland indigenous groups belonging to the Tupian, Ge and Tucanoan language families of modern-day Brazil and lowland Venezuela, Ecuador, Peru and Colombia. Their best-known descendants today are the Shuar, Guaraní, Tucano, Sirionó, Suyá and Mundurucú.

Tribes based on kinship groups lived in large villages on the rivers and tributaries that dissected the region, and in smaller communities inland. They travelled primarily by canoe to hunt, fish and gather wild harvests. Their game were jaguar, deer and peccary although some groups, such as the Warrau of the Orinoco delta, considered such animals 'people of the forest' and stuck to roasted rodents, birds and fish. They practised slash-and-burn agriculture to produce their staples of manioc, plantains, sweet potatoes, tobacco, sugar-cane, cotton, maize and tomatoes – all previously unknown to the invaders from the Old World.

Farther south, in the river plains and grassland pampas of what are today Argentina, Uruguay and Paraguay, lived peoples belonging to the Chon, Charruan, Huarpe and Guaycuruan language groups. At the centre of this region lay the Gran Chaco, an arid plain which became a dense swamp whenever its rivers overflowed. The seasons dictated a semi-nomadic existence here, the competition for food spurring sporadic warfare, particularly among Guaycuruan peoples.

To the south of the pampas lay Patagonia, the Land of Big-Footed People, as Magellan's sailors labelled the Tehuelche people who lived here. They shared their treeless, wind-swept wilderness with the Ona and the Yahgan, the

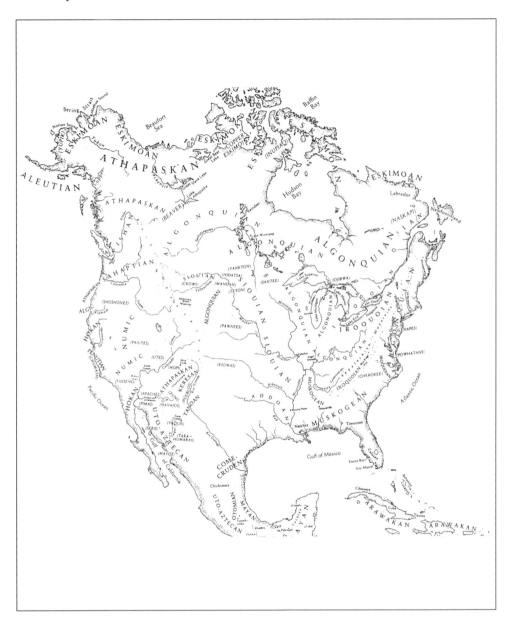

Indigenous America 1492: Indian language groups at the time of Columbus.

Based on Alvin, J. (ed.) *America in 1492*. Vintage Books, 1993

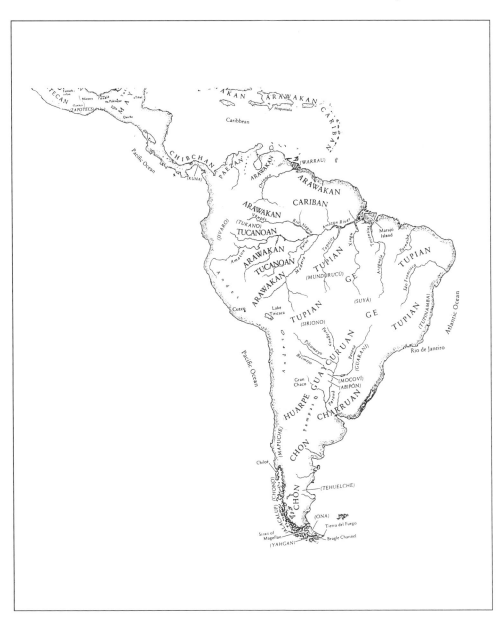

11. *British Guiana (now Guyana): Caribs crushing sugar-cane and making cassava bread, c. 1840.*
COURTESY OF SOUTH AMERICAN PICTURES

inhabitants of what is today Tierra del Fuego. Cloaking themselves against sub-zero temperatures in guanaco, wildcat and jaguar skins, the latter two groups lived on game, shellfish, sea-birds, seals and even beached whales.

Some of the fiercest resistance to the invaders emerged from the southern cone of South America. At the forefront of such resistance were the Mapuche, the 'People of the Land' of south-central Chile. A widely varied people who still number more than a million today, they had successfully resisted conquest by the Inkas to the north by means of wood forts and palisades. Yet in a development that would come to typify indigenous resistance during the next five hundred years, the Mapuche had also taken full advantage of the agricultural innovations that prompted the Inka expansion. By 1492 the Mapuche were cultivating at least eight types of maize, 30 varieties of potatoes and dozens of other grains and vegetable crops. Impervious to Christian evangelization, the Mapuche continued to worship a pantheon of gods, headed by their own 'Supreme Being'. They successfully resisted the *huincas* (foreigners) until 1884 when, after 15 years of war, they were squeezed on to 3,000 small reservations totalling just 5 per cent of the expanse of their ancestral lands.

In the extreme north of the Americas, where no agriculture was possible, hunting was the only option. The Aleutian and Eskimoan peoples lived on the sea mammals of the Arctic coasts and inlets of Canada and Alaska, and the caribou, moose, wolves, Arctic foxes and hares that migrated seasonally between the Arctic tundra and the sub-Arctic taiga.

Farther south, below the boreal forest tree line of spruce, poplar and jack, people speaking Athapaskan, Salishan and Wakashan languages supplemented their hunting by gathering summer berries, wild plants and tree barks.

Farther south still lived the Siouian, Caddoan, Numic, Sahaptian and Uto-Aztecan peoples of the western half of what was to become the United States, southern Canada and northern Mexico. These peoples of the semi-arid plains were not the mounted bison-hunters of the Westerns, but toiling farmers who hunted smaller mammals and birds. Only the horse, introduced by Europeans, made bison-hunting feasible, while the population pressure of swelling European colonies on the east coast made migration on to the prairies by peoples such as the Sioux and Cheyennes necessary.

Onhatariyo and the Great Civilizations

The eastern half of the United States and Canada as far as the Great Lakes was inhabited by the Muskogean, Iroquoian and Algonquian language groups. They included ancestors of today's Iroquois, Cherokee, Powhatan, Mohawks and Cree, the first three groups being some of the first people to come into contact with Dutch and English settlers or Spanish conquistadores pushing up from Florida.

Here, life was moulded by the woodlands and rivers that studded the landscape and, as elsewhere, was as settled as the varying climates and terrain allowed. Some peoples were true farmers, tilling the floodplains of the region's rivers, others were semi-nomadic gardeners growing vegetables in the ash of their slash-and-burn clearings in the woodlands. Both groups grew beans, corn and squash, the subsistence foods of Mexico and Central America, which, by means of trade and adaptation to cooler climates, had moved up the continent since about the time of Christ's birth and had probably helped fuel a significant population boom since that time.

On the shores of what the Mohawks knew as Onhatariyo (Lake Ontario), five major Iroquoian-speaking peoples came together sometime before Columbus's arrival to form a unique political union. This multitribal confederacy seems to have been a by-product of the population growth brought on by farming and the political frictions it produced. The Five Nations' answer was a representative government enshrining individual rights, a federal system of autonomous government among the five (later six) peoples, and matrilineal lines of descent in the longhouses that served as the basic building blocks of Five Nations society.

What became known as the Iroquois Confederacy or League reached its zenith in the eighteenth century, when the influence of the greatest indigenous political organization in North America stretched from Quebec to Kentucky. Ironically, it was taken up as a model when the European colonists were seeking a constitution of their own. Its principles were recommended by Canasatego, an Onondaga *royaneh* (leader), at the Treaty of Lancaster negotiations in 1744, and one Benjamin Franklin, co-author of the US constitution, took note. In 1751 Franklin wrote:

> It would be a very strange thing if Six Nations of ignorant savages should be capable of forming such a union and be able to execute it in such a manner as that it has subsisted ages and appears indissoluble; and yet that a like union should be impracticable for ten or a dozen English Colonies. (Quoted by Campbell and Campbell, 'Cherokee Participation in the Political Impact of the North American Indian'. Journal of Cherokee Studies 6, No. 2.)

Today, the historical debt to the Iroquois Confederacy is evident on every government building in the United States. The eagle of the US shield is the Iroquois eagle, the 5 bundles of arrows of the Iroquoian-speaking nations in its talons replaced by 13 – one for each of the original colonies.

Other great indigenous civilizations lay farther south in 1492. The first of these was the thriving Aztec Empire, based on an island in Lake Texcoco in the Valley of Mexico, but stretching as far south as what are today the states of Oaxaca and Tabasco. The second was the remains of the Maya Empire, by the late fifteenth century a series of feuding city-states in what is today the Yucatán peninsula of southern Mexico, Guatemala, Belize and parts of Honduras and El Salvador. The third and largest was the Inka empire based in Qosqo (Cuzco), Peru, but stretching the length of the Andes – as far north as Quito, Ecuador and southern Colombia and as far south as Chile's modern-day capital, Santiago.

All three civilizations were the product of thousands of years of cultural development. What is known as the Archaic or Pre-Ceramic period (7000–2000 BC) marked the beginnings of agriculture with small semi-nomadic tribes using simple tilling techniques such as the digging-stick. The Pre-Classic period (2500 BC–AD 1) saw the evolution of a settled agrarian economy based on kinship groups living in villages. They produced decorative pottery and weaving, and towards the end of the period were increasingly ruled by priestly élites who held public ceremonies in wooden temples built atop mounds of earth. The most notable examples were the Olmecs (1500–400 BC) around Veracruz on the Gulf of Mexico, whose huge stone figureheads and stelae show development of hieroglyphs and calendar systems.

The Classic period (AD 1–900) saw the emergence of cities, ceremonial centres built of stone, and the evolution of a powerful state ruled by a king and priestly caste. The best-known example of this period is the ruins at Teotihuacán, about 30 miles north of Mexico City, where the huge temple pyramids and the 2½-mile-long avenue bisecting a regular grid testify to the size and order of this society. At its zenith in the fifth century, Teotihuacán had a population of about 50,000 covering an area of 15 square miles. Here were worshipped Tlaloc and Chalchiuhlicue, Lord and Lady of the Waters, Xiuhtecuhtli, Lord of Fire, Xochipilli, Prince of Flowers, and above all Quetzalcoatl, the Feathered Serpent god.

Other notable Classic civilizations were those based on Monte Albán (AD 500–800) near what is today the state capital of Oaxaca in southern Mexico; the Moche and Nazca civilizations on the northern and southern Peruvian coasts respectively; and two Andean highland civilizations, Tiawanaco, near Lake Titicaca, and Huari, which extended its influence north and south from Ayacucho.

The Maya and the Fate of the Cosmos

Perhaps the most outstanding culture of the Classic period, flourishing in Middle America or Mesoamerica in the dense jungles and rain forest of southern Mexico, Belize and Guatemala, was that of the Maya, often called the Greeks or Egyptians of the 'New World'. Between AD 300 and 900, the Maya built a civilization based on a series of city-states at what are today the ruins of Tikal, Uaxactún and Piedras Negras in Guatemala; Copán and Quiriquá in Honduras; Lamanai and Nakum in Belize; and Yaxchilán, Palenque, Chichén Itzá and Bonampak in Mexico. Even now, two and half thousand years later, crumbling and endlessly choked by the encroaching jungle creepers of the Petén forest, the splendour of somewhere like Tikal is awe-inspiring. It was the Manhattan of its day. Five steep 200-ft pyramids, topped by stone temples whose doorways peer out over the forest canopy, dominate more than 20 square miles of ruins. Much of Tikal has yet to be properly excavated, but at its peak it is believed to have been as large as Rome, then Europe's largest city, housing perhaps 120,000 people.

Architecture was only one of the Maya's skills. Their outstanding achievement lay in mathematics, in particular their development of the concept of zero and place-system numerals, concepts that eluded both the Romans and Greeks. Their mathematics allowed them to measure the lunar month and solar year to within seconds and to chart timespans of millions of years for calculations in astronomy and astrology. Their calendar (Plate 12) was more accurate than the Julian calendar used in Europe until 1582.

39

POP   UO   ZIP   ZOTZ   TZEC

XUL   YAXXIN   MOL   CHEN   YAX

ZAC   CEH   MAC   XANXIN   MUAN

PAX   XAYAB   CUMXU   UAYEB

12. *Maya months. The Maya calendar had eighteen 20-day months, with five ominous days added at the end of the year.*

The Maya's interest in astronomy and time was a by-product of their obsession with the fate of the cosmos and the need to understand and interpret it. It is a tradition kept alive today by Maya 'daykeepers', who still use and are now busy re-establishing the Maya calendar. They believed that a succession of worlds had been created and destroyed and that their era would end in apocalypse, a constant theme in Maya literature and oral tradition.

To postpone the day of reckoning, the Maya practised various forms of expiation, including human sacrifice. In recent years, scholars have begun to unravel more of Maya life as they have started to decipher the hieroglyphics (Plate 13) inscribed on stone stelae, lintels, murals and the three books or codices of amate tree bark that survived the bonfires of the Spanish Inquisition. Maya hieroglyphs were a highly developed system combining phonetics and ideographs in which a nucleus is complemented by affixes and suffixes. The pattern corresponds to the linguistic structure of the 30 or more Maya languages in use today.

13. *Honduras: Maya hieroglyphs at the ruins of Copán. At their height, Maya science and architecture surpassed anything in contemporary Europe.*
© CHRIS SHARP/SOUTH AMERICAN PICTURES

This was complemented by an elaborate oral tradition, rich in mythology and legend, some of which is now accessible through the *Popul Vuh* (Book from the Seat of Authority or Book of Counsel) of the Kʼicheʼ Maya. The text was transcribed into the Roman alphabet shortly after the conquest of Guatemala. The *Popul Vuh* is a sacred, cosmological text, the equivalent perhaps of the Old Testament or the Sanskrit Vedas, and a major work of world, not just 'New World', literature. The detail of its story of genesis and the fact of its origin in the middle of Mesoamerica – a central geographical reference point for texts from North and South America – have led to its being labelled the Bible of the Americas.

'Offering a critique of the *Popul Vuh* means searching for the heart of native America,' observes Gordon Brotherston, professor of Spanish and Portuguese at Indiana University and author of the *Book of the Fourth World: Reading the Native Americas through their Literature*. The narrative starts at the beginning of time, moves through the creation of man from maize flour and on through the four ages of the history of the Kʼicheʼ Maya to the arrival of the *conquistadores*, led by Hernán Cortés's lieutenant, Pedro de Alvarado, who stormed into Guatemala in 1524.

41

Maya prophecies about an apocalyptic end to their era seem to have come true. Classic civilization throughout Mesoamerica went into a mysterious and as yet unexplained decline from about AD 750. By AD 950, what is now described as a dark age had spread to the city states and empires of the Andes.

In the Maya case the archaeological evidence indicates quite sudden collapse, with experts now suggesting anything from disease to ecological disaster brought on by soil erosion and deforestation. There is little evidence of external attack or internal revolt. Whatever the reason, one by one the peoples of the Classic civilizations seemed to fulfil the Maya prophecies of the 'coming of another time' as they abandoned their capitals and reverted to the smaller, localized tribal groups from which their civilizations had emerged. Perhaps only the Maya were destined to understand their own passing. In the words of the *Popul Vuh*:

x kizk etamah ronohel	x ki muquh	they understood everything	they saw it
kah tzuq kah xukut		the four creations	the four destructions

Although the decline set in somewhat later in the Andes, the 'dark age' seems to have engulfed the whole of the Americas. It was followed by a Post-Classic age running from about AD 900 until the arrival of the Spaniards in its main centres, Mexico and Peru, in the 1520s. The dispersal of the population from places like Teotihuacán saw the ideas and concepts of their civilization spread through other empires.

The Aztecs and the Age of the Fifth Sun

The first to arise from the ashes were the Toltecs, who established a large empire in central and southern Mexico between AD 1000 and 1200. From Tollán, about 50 miles north of present-day Mexico City, they spread the rule of their sage high priest, Quetzalcoatl, the Plumed Serpent, to the Mixtecs and Zapotecs of Oaxaca and to the edge of what had been the Maya Empire.

The Toltecs were succeeded by the Mexica, one of the best-known pre-Columbian civilizations. Originally from Aztlán, 'the place of the herons', somewhere in northwestern Mexico, the Aztecs, as the Mexica became known, entered central Mexico in the middle of the thirteenth century looking for a land promised by their high priest, sun and time god, Huitzilopochtli ('The One Who Makes the Day'). The sign was to be a powerful eagle devouring a snake while perched on a prickly pear, a sight the wanderers encountered on an island in Lake Texcoco in the Valley of Mexico. As with the Iroquois eagle in the United States, the Aztec symbol remains Mexico's national emblem, visible to the

42

modern visitor on postage stamps, the national flag and government buildings.

Tenochtitlán, 'the place of the cactus', became the Venice of the Americas (Plate 14) and the Aztecs thrived. They developed a unique system of land reclamation for agriculture using earth and silt with wickerwork to form soil-beds called *chinampas*, or floating gardens. Year-round harvests of maize and vegetables and alliance with two neighbouring city states, Texcoco itself and Tlacopán, allowed the population of Tenochtitlán to grow to about 225,000 by the end of the fifteenth century, more than that of any contemporary European capital.

From the canals and causeways that were Tenochtitlán's streets and highways, the Aztec Empire expanded south and east to rule perhaps 10 million people. Defeated tribes yielded the tribute and labour that drove further expansion and boosted the wealth of the Aztec aristocracy or *pipiltin* ('those of lineage'), comprising warriors, priests and state officials. Land, jade, gold, precious stones, quetzal feathers and jaguar skins were the booty most craved by the élite, much of it used to decorate the flat-topped pyramid temples used to worship some 126 principal gods. Imperial expansion was thus motivated as much by religious as economic imperatives, in particular the need to satisfy the gods with a constant supply of human blood and, in the case of the sun god Huitzilopochtli, human hearts.

Commoners were organized into *calpulli*, originally kinship groups but later clans performing specific social and economic tasks. In the cities, the *calpulli* became an artisan or merchant class, a sort of middle stratum which often played a role similar to that of the contemporary medieval guilds in Europe. In rural areas, they tended to be labourers or *macehuatlin*, with their chiefs responsible for collecting Aztec tribute, spreading Aztec religion and culture, and promoting the Nahuatl language. They were also responsible for ensuring that their subjects took their turn in performing *coatequitl* service, working state lands, doing military service or labouring on state construction projects.

The *macehuatlin* farmed land held by the community and allocated to individual families according to need. Such land could not be sold but could be passed to the next generation. Below them were landless *calpulli*, a serf class working on the estates or in the households of nobles. Beneath them in the social pyramid was a large slave class, mostly captured in battle.

Ruling over this society was the Aztec emperor or *tlahtoani*, 'the Great Speaker', treated and obeyed as a god, religious belief underpinning his authority and status. The Aztecs skilfully adapted the myths and religions of conquered tribes to their own ends, styling themselves the heirs of the Toltecs to give their rule a sacred justification, as forms of Toltec religion were common to many of the peoples of Middle America at this time.

Many of their own gods, such as Tlaloc, the rain god, traced their lineage back beyond the Toltecs to the civilization of Teotihuacán. The Aztecs conceived of

43

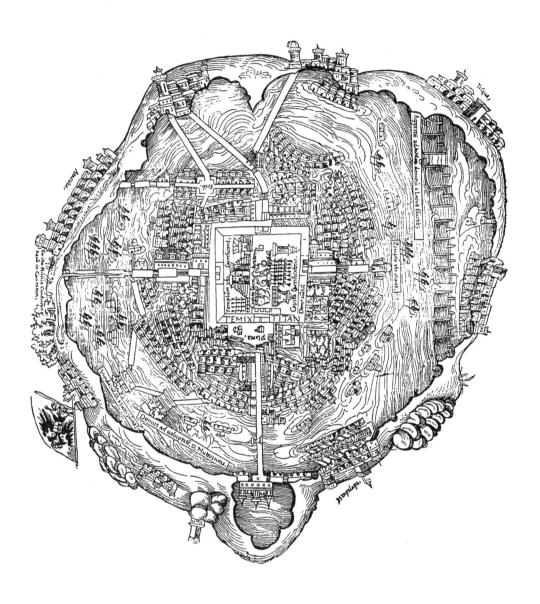

14. *Mexico: Plan of Tenochtitlán, capital of the Aztecs and home to about 225,000 people at the time of the conquest. The Spaniards destroyed it in 1521 and built Mexico City on the ruins.*

the world as an island, their capital a microcosm of the whole. Their cosmology taught that there had been four worlds or 'suns', each the creation of one of the four sons of the originator of the Universe, the god Ometeotl. They lived in the age of the Fifth Sun, which had begun with the founding of Teotihuacán, the city of the gods. Human sacrifice sustained the Fifth Sun but, as in Maya belief, only postponed what they believed was inevitable, its destruction and the end of their world and empire. Destiny was determined by time, ruled by Huitzilopochtli, and measured in days in groups of 13, 20, 260 and 360, plus five ominous days at the end of the solar year.

Cosmic destruction and renewal and a presentiment of doom dominated Aztec thinking and probably contributed to the empire's overthrow by a handful of Spanish adventurers. When he heard of the arrival of the strange band of foreigners led by Hernán Cortés, the Aztec emperor, Moctezuma II, apparently a particularly mystical *tlahtoani*, was worried. Legend told how Quetzalcoatl, the god-made-man Plumed Serpent (Plate 15), had been driven out of Tollán, the Toltec capital, by his enemies despite having brought law and good government to his people. According to myth, Quetzalcoatl had sailed away eastwards vowing to return to reclaim his own in *Ce Acatl*, One Reed year.

Like every year in the cyclical Aztec calendar, *Ce Acatl* occurred every 52 years. Incredibly, *Ce Acatl* had begun in February 1519, the very year in which Cortés's ships and men were first sighted by Aztec scouts. There seems little doubt that Moctezuma feared that the prophecy was being fulfilled by Cortés's arrival and that he and his people, upstarts and to some extent usurpers of the Toltec legacy, were about to suffer the long-anticipated end of the Fifth Sun. He was right about the end, if not the means and cause. Hesitation and foreboding about how to deal with the foreigners who marched over the causeway into Tenochtitlán were to play a key role in making the fate of the Aztec empire a self-fulfilling prophecy.

The Inkas and the *Tawantinsuyu*

In the central Andes, the Post-Classic age evolved similarly to that in Mesoamerica. Of several powerful kingdoms, the most important was that of Chimu at Chan Chan on the northwest coast of Peru. Today, the remains of a capital of an empire that stretched for a thousand miles along this coast are visible some three miles northwest of the Peruvian city of Trujillo, where 20-feet-high perimeter walls enclose 11 square miles of decorated adobe palaces, temples, burial mounds, workshops and houses. Despite the crumbling state of the remains, further battered by flooding in 1983, Chan Chan remains the largest adobe city in the world.

15. *Mexico: Temple of Quetzalcoatl, the Plumed Serpent god, at Teotihuacán.*
The Aztec emperor Moctezuma II seems to have believed that Hernán Cortés was
Quetzalcoatl, returning as prophesied in the year 1519.
© JENNY PATE/HUTCHISON

Around AD 1450, an even stronger imperial power conquered, but did not despoil, Chan Chan. In the late fourteenth century, the Inkas had emerged as the most dominant of several tribes that lived in the Qosqo (Cuzco) valley in the central highlands of the Andes. The primary meaning of the word 'Inka' is 'archetype' or 'original model of all things'. Yet as in Mesoamerica, the Inka empire was rooted in the cultural and physical remains of earlier cultures. Indeed, the key to the Inkas' rapid expansion was their skill in refining existing Andean social structures in order to extend their control over ever-greater numbers of ethnic groups.

By the time Francisco Pizarro, the Spanish *conquistador*, first set foot in the Inkas' northern port of Tumbes in 1527, their empire included what is today Ecuador, Peru, Bolivia, the northern half of Chile and northwestern Argentina. To the Inkas it was *Tawantinsuyu*, the realm of the Four Quarters, reflecting their own administrative division of the empire into four divisions or *suyus* (cardinal provinces) and their belief that they had conquered the whole Andean world.

The symbolic division of this world began with the four roads that left Qosqo ('navel' in Quechua, the language of the Inkas and their descendants today) where, at over 10,000 ft, heaven met earth in the form of the Inka, or Sapa Inka (Unique Inka), the emperor. Like the Aztecs, the Inkas worshipped the sun, of whom Manku Quapaq, their first ruler, was a direct descendant. As in the Aztec Empire, this connection gave the Inkas a semi-divine status and authority. Also like Mesoamerican cultures, the Inkas believed in a supreme creator, Pachakamaq, the 'Soul of the Universe' and a pantheon of gods, of whom the most important was Pacha Mama, Mother Earth, who is still worshipped today throughout the Andes.

The *ayllu* was the exact equivalent of the Mesoamerican basic social unit, the *calpulli*. This kinship group or clan enjoyed an inalienable right to land and served as a framework for the extraction of tribute, mostly produce and textiles, and the *mit'a*, obligatory or forced labour.

There were however important cultural differences between the Aztecs and the Inkas, based largely on their differing environments. The Aztec Empire was an urban, entrepreneurial world with a large merchant class and a relatively sophisticated monetary system based on copper and cacao. The Inka Empire was rural, with even the largest cities housing only 15,000 people, while Qosqo, the capital, was barely one-third the size of Tenochtitlán. The most common means of exchange was labour and foodstuffs. Reciprocity and redistribution, the best means of guaranteeing food security in the hostile mountain and desert environments, were the basic organizing principles of the whole empire.

Interdependence was based on the Andean environment, where crop production and natural resources varied according to altitude. Social organization came to revolve around ensuring access for any group to the maximum number of ecological zones, creating what has been called a vertical economy. In a land where a third of crops were lost to frost, hail, wind or drought, not to mention the difficulties of transport over soaring mountain passes, *ayllus* could ensure a balanced diet only by exchange or alliance with other *ayllus* in the three separate climatic zones: the high pastures, the hot lowlands and the temperate zones in between.

In practice, most of the population at the heart of the Inka empire in the highland basins over 9,000 ft could raise little else but high-altitude tubers (potatoes, *oca*, *ulluca* and *mashwa*) along with their unique grains, *quinoa* and *caniwa*. These they exchanged for the fruit, vegetables, maize and, above all, coca (their main ritual plant) of the temperate and lowland zones.

The basis of the Inka empire and its phenomenally rapid growth was the centralized organization of such interdependence. Huge public warehouses stored grains and other foodstuffs in case of famine. Archaeologists have calculated that the Inka ruins at Huanuco contained 500 warehouses with a total capacity of one

47

million cubic feet. The tacit deal between state and people – food security in exchange for tribute and labour – allowed the Inka Empire to control more than 200 separate ethnic groups, ranging from hunter-gatherers in the Amazon basin to powerful kingdoms on the Pacific coast. Although the Inkas maintained a large standing army and completed large infrastructural projects (the empire boasted perhaps 20,000 miles of paved roads including two north–south arteries over 3,000 miles long), many tribes and kingdoms joined the Inka state voluntarily.

Yet the Inka state remained an empire. What many historians have portrayed as a welfare or even socialist state was no more than royal paternalism and enlightened self-interest. In a society in which people and their labour rather than goods and possessions represented wealth, the welfare of subjects was a natural and essential priority.

Given the size and geography of their empire and the importance of tribute and the *mit'a*, it is hardly surprising that Inka civil administration was far in advance of anything in Mesoamerica. The Inkas counted households in multiples of ten, *chunka* (10) being the smallest unit and *huna* (10,000) the largest. Each unit was headed by an official of appropriate rank, with harvest, tribute and census records kept by means of *khipus*, knotted strings tied in long fringes which reflected Inka weaving in making elaborate use of colour and plaiting (Plate 16). Spanish conquerors destroyed thousands of these *khipus*, and the system died out along with the relatively few state chroniclers who could understand them. We can only speculate about how much they might have told us about Inka history and thought.

One legacy of the Inka empire is the supremacy of the Quechua language, the most widely spoken indigenous tongue in the Americas. Most indigenous groups have their own language which is part of their ethnic identity. Most Quechua speakers, however, are the descendants of peoples who dropped their native languages to adopt the *lingua franca* of the Inka empire. As a result, Quechua speakers tend to be disparate with little in the way of a common identity. Some groups however remain bilingual – speaking Quechua and their original language. This is most obvious in Ecuador where highland peoples define themselves primarily by their historical identities as Cañaris, Salasacans, Chibuleos or Otavaleños.

Common Themes: A Community of Creatures

It is difficult to generalize about the wide variety of cultures and social systems in place in the Americas when Europeans began to arrive at the beginning of the sixteenth century. Yet it is possible with the help of archaeology, the few surviving indigenous texts, hieroglyphics and the testimony of a few European

48

16. *Peru: Señor Yucra, of Taquile Island in Lake Titicaca, still uses the Inka* khipu *record-keeping system, using knotted string to record deaths, weddings and other local events.*
© M. S. FINI/TUMI LATIN AMERICAN CRAFT CENTRE

chroniclers to look at the common themes running through such cultures. Like an Inka *khipu* perhaps, these strands can be woven together to produce an impression of the cultural clash that now took place with the invaders.

The first theme was the kinship group or household, which formed the basic social building block of often larger social structures. From Alaska to Chile, hunter-gatherers, farmers, or even merchants and artisans in the more sophisticated societies were bound together in a complex interweaving of social relationships based on a variety of ties such as lineage, clan and family connections. Such ties were built on generations of interdependence and co-operation that had always been the basis of survival, especially in the continents' harsher environments.

The social did not necessarily eclipse any sense of the individual; the two were intimately interwoven. In many societies, the space and security provided by the sense of community allowed the concept of the individual, competition and rivalry to flourish. It is an interrelationship that continues to this day. 'For us, the individual has no clear right to self-determination that can be exercised without a collectivity,' says Robert T. Coulter, the Potawatomi director of the Indian Law Resource Center in the United States. 'We Cherokees have always known that a free people speaks both with the voice of the whole people and with the voice of each individual person. Among Cherokees, each man has his own way of thinking ... We do not speak as a people until we can speak for every single Cherokee,' stated the Declaration of the Five County Cherokees, published in 1972.

Most indigenous societies measured an individual's status by their contribution, participation and accountability rather than material possessions. Those values remain the key litmus test for indigenous culture today. 'For me that value system is a key part of my personal definition. Much as they may like digital watches or colour televisions, to me the real Mixtec, Nahua or Tzotzil would always rather *be* someone than *have* something,' explains one indigenous doctor in Mexico.

The invaders who now began arriving in the Americas had a very different value system; they came to enrich themselves precisely because many of them were 'nobodies' back in their own countries. They were desperate for land, gold and slaves in the New World to achieve the status symbols of the aristocracy and their rulers in the Old World.

Indigenous people put their own interpretation on this acquisitiveness. 'This love of possession is a disease with them,' remarked the famous Sioux chief Tatanka Yotanka (Sitting Bull – Plate 17) in 1877. For many, it has remained an alien value system. 'What it takes to be a good businessman or entrepreneur is so opposite to what it takes to be a good human being,' observes Leonard George, a Burrard Indian from Canada.

50

17. *USA (undated): Last of the great chiefs.*
From left to right, back row:
Julius Meyer (interpreter), Oglala Sioux chief Mahpiua Luta (Red Cloud).
Front row: Sioux chief Tatanka Yotanka (Sitting Bull), Swift Bear and Spotted Tail.
COURTESY OF HULTON DEUTSCH

The indigenous peoples of the Americas saw themselves as an integral, albeit individual, part of a whole community, their lives a part of a seamlessly woven web of history and place. The soldiers of fortune who now invaded their continent had no sense of identity, and not only because as poor, landless yeomen they actually had no status at home. In what they saw as a hostile environment without reference points they soon lost any sense of their cultural bearings.

After 1492, the clash of identities and values between community and individualism in the Americas intensified. The growth of capitalism, the Reformation and political change in the seventeenth and eighteenth centuries all encouraged a European sense of self, private property and individual rights. Ironically, the wealth of the 'Indies', largely shipped back to Europe, was a key factor in spurring such developments, one reason many scholars date the birth of the modern world to 1492.

The second common theme connecting indigenous societies was their naturalist, what today might be termed environmental, perspective. To them, animals and plants were part of society; in many cultures they had spirits just like humans. The reverse was also true; people were part of the natural kingdom. This holistic approach was based on evolutionary experience. Environmental scientists are now convinced that the environment of the Americas, particularly its forests, both moulded and was moulded by its peoples. 'The monuments of their civilization are not cities and temples but the natural environment itself,' claims North American anthropologist Darrell Posey.

People, animals and plants could change the form in which they appeared, a transformation recorded in myths and stories and represented today by the use of animal masks in dances and rituals. In many indigenous cultures, human beings were simply mediators of complex relationships between plants, animals and themselves, touching and consuming the spirits of those they hunted and cultivated.

Part of this environmental perspective was proximity. People were born, had their children and died in the same locality, even if they moved around as semi-nomadic hunters. Most indigenous people believed that they lived and died where their ethnic group, or even humanity itself, had originated, and could see manifestations of their gods – the sun, rain, the earth, the mountains, the forest – all around them (Plate 18).

As a result many indigenous peoples' bond with their environment was deeply mystical. 'Healthy feet can hear the very heart of Holy Earth,' observed Tatanka Yotanka (Sitting Bull) in the late nineteenth century. 'In the Indian, the spirit of the land is still vested; it will be until other men are able to divine and meet its rhythm,' wrote Chief Luther Standing Bear of the Lakota Sioux in his autobiography, published in 1933.

Indigenous peoples performed customs and ceremonies in honour of

18. *Peru: Sun Rock at the Inka ruin of Machu Picchu.*
© ERIC LAWRIE/HUTCHISON

ancestors buried nearby who linked their world to the afterlife. To native Americans, theirs was not just the old world, it was the only world, the centre of the universe; to some the bond of belonging included reincarnation. Chief Luther Standing Bear again: 'Men must be born and reborn to belong. Their bodies must be formed of the dust of their forefathers' bones.'

For the *conquistadores*, this world was best described by Amerigo Vespucci, the Italian whose name the Americas now bear. He called it '*mundus novus*', the 'New World'. They were men of their time, distorting what they encountered to fit their preconceptions and prejudices just as Columbus himself had done. Yet in many respects, they were worse than men of their time, for they were unrestrained by the conventions or norms of the authorities they had left behind. Indeed, the *conquistadores* often openly defied such authorities while acting in their name. They came to conquer nature as much as the native savages they saw as part of it, driven by their own quest for gold. Most were to be as disappointed here as they had been at home.

Science, Spirits and Standing Stones: Ordering the Cosmos

The third common trend in indigenous societies in the Americas was their under-standing of science and technology. There is evidence that different indigenous peoples used all five devices that formed the basis of European technology at the time: the wedge, the inclined plane, the screw, the pulley and the level. However, there is little evidence that they theorized or experimented to see why such devices worked. Their main interest in the practical was the spiritual, the basis of their science being the effort to harness the inner forces which gave meaning and life to outer forms. Thus gold, which represented material wealth to the invaders, often represented spiritual and political power to indigenous peoples, but only when it had been crafted and infused with some special property such as the life spirit represented by the sun, *camay* in Quechua. This process transformed its inner form, which was more important than the outer one.

Such differences of understanding and interpretation led the Europeans who started landing in the Americas from the end of the fifteenth century to see indigenous societies as being in the Stone Age. After all, it was Spanish tech-nology in the form of gunpowder, swords and armour that had been decisive in the conquest. The Indians had little bronze and no iron, the two metals that had transformed Western society in the shape of weapons and tools. Most made no practical use of the wheel; they had no phonetic alphabet or literacy, despite quite sophisticated record-keeping systems. These were oral cultures. 'Why does it not speak to me?', asked Inka Atawallpa, leafing through the pages of the Bible presented to him by Friar Vicente, Francisco Pizarro's priest.

It was thus ironic that it was probably in the fields of science and knowledge that indigenous and European thought came closest. Although they understood the natural environment differently, both societies had similar ends: to be able to control the outcome of events around them. It should be recalled that late-fifteenth-century Europe abounded with philosophers' stones that could trans-mute base metals into gold, witches and spirits who could cause illness or bad luck, and invisible forces that could move between objects.

Nowhere were views more similar than in medicine. Both societies believed plants and natural substances could cure illnesses. The difference lay in the reasoning. To indigenous peoples, the cause was not chemical but the inherent spiritual power the plant possessed and its ability to react with body and soul. 'For a Western-educated audience, a tree with a spirit, a universe alive, is a dif-ficult concept to grasp,' points out Dr Pam Colorado, an Oneida. Yet she insists that with a little thought or cultural transference, all kinds of insight become possible. 'A Native speaking with a tree is not a case of mental instability. On the contrary, this is a scientist engaged in research!'

In renaissance Europe nature was steadily becoming less spiritual and more material, belief was becoming more rationalist, with everything and everyone governed by one omnipotent God. It was a trend that would accelerate throughout the seventeenth and eighteenth centuries, widening the gulf between indigenous and European culture.

A fourth common thread running through indigenous cultures in the Americas was their conscious ordering of their cosmos, seeking to explain, define and interpret events and their world. Many saw their own community as linked to other Indian communities in the heavens and underworld. Earth, sky and the underworld represented 'the three earth spaces where our family, past, present and future, resides,' in the words of Shuar leader Miguel Puwainchir.

Balance and opposites were an essential feature of this vision. Hot had to be balanced by cold, male by female, upper by lower, and, in some cultures, white men's influence soon had to be balanced by that of Indians. In many cultures life on earth and in the upper world had to be regulated by ritual and sacrifice to keep the influence of the disorder, chaos and uncertainty of the lower world at bay.

The belief of many indigenous peoples was based on a very literal understanding of the world around them. You were what you ate; if you did not eat indigenous staples, such as maize, potatoes or game, you would in some sense lose your essential Indianness. Things that were the same shape were to many peoples related to each other, so the sun and moon were a natural association, while representing the two 'balances' or 'opposites' of night and day.

Even inanimate objects, such as stones, had such properties. 'Things that are alike in their nature grow to look like each other and these stones have lain there a long time looking at the sun,' Tatanka Ohitika (Brave Buffalo), a prominent nineteenth-century Sioux medicine man, observed in reference to a dream about large stones on Standing Rock Reservation.

Many indigenous peoples in the Americas employed this understanding of the world to explain what the whites were doing to them. The white man seemed literally to grow, taking up their space, as he gorged himself on their resources. According to Speckled Snake, a Creek Indian reputed to be more than 100 years old in 1829 when he made this statement:

> Brothers! When he first came over the wide waters, he was but a little man ... His legs were cramped by sitting long in his big boat ... But when the white man had warmed himself by the Indians' fire and filled himself with their hominy, he became very large. With a step he bestrode the mountains and his feet covered the plains and the valleys. His hand grasped the eastern and western sea and his head rested on the moon ... he said 'Get a little further, lest I tread on thee ...' (Turner, *Red Men calling on the Great White Father*. Norman: University of Oklahoma Press, 1951)

Myths and Beliefs: 'Do You Eat this Gold'?

Much of this interpretation, divination and ordering was carried out by 'shamans', a generic term now used to describe every type of priest, ritual specialist, healer or sorcerer (Plate 19). Shamans possessed extraordinary psychic powers and used these to influence or interpret the indigenous world, often mediating between the visible and invisible world by travelling between the two. As repositories of valued cultural and mythical knowledge, shamans were guardians of the past. But as soothsayers and prophets, they were also the main channel to the future. Song, ritual and dreams were their medium, shamanism being a combination of acquired knowledge and personal calling which underpinned the deep mysticism of indigenous societies.

The words of one Chamacoco shaman from Paraguay underline some of these features: 'When I cease to sing I fall ill. My dreams have nowhere to roam and they torment me. At the end of the day, what good has it done to deny who I am?' Many shamans have described themselves as spirits seeking out greater spirits: ancestors, gods or life forces.

19. Brazil: Yanomami shaman.
© VICTOR ENGELBERT 1980/SURVIVAL INTERNATIONAL

Such mysticism and religious belief were part of everyday life. Often there were no separate words for them, which is what Indians mean by living their beliefs. Disharmony in the community, breaks with tradition or moral offences could cause a disturbance or imbalance in the spirit world which in turn could result in illness, natural disaster or general misfortune.

Even as the Old World in the form of the *conquistadores* began to pillage the cultures of the 'New World', indigenous societies, often through priests or shamans, sought to interpret these events. Moctezuma, the Aztec emperor, suspected that the hairy men from the east were gods reclaiming their inheritance. Inka Wayna Qhapaq was seeking to explain the Europeans' lust for gold and silver when, according to the chronicler Felipe Guaman Poma, he asked the Spaniard Pedro de Candía, '*Kay qoritachu mikhunki?*' – 'Do you eat this gold?'

As temples were stripped to fill one room with the sweat of the sun (gold) and two rooms with the tears of the moon (silver), the ransom demanded for Inka Atawallpa, other interpretations became common. Many feared that this was the *pachakut'i*, the cosmic rupture and catastrophe predicted by Inka priests. When Atawallpa was garrotted, despite raising the ransom and submitting to baptism, their worst suspicions were realized.

Interlaced through all this were myths which explained the past, present and future, reinforced belief systems, satisfied a need for miracles and legitimized the norms of rulers or society, usually by means of some mystical, religious origin. Common myths revolved around the origins of the world, the creation of man and myths purporting to explain the origin of tribes, dynasties, rituals, animals or natural features.

Common themes abound. Renewal and rebirth of both the world and individuals is one; divine punishment by a Great Being, god or variety of gods, often by means of a natural disaster, is another; role reversals, animals becoming human or acquiring human properties and vice versa is a third. In one Kayapó legend, animals had fire before humans, who had to acquire it from them; in another forest tale animals once ate cooked food, humans raw. Many myths involved a 'culture hero', half god, half role model, enshrining the best of the culture in question.

Such tales were soon adapted to the arrival of the white man. In the Andes, the invaders were thought to need Indian sweat and fat to grease their machines; the culture hero would come down from the sky or mountains as he had always promised and liberate the Indian from the oppression of the whites in Central America; sufficient chanting of the Cheyenne Indian Ghost Dance chorus '*hi-niswa' vita'ki'ni*', 'We shall live again!', would bring the dead ancestors and buffalo back to life on the North American Plains (Plate 20).

The whites introduced their own beliefs and myths. Some biblical beliefs and stories were so similar to those of the Indians that the Europeans even

57

20. *USA: Ghost Dance of the Indians of the northern Plains.*
COURTESY OF MARY EVANS PICTURE LIBRARY

speculated that the indigenous peoples might be descended from a lost tribe of Israel. Many of the Creation stories were similar to the tale of Adam and Eve in Genesis; the divine punishment tales were the banishment from Paradise; the deluge was Noah and the flood; the culture hero, Jesus. The Maya even used the cross in religious ceremonies.

But the myth that drove the white man above all other in the Americas – the search for El Dorado, the Golden One – had no place in the Bible. The original legend centred on Lake Guatavita, 10,000 feet up in the mountains behind Santa Fé de Bogotá, the capital of what is now Colombia. Every year the local king was supposed to cover himself in gold dust, take a barge loaded with golden objects into the middle of the lake and offer them to the god of the lake, swimming to wash away his golden skin (Plate 21).

The myth has continued to seduce from the time of *conquistador* Gonzalo Jiménez de Quesada, who sought to discover the secret by roasting the local Chincha chieftain over a slow fire in 1569, to the British company which in 1913 spent a small fortune in a vain attempt to drain the lake. El Dorados have sprung up everywhere. Expeditions setting out from as far south as the river Plate to the Orinoco in the north were sent farther and farther into the forest by indigenous groups, who had also heard the rumours. Ironically, most of these

21. *Colombia: model of the raft of El Dorado.*
© TONY MORRISON/SOUTH AMERICAN PICTURES

probably referred to the mythical wealth of the Inkas in Qosqo, from where many of the expeditions departed.

Such beliefs illustrated the profound differences in Indian and white value systems, the subject of an adapted Cherokee myth. At the time of Creation, the Cherokee say, the white man was given a stone, the Indian a piece of silver. The white man threw his stone away in disgust. Finding his silver equally worthless, the Indian did likewise. Later the white man found the silver and seeing material wealth quickly pocketed it. The Indian found the stone and carried it everywhere as a source of sacred power.

Indians, at home in the Americas, did not want to change; indeed, most of the culture was designed to prevent anything other than evolutionary change. The new settlers, far from home and its comforting norms, wanted change. They believed they could lead the perfect life only if they strove hard enough to change their alien environment and its indigenous people. In the process, they were to launch themselves personally and collectively into what might be termed an endless process of 'becoming', uncertain of who they were and of what they wanted to be.

The attempt to impose that culture of striving, those values of 'achievement', formed the basis of the conflict of cultures. Five hundred years later, little has changed. 'We are compelled by Western culture to have a plan, to execute, to move on some orderly schedule,' complains Gene Keluche, a Wintu Indian. 'That's baloney! It's OK to do nothing. Sometimes you'll infuriate your Western counterpart. They'll think you don't care or have a secret. The reality is you do!'

Bibliography

Brotherston, Gordon, *Book of the Fourth World: Reading the Native Americans through Their Literature* (Cambridge: Cambridge University Press, 1992).

Inventing America 1492–1992, NACLA Report on the Americas (New York: North American Congress on Latin America) vol. 24, no. 5 (Feb. 1991).

Josephy, Alvin M., Jr (ed.), *America in 1492: The World of the Indian Peoples before the Arrival of Columbus* (New York: Vintage Books, 1993).

Koning, Hans, *The Conquest of America: How the Indian Nations Lost Their Continent* (New York: Monthly Review Press, 1993).

Luther Standing Bear, *Land of the Spotted Eagle* (Boston: Houghton Mifflin, 1933).

Todorov, Tzvetan, *The Conquest of America: The Question of the Other* (New York: Harper & Row, 1984).

Wachtel, Nathan, *The Vision of the Vanquished* (New York: Barnes & Noble, 1977).

Wolf, Eric, *Europe and the People without History* (Berkeley: University of California Press, 1982).

3
Human Rights, Human Wrongs

With the true God, the true Dios,
came the beginning of our misery.
It was the beginning of tribute,
the beginning of church dues ...
the beginning of strife by trampling on people,
the beginning of robbery with violence,
the beginning of forced debts,
the beginning of debts enforced by false testimony,
the beginning of individual strife.

(Katun II Ahau (1539–59), Book of Chumayel, *Chilam Balam*)

It reads like the beginning of the Book of Genesis, but the Maya Book of Chumayel tells a story more like the Apocalypse. In their initial onslaught, the invaders turned much of the Central and South American indigenous world so upside down that by the second half of the sixteenth century its continued survival was in genuine doubt.

The books of the *Chilam Balam* (in Yucatec Maya 'chilam' means 'jaguar' or 'godhead' and '*balam*', 'priest' or 'oracle') are community chronicles that were constantly updated during three hundred years of occupation. Although in Roman script, their stories are laced with coded allusions and riddles that make them impenetrable to non-Maya, a feature which helped them escape the Spanish Inquisition's bonfires. They are a perfect metaphor for the subtle subversion that ensured the Indians' physical and cultural survival.

All the abuses listed in the *Chilam Balam* continue today, some in a different form, but most remarkably unchanged. Any understanding of indigenous society in the Americas today must take into account the conquest and resistance to it as continuing processes. The conquest was not completed in a few decades and neither were its abuses.

In the 1990s, the threat to physical human rights remains as real for many indigenous people in the Americas as it was for their ancestors. Imported, preventable diseases kill indigenous people today just as they did in the sixteenth century. Debt peonage and food-for-work schemes are the modern versions of early colonial slavery and forced labour. Aggressive Protestant evangelization in many areas poses the same sort of cultural threat to indigenous peoples today as the Roman Catholic Inquisition did half a millennium ago (Plate 22).

Indigenous communities in the Americas have suffered a triple abuse of human rights since the Europeans arrived. First, they suffer the full range of physical abuses that form the common picture of human rights violations: arbitrary arrest, eviction, forced relocation, detention, torture, rape and murder. Second, they are denied social, legal and economic rights, and rights to health care, education, legal wages and market prices for their products. Third, they suffer cultural abuse and racial discrimination, abuse directed against their collective identity as peoples or nations. Indigenous peoples have been denied the right to a different manner of dress, lifestyle, language, religion and outlook, rights of 'cultural conscience'.

In Brazil today, Indians have few legal rights. The Brazilian Civil Code considers them 'relatively incapable' in civil legal terms, placing them on a legal par with minors and the mentally ill. Indians must therefore have legal guardians, and their guardian, ironically, is the Brazilian state, which through FUNAI, the government's National Indian Foundation, legally holds their territories. It is the same state against which all the country's indigenous nations within the borders of modern Brazil would have a strong legal case for theft, abuse and maladministration, if only they had any real legal rights. 'It is the President of FUNAI, not the Indians, who should be a ward of state,' complains Ailton Krenak, co-ordinator of Brazil's Union of Indigenous Nations (UNI).

Some such rights, including those of language, dress, customs and freedom from discrimination, are obvious and are sometimes endorsed (although seldom upheld) by the governments of the states concerned. The other rights claimed by many indigenous people, such as self-determination, autonomy, rights to land and resources and their own judicial and administrative systems, are more commonly disputed both in law and practice.

More than five centuries after the Europeans' arrival in the Americas there is only one current international convention on the rights of indigenous people, the International Labour Organization's Indigenous and Tribal Peoples Convention no. 169 (1989). Since it came into force in September 1991, only six governments in the Americas have ratified it; even fewer have made genuine efforts to implement it.

Physical, socio-economic and cultural rights are interlinked and are often impossible to disentangle. Physical abuses are often intended to suppress demands for cultural or socio-economic rights, as thousands of indigenous organizations whose leaders have been detained, tortured and murdered in different

62

22. *Remembering Columbus: ironic memorial to '500 years of evangelization of the New World, 1492–1992'. Protests against the Columbus quincentenary proved a watershed for the pan–American indigenous movement.*
© PAUL SMITH

countries could testify. Because Quechua, Maya or Tucano communities enjoy no distinct cultural recognition, they suffer particularly severe denials of economic and social rights. Conversely, because indigenous groups have no socio-economic rights, their culture is under attack.

Just one example highlights this interconnection. Without the legal right to testify in your own language, you are unlikely to be able to defend yourself properly in court. The problem was illustrated in a cartoon which appeared in the Mexican press shortly after the largely indigenous Zapatista National Liberation Army took over four towns in the southernmost Mexican state of Chiapas in January 1994. A detained Maya Indian stands in front of a police official who says, 'So you don't speak Spanish, eh? First charge then, treason.'

The reality of indigenous human rights abuse in the Americas today is the reality of continuing conquest. What has been taken by force from indigenous peoples over the past five hundred years – land, resources, liberty, even culture – can be held only by force or the threat of force. This remains the primary reason why killing, exploitation and discrimination have never stopped in the Americas. Upholding the status quo can be done only as it was introduced – by force.

Today, the conquest of the Americas is enshrined in the inequalities evident throughout the region. Indeed, the main reason that there has not been even more violence in the Americas is simply that most of the inequalities and means of enforcing them have become institutionalized, through the army, the economy and the government.

Invariably, repression is at its fiercest where the challenge to the status quo is at its strongest. That challenge often involves indigenous people reacting to incursions on to their land or to economic policies that threaten their way of life. Although almost any country in the Americas today could proffer good examples, the Amazon regions of Peru, Brazil, Ecuador and Venezuela, the Cauca region of Colombia and the highlands of Guatemala are among the most obvious.

The sad truth is that in most states in the Americas, the scale of the perceived threat that indigenous people or other opponents represent can be measured by the annual, monthly or even weekly body count. 'Innocent men of our nation are killed, one after another. Are you determined to crush us?', asked Seneca chief Cornplant of George Washington in 1791 in a plea that has echoed down the generations.

Institutionalizing Racism: Half a Soul Each

It may seem incredible that anyone in the Americas should perceive the continents' impoverished, largely marginalized indigenous peoples as a threat, but individuals and states are products of their history, even if they deny it. In countries where indigenous people form the majority or a substantial minority, the white, Western élite and the governments they dominate show the classic psychology of rich exploiters who have grown paranoid through fear and greed. 'They know only too well what they have done to the Indian, and are paranoid that the Indian might one day do the same to them,' says one Bolivian aid worker.

A complex racism was part of the institutionalization of the conquest, providing the historic rationale for human rights abuse. Medieval Hispanic concepts of 'purity of blood' (*limpieza de sangre*) were transferred to the Indies, and American Spaniards became obsessed with classifying the various permutations of race. Racism, including cultural discrimination, became the ideological framework that justified the domination of the invaders and the subordination of the conquered.

64

Indigenous people established their own post-conquest racial vision, if only in their myth and oral tradition. Just one of many good examples comes from the Shipibo people of the Amazon basin, who tell how the creator made three ancestral humans out of fired clay. One is underdone and becomes the white man; one is overdone and becomes the black man, and one comes out just right and becomes the Indian.

The legacies of this apartheid-like social hierarchy, with whites at the top, various grades of *mistis*, *mestizos* or *castas* (people of mixed blood) in the middle, and indigenous people and blacks at the bottom, are still obvious today. Throughout the Americas, the racial/cultural hierarchy has, over the years, tended to mirror the class/social hierarchy, so that culture and class have become largely interchangeable.

The Europeans' first encounter with American indigenous society stimulated a serious debate in Spain and Portugal as to who these people were, whether they were capable of rational thought and if they had souls (some suggested they might have half a soul each). In essence the debate was whether Indians were human or not and therefore possessed any human rights. The controversy reached its apogee in 1550 in a month-long public debate in Valladolid, Spain, between the liberal friar Bartolomé de las Casas, who had condemned the treatment of the indigenous people in his book, *A Short Account of the Destruction of the Indies*, and the eminent humanist, Juan Ginés de Sepúlveda. Sepúlveda cited Aristotle in arguing that Indians were barbarians and so should be hunted down and enslaved in a 'just war'. De las Casas put the case for spiritual tutelage instead of force.

Whether official policy was based on paternalism or repression, in practice it made little difference. The best status indigenous people achieved under colonial powers or the governments that replaced them was to be declared wards of the state, judged incapable of making decisions for themselves. Concepts of citizenship and nationality specifically excluded them, particularly in the post-colonial era.

The debate over the rights of indigenous people simmered on for more than two centuries before coming to a head in North America as settlers began mass migrations on to the plains of the Mid-West. By the nineteenth century, social Darwinism was being used as a scientific rationale for colonialism. Evolutionary theory lent itself to the argument that the 'superior' Europeans had the right to replace 'inferior' native peoples, and that it would be going against nature not to do so. In North America, the pattern followed that in the rest of the hemisphere.

The conviction that the indigenous people of the Americas were barely, if at all, human made the most blood-curdling atrocities possible. Death as salvation, the crux of the Christian message, became a common sentiment throughout the Americas. 'Kill the Indian, save the man!', went a common war cry. Now as

65

23. *Peru: colonial painting of an Inka noble after the conquest, showing a syncretic mixture of Christian and Inka symbols.*
© H. R. DÖRIG/HUTCHISON

then, stereotyping justifies such racism. 'Indians' are dirty, lazy, indolent, stupid and, above all, primitive or backward. They are easily led, need forcibly 'civilizing' and are completely untrustworthy. The very word *indio* (Indian) or *indito* (little Indian) is an insult in much of Latin America.

Today, as the Uruguayan writer Eduardo Galeano has pointed out, the racism that denies indigenous people status as people or nations has seeped deep into the languages the invaders brought with them. Indigenous people have folklore, not culture, superstitions rather than religion, dialects instead of languages, handicrafts, not art.

In recent years, much of the racism experienced by indigenous peoples in the Americas has become more subtle, the means of discrimination more ambiguous. In a witty speech, entitled 'Twenty-one Ways to Scalp an Indian', delivered at a conference on human rights in 1968, Jerry Gambill, a Mohawk scholar and editor of the pioneering Indian periodical *Akwesasne Notes*, claimed that the art of denying indigenous peoples their human rights had been refined into a science.

In his list of commonly used official techniques, he cited 'setting yourself up as protector of the Indian's human rights'; 'pretending that the reason for loss of human rights is for some other reason than that the person is an Indian'; 'making the Indian believe that things could be worse'; and 'removing rights so gradually that people don't realize what has happened until it is too late'. Such techniques, he pointed out, are much more successful if the Indians' confidence is won first. 'It is much easier to steal someone's human rights if you can do it with his own co-operation,' Gambill explained, 'so make him a non-person. Human rights are for people. Convince Indians their ancestors were savages, that they were pagan ... make a legal distinction between Indians and people.'

The perception of human rights among indigenous people in the Americas when the Europeans arrived varied almost as much as any other aspect of their culture. Yet the observation (made in 1967 on the anniversary of Canada's 'centenary') of Chief Dan George, a hereditary chief of the Coast Salish tribe of what became British Columbia in Canada, might stand for many:

> In the hundred long years since the white man came, I have seen my freedom disappear like the salmon going mysteriously out to sea. The white man's strange customs pressed down on me until I could no longer breathe. When I fought to protect my land and home, I was called a 'savage'. When I neither understood nor welcomed the white man's way of life, I was called lazy. When I tried to lead my people, I was stripped of my authority. (T. McLahan (ed.), *Touch the Earth: A Self-Portrait of Indian Existence*. London: Abacus, 1973)

The concept of natural rights and justice varied according to political structures and social hierarchy. The Aztecs thought nothing of mass human sacrifice – indeed to them it was essential to keep the sun in the sky – whereas other indigenous peoples would have abhorred such slaughter.

The attitudes of the Europeans who began arriving in the Americas from the beginning of the sixteenth century were similarly varied. Despite the prevalence of slaughter and slavery, the English, Spanish and Portuguese crowns all upheld a concept of communal indigenous rights that was abandoned only after the territories concerned gained independence. It was, as Jerry Gambill pointed out, more effective to encroach on Indian rights or property with a minimum of consent.

Indian Morals: Exposing European Hypocrisy

Yet from the hunter-gatherers of the Amazon to the sophisticated empires of the Inkas and Aztecs, native Americans have always had a strong moral sense of justice rooted in their own cultural norms. Many of the structures responsible for maintaining such justice – community police, councils of elders, community courts and sanctions – still exist in many largely self-regulating indigenous societies, although some, at least, are the product of the colonial period.

From the hierarchical empires of the Aztecs and Inkas to the more egalitarian societies of tribal or extended family groups, rights were based on responsibility, accountability and reciprocity. Some peoples used a relatively broad range of simple rules not unlike the ten commandments. '*Ama sua, ama llulla, ama khella, ama llunk'u*' – 'Do not steal, do not be lazy, do not lie, do not give false praise' – ran the traditional commands of the Aymara. Others had much more complex laws and rights based on unwritten customs, precedents and codes underpinned by culture, namely shared perceptions and world-views.

To indigenous peoples the invaders seemed largely impervious to such concepts; indeed, most of them seemed to act in direct contradiction to them even if the European monarchs nominally recognized and respected many indigenous communal rights. In failing fully to protect their subjects, honour many of their treaty agreements and redistribute at least some of the wealth they extracted, the white rulers violated most indigenous peoples' understanding of the legitimate exercise of power. The whites took, in the shape of tribute, labour, minerals and land, but gave little or nothing in return but the repression and death necessary to extract such gains by force. 'We gave them forest-clad mountains and valleys full of game. What did they give us? Rum, trinkets and a grave,' recalled Shawnee leader Tecumseh (Cougar Crouching for His Prey) in 1812.

Such behaviour mystified indigenous peoples, and their confusion about the nature of the people they were facing impeded their resistance for generations. Indigenous cultural norms were based on sharing and consensus, because that had traditionally been the best guarantee of survival. Those who gave today received tomorrow. Respect and status were traditionally based not on what you had but on who you were, and who you were was at least partially based on your willingness to circulate wealth, often through ritual or ceremonies linked to major milestones in life: puberty, marriage, death or accession to a leadership position. This redistribution of wealth strengthened kinship ties and group solidarity at the same time as conferring status. Its roots run deep and probably originated with food distribution. As Daniel Ashini, an Innu, explains, 'A hunter's prestige comes not from the wealth he accumulates but from what he gives away. When a hunter kills a caribou, he shares with everyone else in the camp.'

In many societies, the indigenous sense of justice is an extension of their belief in the need to ensure that an imbalanced universe achieves some sort of equilibrium between opposing forces. People, society, the cosmos, everything in life is divided into two complementary parts, the harmony of the universe depending on the controlled interrelationship between the two halves: the human and spirit worlds; the highlands and lowlands; heaven and earth; male and female; sun and rain; heat and cold. Disturbing these complementary forces can cause sickness, drought, crop failure or the sort of *pachakut'i* – cosmic upheaval – that described the conquest for Andean peoples. In the Andes, where the Inka had personified the order of the universe by transcending its opposing forces, keeping them in order by epitomizing the contract of reciprocity between ruler and ruled, it was understandable that his overthrow and death would create havoc.

But that did not bring indigenous people any closer to an understanding of their new rulers' claim to the right to govern. Felipe Guaman Poma, a late-sixteenth-century Quechua author, articulated a complaint which has echoed down the centuries. In a 1,200-page treatise on the Andes entitled *The First New Chronicle and Good Government*, addressed to Philip III of Spain, he asked, 'Why do you wish to run the lives of foreigners when you cannot run your own? Why do you demand from the poorest man his mule, but never ask if he needs help?'

Although this has been a constant refrain in indigenous–European relations, most obviously reflected in the different legal systems that enshrine the various concepts of rights, the difference between oral and written legal systems is often more one of appearance than reality. As Sharon Venne, a Cree attorney, has pointed out, 'Our legal systems may be built on custom, but so, too, are most other peoples' legal systems. The British have no written constitution. Likewise, our legal system is not written and our laws are just as valid and principled as the non-indigenous laws.'

Most Indians would say more so. Over the years indigenous people became convinced that the invaders' laws were simply a means to an end with two very different standards of application. 'So-called civilized legislation only functions

24. *USA: squeezed between Florida's citrus farms and conservationists, who have declared the remaining Everglades a protected area, Danny Billie finds he is now a trespasser on the land where the Seminole traditionally perform their sacred corn dance.*
© SABINE PUSCH/HUTCHISON

when it benefits the invaders,' noted José Payo, a Kalihna leader from Venezuela, after a recent spate of land invasions. 'They spoke very loudly when they said their laws were made for everybody; but we soon learned that although they expected us to keep them, they thought nothing of breaking them themselves,' said Crow chief Aleek-chea-ahoosh (Plenty-Coups) in his autobiography. He continued:

> We saw that the white man did not take his religion any more seriously than he did his laws and that he kept both of them just behind him, like Helpers, to use when they might do him good in dealings with strangers. These were not our ways. We kept the laws we made and lived by our religion. We have never been able to understand the white man, who fools nobody but himself.

The Whole and the Self: Rights as Responsibilities

Reciprocity and responsibility were rooted in indigenous conceptions of collective rights. In societies where everyone was part of a whole, where everyone played a role, individuals found full expression only within the collective whole. In contrast, the Western concept of human rights, which evolved both during

25. *USA: an Indian council meets.*
© HULTON DEUTSCH

and after the colonial period in the Americas, was based on personal property and individual liberty. Such a vision could not have clashed more dramatically with the dominant indigenous concept of community rights and responsibilities. Private acquisition and unbridled competitive individualism was to them the road to impoverishment, not enrichment, a philosophy thoroughly borne out from an indigenous perspective by the processes set in train by the arrival of Europeans.

Although 'group' rights remain largely undefined in international or national law, the issue of community versus individual lies at the heart of the philosophical, even spiritual, confrontation that underpins the continuing conquest. For many, like the Sioux author and activist Vine Deloria Jr., white man's laws are a matter of both cultural and physical life and death. 'Some day this country [the United States] will revise its constitution, its laws, in terms of human beings, instead of property,' he wrote in the 1970s. 'What is the ultimate value of a man's life? That is the question.'

In the early years of the conquest, Western concepts of individual rights underpinned the development of international capitalism and the demise of feudalism in Europe. They were further refined through the age of Enlightenment, the American and French Revolutions and the growth of Protestant Nonconformism during the eighteenth and nineteenth centuries. Yet indigenous concepts of cultural communal rights persisted, indeed in some cases were reinforced by the impact of the conquest, simply because community solidarity sometimes became the sole means of resistance. 'It's very simple. Together we can achieve a lot, alone or divided it's hopeless,' says Ailton Krenak, the co-ordinator of the Union of Indigenous Nations in Brazil.

Nothing epitomizes the cultural struggle accompanying the conquest better than efforts to impose concepts of individual rights, in particular individual land ownership, on indigenous communities: Indian resistance on the other hand is epitomized by Indians' efforts to hold on to a sense of communal rights, in particular communal landholding rights and a communal identity (Plate 26). A United States Commissioner of Indian Affairs wrote in 1886, 'The Indian must be imbued with the exalting egotism of American civilization so that he will say "I" instead of "we" and "This is mine" instead of "This is ours".' As one Maya refugee in Mexico observed, as if in reply, 'They kill us because we work together, eat together, live together, dream together.'

As in much else, many native American societies were well ahead of their conquerors on the issue of rights. Many elected their leaders in open meetings in which women took part as equals, centuries before universal suffrage became the norm in Europe. As long ago as 1523, a *cacique* (chief) on the coast of what is today Nicaragua asked some *conquistadores*, 'As for your king, who elected him?'

Today, ancient democratic structures and legal systems, based on custom and enshrining both individual and collective rights, abound throughout the

Americas. Indigenous community meetings will try to reach a consensus, even if it takes days for everyone to have their say. The exercise combines consultation, opinion-sounding and decision-making. 'We talk, and talk and talk until we agree. That is what talking is for,' says Kuna leader Léonidas Valdez from Panama.

Such collaborative consultation is a tradition rooted in indigenous society, as the *Popul Vuh* suggests: 'Then they spoke and consulted together; they came to an agreement. They joined their thoughts and words.' This remains to some extent an alien concept to the societies which came to dominate indigenous nations, based as they are on military might, competitive individualism and accusatory legal systems. Equally alien is custom, unwritten tradition, as the basis of the legal system. 'I've lost count of the number of times we've been told custom is not the law in legal disputes. Whose law? Not ours!' says Alberto Esquit, a Maya archivist.

In the legal sphere, rights based on custom have been replaced by alien laws

26. *Ecuador: Women take part in a* minga, *or collective work session, preparing the land for planting on an occupied hacienda. Indigenous groups in Ecuador regularly seize under-used farmland for their communities.*
© JULIO ETCHART/REPORTAGE

which, even when offering some nominal protection, do not seem to apply to Indians. White men were free to seize land; Indians were massacred or rounded up for doing the same thing. White men were free to roam the jungles, plains or mountains of the Americas; Indians were hunted down for doing so.

The distinction over rights also stems from the difference between rights as responsibilities or obligations and rights as demands or aspirations. An indigenous seminar in Guatemala in 1994 offered this collective view, which is worth quoting in full:

> For us the word 'right' refers to something which belongs to us. When someone is abiding by the norms of our community we say they are practising this 'right'. When the *ladinos* [*mestizos*] speak of rights, however, they mean what any person wants or can have. When we deal with *ladinos*, we claim our rights under their laws, in the way they understand. They do not value our rights and the law clearly establishes that custom does not make law when we have organized our community life on the basis of custom.

Today there is growing acceptance of the need for real recognition of collective rights in both international legal instruments and in human rights campaigning. The most obvious manifestation of this following the adoption of the International Labour Organisation's Convention no.169 has been the discussions around the United Nation's Draft Declaration on the Rights of Indigenous Peoples. The proposed declaration, drafted over more than decade of deliberation by a UN Working Group on Indigenous Populations, has benefited from the input of hundreds of indigenous people. Collective rights run through the declaration's 45 substantive articles, which are expected to come before the UN General Assembly sometime in 1996.

The issue of collective rights has also been studied or adopted by aid agencies, environmental groups and major human rights organizations such as Amnesty International. Taking a lead from groups like Survival International, the International Work Group for Indigenous Affairs (IWGIA) and Cultural Survival, organizations which have always specifically campaigned on indigenous rights, these groups have begun to publish reports on vulnerable peoples or lobby government or multilateral agencies such as the World Bank on their behalf.

Disease and Disaster: The 'Great Dying'

Although continuous, the processes unleashed by invasion have not been even in terms of time or place. Some societies, particularly those with the wealth and land the invaders sought, were utterly destroyed. Others, such as the Tlaxcalans in Mexico and the Huancas in Peru, chose to ally themselves with the invaders, affording themselves some protection.

A few societies were actually liberated by the conquest. The destruction of pre-invasion empires released their subjugated ethnic kingdoms, reinforcing their identity. Still other groups, such as the forest peoples of the Arctic North, Amazon basin and Central America, remained relatively untouched until recent times, although at least some of the latter are the descendants of peoples who fled into the forest to evade the colonists.

One impact, however, was universal. The *conquistadores* brought with them a devastating array of Old-World diseases – smallpox, measles, bubonic plague, influenza and yellow fever – that wiped out the vast majority of the Indian population. The Spanish troops, though better equipped, were far too few to defeat mighty civilizations such as the Aztecs or Inkas. In fact, not one of the major mainland states and empires was conquered until after an unprecedented plague had killed the rulers, many military leaders and about half the general population.

In Tenochtitlán, the Aztec troops trounced the Spanish in their first major battle, killing three-quarters of the invaders on what became known (to the Spaniards) as '*la noche triste*', the sad night. The invaders were unable to regroup and defeat the Aztecs until a massive smallpox plague broke out a few weeks later, turning the city into a death camp and influencing other groups, such as the Tlaxcalans, to change sides.

Within 35 years of Columbus's arrival in Hispaniola, the Arawak peoples of the Greater Antilles (Cuba, Haiti, the Dominican Republic, Puerto Rico and Jamaica) were all but extinct. Perhaps as many as 10 million perished. Today, a few hundred people of Taino-Arawak descent inhabiting the eastern tip of Cuba are the last remaining link with the people who greeted the first Europeans so hospitably. 'We don't live exactly like they did but we are still here,' says one, Pedro Hernández Cobas. 'It is only in recent years that we have discussed who we are openly with other people.'

Their Kwaib (Carib) neighbours of the Lesser Antilles have fared little better. A few thousand farm communally and boast some autonomy on a 3,700-acre reservation, whose boundaries are currently in dispute and subject to encroachment, on the rugged Atlantic coast of Dominica (Waitukubuli in Kwaib). There are two other clusters of Kwaib population around Sandy Bay and the village of Greggs on the island of St Vincent (Yurimein).

In recent years there has been a perceptible resurgence in pride in being Kwaib in both Dominica and St Vincent, according to social worker Nelcia Robinson of the Yurimein Association for Rural Development (YARD). Through the Caribbean Organization of Indigenous Peoples (COIP), Kwaib children have begun writing to other Kwaibs in Belize and Guyana; Kwaib names and language have started to make a comeback. 'Through the pen-pal system we have re-introduced basic words and phrases,' explains Robinson.

The 'great dying' spread with the Europeans into South America and Mesoamerica. Perhaps 90 per cent of the population perished, up to 95 million people, nearly 20 per cent of the world's population at the time and the equivalent of over a billion people today. Figures are inevitably informed guesses, but there is little doubt about the scale. The Mesoamerican population, perhaps 25 million before the conquest, was a mere 1.5 million by 1650; the population of the former Inka Empire at the time of the conquest, anything between 9 and 18 million according to the latest research, had fallen to 1.3 million by 1570 and just 600,000 by 1630.

Besides disease, military conquest killed thousands. Slaughter, usually with great cruelty, became the norm. Muskets, cannon, armour, horses and fighting mastiffs (Plate 27), which it was considered prudent to give 'a taste for Indian flesh' according to Bartolomé de las Casas, gave the Spanish, English, Dutch, French and Portuguese a technological advantage that indigenous nations could never overcome. This technology and the sheer force of the lust for gold lent the conquest a ferocity that the continent's first peoples, used to waging war for ritual purposes as much as for military gain, could not comprehend. War and killing to the bitter end left them stunned, disoriented and in many cases lacking the will to live.

There were relatively few pitched battles. Massacres and sometimes long-running guerrilla struggles were mixed with political manipulation. Some 5,000–10,000 unarmed Inka soldiers were slaughtered in the town square of Cajamarca in November 1532 (Plate 28), but it was the Inka civil war waging between Waskhar and Atawallpa and the latter's overconfidence that made such a massacre by so few Spaniards possible.

Yet the Inka civil war itself stemmed from the Spaniards' inadvertent germ warfare against indigenous America. It was the direct result of Inka Wayna Quapaq's death in the first wave of plague, which swept through the Inka empire just ahead of the Spaniards themselves.

In the North, technology played its role, but so did the enforced treaties that followed each defeat and the dependence built up by trade. Nothing proved more destructive than the European demand for fur and the indigenous hunters' need for metal traps, guns and gunpowder to satisfy the craving for beaver, muskrat and other pelts.

Unrecorded skirmishes and countless acts of individual abuse by European settlers acting like 'ravening and wild beasts' (de las Casas) were probably as significant as the recorded acts of slaughter during the conquest. 'Spaniards lance Indian men, women and children they meet on the road, from their horses, at the slightest provocation or indeed without any provocation,' wrote one sixteenth-century governor. In the North, the seventeenth-century Puritan settler Dr Cotton Mather had a nice line in religious euphemisms for such killing,

27. *During the conquest, the Spaniards used fighting mastiffs, which it was considered prudent to give 'a taste for Indian flesh', according to Bartolomé de las Casas. Illustration by Theodor de Bry, 1592*
COURTESY OF SOUTH AMERICAN PICTURES

once recording in his diary, 'Today we sent six hundred black souls to hell.'

De las Casas wrote that the aim of the Spaniards was to 'carry out a massacre or as they called it, a punitive attack in order to sow terror'. Five hundred years later, that objective remains unchanged. In Mexico, Peru, Guatemala, Colombia, Ecuador, Brazil, anywhere indigenous peoples are trying to assert their rights or simply defend their territory or culture, Indians run the risk of being targeted individually or collectively to sow terror and deter others from trying to do the same.

In one week in August 1993 (the UN's Year of Indigenous People), during the course of research for this book, two massacres of indigenous people were reported. On the Ene River in Peru's Amazon, Shining Path guerrillas left about 60 Ashaninka dead, and in the Brazilian state of Roraima near the Venezuelan border, *garimpeiros* (wildcat gold miners) killed about 70 Yanomami.

77

28. *Peru: the slaughter by the Spaniards of 5–10,000 unarmed Inka soldiers in Cajamarca in November 1532, depicted by Theodor de Bry, 1592.*
COURTESY OF SOUTH AMERICAN PICTURES

More frequently it has been the national armies of states which have sought to sow terror and, in one Guatemalan officer's words, 'teach Indians a lesson'.

- In Accomarca, Ayacucho, Peru, about 70 Quechua, including women and children, were slaughtered by the army in August 1985, in just one of countless massacres in the Peruvian highlands during the 1980s.
- On Finca San Francisco, Nentón, in Guatemala, more than 300 Chuj Indians were massacred in July 1982, one of 440 Maya villages wiped off the face of the map in the early 1980s. What happened in Nentón was remarkable only in that it was so well chronicled; most massacres in this period went unreported.
- In 1932 indigenous people were particular targets when a peasant uprising in El Salvador was put down at the cost of 30,000 lives, a local genocide which led many to take the precaution of dropping the indigenous dress and language, which remain comparatively rare in El Salvador today.
- In North America, where atrocities against indigenous people began later and ended earlier, there was the famous massacre in 1890 at Wounded Knee,

78

South Dakota. Some 200 Oglala Sioux were surrounded and wiped out by a US cavalry contingent, in what was the last of the massacres that punctuated the nineteenth-century 'Indian wars'.

At Wounded Knee the victims, including women, children and one of the few surviving traditional chiefs, Big Foot, were, ironically, performing the Ghost Dance, believed to be capable of restoring dead relatives, animals and Sioux lands. History was once again rewritten as the government in Washington defined the incident as a 'battle'.

Such incidents, and their interpretation, made indigenous leaders increasingly cynical. As the Sioux leader Tatanka Yotanka (Sitting Bull) remarked three years before the massacre at Wounded Knee, 'This government is giving my country a bad name.' As the Sioux writer and activist Vine Deloria Jr. observed in US Senate hearings one hundred years later, 'Indian affairs are comparable to a Grade B movie. You can go to sleep and miss a long sequence of the action but every time you look at the screen its the same group of guys chasing the other guys around the same rock.'

Militarization: Division and Death

Today, the military remain the greatest source of abuses against indigenous people. Military incursions into indigenous communities or land take place in many guises: in the Andes as part of the war on coca, the raw material for cocaine; as part of counter-insurgency efforts against left-wing guerrillas in the Andes and Central America; as part of efforts to secure national frontiers in border disputes or assert control over resources in the Amazon basin; as military exercises or nuclear tests in the 'empty territories' that are the indigenous homelands of peoples such as the Innu in northern Canada or the Western Shoshone in Nevada in the United States.

Militarization can be a physical, ideological or cultural assault; often it is all three. All states in the Americas have depended on their armies to establish them as nation-states, to integrate their peoples, enforce government writ and secure national borders. Today that process continues and has even intensified, the only difference perhaps being that there is now more emphasis on cultural conquest and integration than there is on physical elimination.

To many army officers this remains a core mission. 'The existence of ethnic groups demonstrates that we are not an integrated society,' explains Colonel Marco Antonio Sánchez of the Guatemalan School of Ideological Warfare. 'Who better than the men in uniform to project the message of nationalism to every last corner of the Fatherland?' Nowhere have the effects of militarization been more obvious in recent years than in Guatemala, where between 1981 and 1983 the army slaughtered thousands of Maya Indians and forced tens of thousands into exile in one of the most brutal counter-insurgency campaigns ever seen in Latin America. It was followed by a co-ordinated effort to reshape Maya society as the army occupied the highlands, built model villages (Plate 29) from the ashes of those they had burned down, set up re-education camps for those tainted by rebel teachings and recruited (often forcibly) nearly a million Maya men for military training in civil militias – 'development as counter-insurgency', as one Guatemalan officer described it.

What happened in Guatemala was full-frontal cultural assault, first by means of direct repression, then by what the army came to call 'permanent counter-insurgency' or 'war by other means'. The logic was simple: if culture had been the basis of indigenous resistance for five hundred years, then culture must become the target. 'The military seek to destroy and shatter our cultural identity as Indians because the regime knows that our identity constitutes a part of our strength to resist and organize,' Francisca Alvarez, a Maya delegate, told the United Nations Working Group on Indigenous Populations in 1983. Guatemala is typical of many Latin America states where the military is perhaps the only real national institution. Such a role has allowed it to become an independent political force, seizing power, building up large economic interests and defining its own national vision, particularly in remote indigenous regions far from the national capital.

Brazil, a country where the military left power as recently as 1985, is a recent example of militarization for such ends. The Calha Norte project, announced in 1985, planned a string of military posts along 4,000 miles of border. Their dual function was to establish a state presence on the country's jungle borders and control Brazil's 'internal borders', including the territory of the country's indigenous peoples. The threat of a 'Yanomami state' was specifically cited as a motive in the initial Calha Norte plan, but far more important was the Calha Norte's role in the 'Plan for the Development of Amazonia', a US$640 million scheme for the exploitation of minerals, timber and cattle ranching. 'The army knows the Amazon is green but the green they see is the green of the dollar,' complains Ailton Krenak, co-ordinator of Brazil's Union of Indigenous Nations.

Most armies in Latin America see their primary mission as domestic, implementing the doctrine of national security: defending the existing social order, integrating ethnically distinct groups and protecting the state against internal subversion. Indigenous people, especially increasingly organized indigenous people, qualify as enemies on almost all fronts. Indeed, in Brazil there was effectively no distinction between domestic and foreign military action as far as the country's indigenous people were concerned. The Brazilian state has classified Indians as foreigners in court actions such as that brought against two

29. *Guatemala: thousands of Indian families were herded together into 'model villages' as part of the army's counter-insurgency campaign in the 1980s.*

Kayapó who protested against the construction of the Xingu River dam.

Many states use disproportionate numbers of indigenous recruits to wage domestic wars on their own peoples. Forced recruitment, elaborate 'de-culturation' and the sheer brutality meted out in training have ensured that many of the worst atrocities against indigenous communities in countries such as Peru, Guatemala and Colombia have been carried out by indigenous soldiers (Plate 30). There is nothing new in this. Indians have fought Indians in European wars since the sixteenth century. 'No matter who wins in these battles, the Indians lose,' observed one indigenous leader after allying himself with the British during the American War of Independence.

That eighteenth-century sentiment has been equally true of foreign wars. There were huge numbers of indigenous casualties among North American forces in both world wars and in Vietnam, among Mexican forces in their war with the United States (1845–7) and on both sides in the War of the Pacific between Chile and Peru (1879–3).

On being demobbed, many indigenous soldiers have found it impossible to reintegrate themselves into either indigenous or white society. Military service intensifies the identity crisis many already suffer. 'The officers came to me when I was overseas and said, "You're all right. You fought for your country." I just gave them a smile and thought to myself, "Where is my country?",' recalled Robert Spott, a Yurok Indian from northern California who fought in the trenches in World War I.

Drunkenness, crime and destitution became the lot of many indigenous veterans. The tale of Pima soldier Frank Hayes, who helped raise the US flag on Mount Suribachi at Iwo Jima, immortalized in one of World War II's most famous photographs, was typical. He died of alcohol poisoning and exposure on his reservation in Arizona. For other returnees, their plight illustrated the gulf between the rights they had fought for in the name of others and those they were denied at home. 'I have a false eye, a shattered cheekbone, a silver plate in my head, but I can't even buy liquor in a bar like any other American,' complained one Indian veteran.

Military recruitment remains one of the most potent means of 'de-culturation' in the Americas today, particularly in the numerous Latin American states where military service remains compulsory. Indigenous young men are singled out in raids on villages, poor urban *barrios*, church services and sports events. Fleeing the *cupo* (quota) or *leva* (lift) is for many a frequent, albeit deadly serious, sport.

In North America, the abuse of indigenous territory for military purposes remains another contentious issue. Since 1951, when the United States government expropriated their land, more than 800 nuclear tests have been conducted on Western Shoshone and South Paiute territory in Nevada, making

30. *Colombia: indigenous groups demonstrate, demanding 'Paramilitary Groups Out of the Indigenous Communities'. Hundreds of indigenous activitists have been killed in recent years by the military, police,* pájaros *(hired killers) and the guerrillas.*
© JOE FISH/SURVIVAL INTERNATIONAL

them the most bombed nations on earth. Cruise missile testing has been common up the Mackenzie River in Cree and Dene hunting grounds in Canada, while early warning systems and radar, prime targets in any war, are entrenched on Inuit land in the Arctic.

Against all odds, militarization has been fiercely resisted by indigenous peoples in the Americas. The adaptation and even co-option of aspects of the military presence in the highlands have been notable in both Peru and Guatemala. In Santiago Atitlán, an indigenous town in Guatemala, the population managed to secure the removal of the army garrison in December 1990 after a massacre by the troops left 13 residents dead. In the ten years the army had been in occupation, 268 *Atitecos* had been murdered and scores more had 'disappeared'.

In Canada, the Innu people who occupy their land of Nitassinan, comprising 40,000 square miles of Quebec and Labrador, have to date successfully opposed the construction of a US$800 million NATO Tactical Fighter Weapons Training Centre at Goose Bay. Already, low-level flying by bombers is believed to be at least partially responsible for halving the Innu's 600,000 Caribou herd in less than a decade. 'We can't think of a worse denigration of our homeland than to have it used for war games,' notes Innu representative Daniel Ashini. Or indeed of its people, for in the end, the real victims of militarization in the Americas have been the continents' indigenous peoples. Ultimately, the longest war in the history of every country in the Americas has been the war against its own Indians.

'Finishing Us Off': Disease and Forced Labour

Through the ages, disease has been far more lethal than military attack for indigenous people. 'In the old days we worked all winter in the wind and never felt the cold, but now when the wind blows down from the mountains it makes us cough. Yes, we know that when you come, we die,' lamented Chiparopai, an old Yuma woman, at the beginning of the twentieth century.

Indigenous people had no immunity to the new diseases, succumbing rapidly as Europeans spread westwards throughout the continent. From 1520 until the end of the sixteenth century there were 14 major epidemics in Mesoamerica and perhaps as many as 17 in the Andes. Being herded together in relatively confined spaces accentuated the problem. The survivors would soon be looking back in envy as native texts such as the *Chilam Balam* recalled a time when people had 'no aching bones, no burning chest, no consumption, no high fever'.

Today, tens of thousands of indigenous people in the Americas are dying of the same diseases. The victims fall into two categories. First, there are those who fall victim through the lack of basic socio-economic rights, namely access to running water, proper sanitation and, most crucially, health care (Plate 31). These people die of common preventable diseases for 'want of a few cents of medicine or prevention', in one indigenous health promoter's words. Most of these are children. Infant mortality rates of 100 or more per 1,000 live births are still common in the predominantly indigenous rural areas of Latin America.

The second category are those who have only recently come into contact with outsiders seeking to log, mine or raise cattle on their territory and who, like their ancestors five hundred years ago, have no immunity to Western diseases. Foremost among these have been Amazon groups such as the Uru-Eu-Uau-Uau, the Yanomami, the Nambikuara, the Kayapó, the Makuxí, the Tucano and the Pataxo Hahahai, thousands of whom have died in epidemics that have ravaged their forest *shibonos* (communal living places) in the past thirty years. 'They are doing this to finish us off,' said Davi Yanomami, a Yanomami leader, on a recent visit to Europe. It sounds far-fetched, but in 1969 a feature by Norman Lewis in Britain's *Sunday Times* newspaper revealed a secret Brazilian government report detailing how officers from the country's Indian Protection Service had tried to eliminate Indian groups by injecting

84

31. *Canada: citizens of Heart Lake First Nation protest outside the Alberta State Legislature against budget cuts in Indian health care, 21 October 1993.*
© ROY L. PIEPENBURG/SURVIVAL INTERNATIONAL

them with smallpox virus instead of vaccine and issuing them with clothing impregnated with the disease.

The impact of disease was accentuated by the debilitating effects of slavery, forced labour and the overcrowding in which indigenous peoples were forced to live. From the moment Columbus arrived in the Caribbean, Cortés in Mexico and Pizarro in Peru, the mining of gold then silver replaced food production as the organizing principle of society. Slaves were gathered at the mining centres of Potosí, Guanajuato and Huancavelica in Bolivia, Mexico and Peru respectively.

A conical-shaped mountain more than 15,000 feet above sea-level just outside Potosí came to symbolize the economics of conquest. Known to the Inkas as Sumaj Orcko (Beautiful Hill), it was renamed Cerro Rico (Rich Hill) by the Spaniards, as they began to mine what remains to this day the richest deposit of silver ever found (Plate 32). *'Vale un Potosí'* ('It's worth a Potosí'), wrote Miguel Cervantes in *Don Quixote de la Mancha*, in a phrase still used in Spanish.

Throughout the second half of the sixteenth century Sumaj Orcko supplied half the world's silver to Spain via Lima and Panama, causing an unprecedented bout of global inflation and sowing the seeds of a global trade network. Inka emperor Wayna Quapaq had begun to mine Sumaj Orcko silver deposits more

32. *Bolivia: whole communities were forced to work in the silver mine at Cerro Rico (Rich Hill) near Potosí, previously known to the Inkas as Sumaj Orcko (Beautiful Hill). Throughout the second half of the sixteenth century Sumaj Orcko supplied half the world's silver to Spain via Lima and Panama.*
AFTER VANDERAA, COURTESY OF SOUTH AMERICAN PICTURES

than twenty years before the arrival of the Spaniards. However, according to legend the Inka had given up in terror when a voice thundered out of a mine shaft, 'Take no silver from this hill. It is destined for others.' It certainly was. In the three hundred years to 1850 Potosí yielded an estimated US$2 billion in pre-1914 US gold dollars, enough to build a solid silver bridge from Bolivia to Madrid, according to today's miners.

The cost was hundreds of thousands of miners' lives. Many froze, some died in accidents, others succumbed to sheer exhaustion or mercury poisoning. The life expectancy of a miner in the first century of colonial rule was just four years. As Alonso de Zurita, a royal mines inspector, noted in the sixteenth century, 'The mines were easy to find because the bones of dead Indians were so thick along the way.'

New myths sprang up among the miners to explain their hellish plight. The Inka had hidden the minerals in the ground to prevent the Spaniards retrieving them.

The mines were the hell the missionaries spoke of as being underground, a world which became synomous with the Andean *ucu pacha* or underworld. But the mines also became the entry to the world where the pre-conquest order still lurked. Deep underground, the Inkari, the Inka messiah, was preparing a triumphal return; his head was growing a new body to launch the *pachakut'i*, the reversal of upper and lower worlds and, by implication, upper and lower social orders.

Today, Potosí is one of the most indigenous towns in Bolivia and the Americas; once the richest, it is now one of the poorest (Plate 33). The silver has largely gone, but death remains. The day before this writer arrived in Potosí in August 1993, two Quechua miners were killed in a rock fall while trying to scrape a US$2–3-a-day living from the remaining low-grade tin deposits in Cerro Rico. 'We eat the mines and the mines eat us,' one Quechua miner told June Nash, Professor of Anthropology at the City University of New York and author of a book of the same title.

The disruption of slavery and labour tribute played havoc with agricultural production. Seed went unplanted, crops untended, irrigation channels and terraces

33. *Bolivia: Potosí today is the poorest region of the poorest country in South America. The fabled wealth of its silver mines has long vanished overseas. The conical hill in the background is Cerro Rico.*
© TONY MORRISON/SOUTH AMERICAN PICTURES

fell into disrepair. Famine became common, despite the slump in population. Soon the expanding European population began to appropriate land for themselves, not for foodstuffs but for cash crops destined for export. This 'destructuration', the unravelling of the economic, social and ideological structures which gave indigenous cultures coherence and meaning, continues today. Its effects are visible in the high rates of alcoholism and suicide among the dispossessed indigenous people of the continents' urban slums and reservations.

Mining and plantations were both activities initially based on indigenous slave labour. Theoretically, there were distinctions between slaves, who had come with a gift of land or were the product of 'a just war', and vassals, who had to contribute a specified number of days per year of unpaid labour. In practice, the legal niceties made little difference. As the indigenous population diminished and the colonists' activities intensified, slave raids became the norm. Nicaragua alone lost 200,000 of its population to slave raiders in the first half of the sixteenth century, the victims being sold in Peru, the Caribbean or Panama. By the 1560s there were 40,000 indigenous people labouring as slaves on Portuguese plantations in northeastern Brazil. Labour tribute steadily became more onerous as diminishing numbers of indigenous people bore a growing burden in the expanding mines and plantations.

A key figure in this process was the *corregidor de indios*, a Spaniard or American-born Spaniard (*criollo*) responsible to the Spanish Crown for the enforcement of indigenous policy in each administrative district. Collecting tribute and organizing labour drafts, the *corregidores*' position lent itself to abuse. Their pay was minimal and they were given a free hand to engage in trade with indigenous communities, turning them into the precursors of generations of exploitative intermediaries, many of them de-ethnicized Indians. Some, such as the travelling boatmen who ply the Amazon and its tributaries, selling goods to indigenous communities at exorbitant profits and buying their produce at well below market value, still bear the same name, *corregidor*.

Others, such as the labour agents who turn up in Andean or Central American villages to recruit for plantation harvests, are still in the same line of work. They advance small loans just when indigenous farmers need them most for seed, fertilizer or other expenses. In return, the recipients must spend a harvest season amid sugar-cane, coffee or cotton, working off their debt and often incurring others for their overpriced food and accommodation. A cycle of debt peonage or minimal-wage seasonal labour, both modern forms of slavery, is still very common.

The Cross and the Sword: Killing for God

The conquest was carried out in the name of Christianity, one of the main vehicles for cultural abuse or what has been termed 'ethnocide', the cultural equivalent of genocide. The *conquistadores* saw themselves as Christians rather than Castilians, Aragonese or Andalucians, much less Spaniards. Since the Middle Ages, the Church had allowed the import and sale of 'infidel' (non-Christian) slaves, but by the fifteenth century the label was being applied to the slaves' ethnic origin rather than religious belief, another facet of the obsession with race. Religious conversion made little difference for many. Inka Atawallpa found himself trading baptism simply for a more acceptable form of execution. He died Don Francisco Atawallpa in return for being garrotted rather than burned alive.

Churches were invariably built on the ruins of indigenous places of worship, using indigenous labour, symbolizing the way that forced labour and religious conversion went hand in hand. The *encomiendas* (land grants) awarded to leading *conquistadores* fixed an amount of indigenous labour and tribute in return for a commitment to convert the Spanish king's new subjects to Christianity.

The missionaries themselves resettled scattered indigenous groups in *congregaciones* and *reducciones*, specially designed villages where conversion and acculturation could take place. Although many missionaries shielded their converts from the worst excesses of the conquistadores in such settlements, they were often responsible for breaking down ethnic loyalties and traditions in the name of 'modernization' and 'civilization'.

Many clerics embodied the worst of the Inquisition and Spanish state. The Franciscan friar Diego de Landa was one example. He ordered a full-scale *auto-da-fé* (a public burning) in Yucatán in 1562 after discovering idols and the remnants of 'pagan' practices in nearby caves. Thousands of Maya books and artefacts were burnt, while 4,500 Maya were tortured and a further 158 killed during interrogation.

Such individuals set a precedent of ethnocide that has been maintained and even reinforced by the largely North American Protestant fundamentalists of the twentieth century, who regard Latin America, and indigenous people in particular, as their missionary backyard. The New Tribes Mission and the Summer Institute of Linguistics are just two such organizations. The former is a Florida-based establishment with a US$20 million annual turnover and 2,500 missionaries practicing 'tribal evangelism and indigenous church planting'. The latter, one of the largest missionary enterprises in the world, aims to bring 'the Word' to 'Bibleless tribes'. Both groups have deliberately subverted indigenous belief systems, halted traditional ways of life and social organization, and destroyed whole cultures as they 'disguise ethnocide as a blessing', in the words of one anthropologist.

Nowhere has their impact been more devastating than in the Bolivian–Paraguayan Chaco where they have resettled semi-nomadic groups

34. *Paraguay: Eode, a member of the Ayoreo people, with Linda Keefe, a nurse of the New Tribes Mission. Tracked down in a 1979 NTM manhunt he died at the mission shortly afterwards.*
© LUKE HOLLAND

such as the Ayoreo and Ache after 'contact' raids into the forest (Plate 34). Death from disease, trauma and even exploitative labour on nearby farms has become common as indoctrination, dependence and the 'civilizing' process take their toll. 'Is God an American?', asked a report of the same title, which highlighted the cultural devastation.

To many indigenous people, the gap between the Christian values the colonists preached and the reality of what they practised became the most obvious evidence of the Europeans' hypocrisy. Throughout the Americas, missionaries zealously preached 'Thou shalt not kill, Thou shalt not steal' while breaking such commandments with abandon.

In North America the double standards were underlined by the fact that the original settlers had, in one chief's words, 'fled their own country for fear of wicked men, to enjoy their own religion'. As Red Jacket, a famous Seneca leader, noted sardonically to a preacher from the Evangelical Missionary Society in 1828, 'You say you are right and we are lost. How do we know this is true, being so often deceived by the white people?' He continued, 'Brother! You say there is but one way to worship and serve the Great Spirit. If there is but one religion, why do you white people differ so much about it?'

The Spanish conquest was quickly given a quasi-legal religious justification. From 1516 every Spanish expedition was required to carry to the Americas a document known as *El Requerimiento* (the Requirement), which was to be read to any indigenous people encountered. The preamble to the Requirement states that Christ had given St Peter the task of governing the world, a task since handed down to the Popes. The present Pope, it stated, had given all the islands and mainland of the Ocean Sea (the Atlantic) to Spain – a reference to the Treaty of Tordesillas of 1494, by which Alexander VI had divided the 'heathen world' between Spain and Portugal. The document goes on to call on all indigenous peoples to acknowledge the Church, the Pope and the king of Spain:

> If you do so, His Majesty will greet you with all love ... and leave your wives and children free ... He will not compel you to turn Christian unless you wish to be converted to the Holy Catholic Faith. But if you do not, or if you maliciously delay in doing so, by the help of God, I will enter your lands ... and I will take your wives and children and make slaves of them and will sell them as such, and will take all your goods and do you all the mischief I can.

During its short life the Requirement was mocked by those who bothered to comply with reading it. There are tales of its being read to uncomprehending natives or even villages and towns at the dead of night before they were attacked. But its real significance lay in the two precedents it set. First was the quasi-legal justification. For five hundred years many of the worst abuses suffered by indigenous peoples in the Americas, including slavery, land seizures, debt peonage, racism, a myriad of cultural abuses, even torture and massacres, have been justified by laws, edicts or decrees. Halting or reversing such laws and regulations has been a major target of indigenous campaigning.

Second was the precedent of official hypocrisy established. For five centuries governing powers in the Americas have found it politic from time to time to approve legislation and constitutional articles that nominally protect indigenous people yet which remain unenforced or unenforceable.

Today, many constitutions, treaties and laws in the Americas recognize indigenous peoples' right to land, language and even their cultural distinctiveness. The practicalities of enforcing or securing those rights are another matter, however. Five hundred years of betrayal and broken promises have taken an inevitable toll on trust. 'Our people no longer believe. It is as simple as that. Government can promise ... We will no longer believe them,' wrote Harold Cardinal, a Cree Indian, in his book *The Unjust Society: The Tragedy of Canada's Indians* (Edmonton: Hartig, 1969).

Women and Children First: The Most Vulnerable Resist

The most vulnerable always suffer more: women, children and old people. Initially, at least, Spanish men depended on native women for sexual relations. From what we know of the conquest, its brutality and racism, it is clear that rape and forced cohabitation were routine. Abuses were encouraged by the *macho* culture that the invaders imported, a culture which denied women the right to land upheld by many indigenous societies, which separated families as men were recruited for forced labour, and which made a money economy, from which women were largely excluded, the basis of power.

All this was underpinned by the imposition of a religion which worshipped a single male god rather than a range of gods of both sexes, helping to skew the sexual balance of indigenous society, which before the conquest had been largely based on a complementary equality. While such 'ideological colonization', in the phrase of one Mapuche women's organization, continues today, the traditional view of complementarity persists and is now reaching new audiences. 'Our creators are personalized by the figures of a man and woman, Manku Quapaq and Mama Oello who emerged from Lake Titicaca at the same time,' observes Wara Alderete, a Calchaqui from Argentina. 'Men and women were different, even opposed, but complementary, not antagonistic. It's a reflection of the duality present in nature, where forces like day and night, the sun and moon, summer and winter, complement each other to maintain the harmony of the universe.'

The rape of indigenous women epitomized the rape of indigenous culture and land. As one of the most powerful symbols of conquest and degradation, rape remains a powerful weapon of the continuing war against indigenous people, particularly among the armies of Latin American states. As recently as 1986 judicial officials in Ayacucho, the centre of the Sendero Luminoso revolt in Peru, told Amnesty International representatives that incidents of rape were 'natural' when troops were posted to rural areas and that prosecutions could not be expected.

The racism and ethnocide underlying such campaigns often mean that women and young children, the symbols of any ethnic group's ability to reproduce and continue in existence, are singled out. Old people, the traditional repository of a group's oral history, religious beliefs and myths, are also common targets. 'We are going to leave them with no seed,' a Guatemalan colonel, Horacio Maldonado Shadd, boasted during a ruthless counter-insurgency campaign that killed at least 40,000 indigenous people, thousands of them children, in the early 1980s. 'If you pursue a wolf you have to go after the whelps,' US President Andrew Jackson assured his followers after winning the presidency in 1828 on his record as an 'Indian fighter'.

From the moment that Manku Inka Yupanki was forced to watch the Inka

35. *Guatemala: Women at the exhumation of relatives from a clandestine cemetery in Baja Verapaz, 1994.*
© PAUL SMITH

women of his family being raped by Spaniards in the 1530s, the women who clothed, fed and gave life to potential indigenous resisters have been singled out for abuse. Yet that very abuse helped inspire some of the fiercest resistance from women, and in some cases guaranteed the survival of indigenous culture. 'Men are more susceptible to taking up the vices of the colonizer. Indian women are stronger, more responsible and hold on to our moral values,' says Wara Alderete. 'Maybe our women are more active because they have more need to survive,' muses Patricia Gualinga, a Quichua from Ecuador.

Today the mixed-race product of the conquest is most evident in Mexico, the country with the largest *mestizo* population in Latin America. Here, government efforts to make the cultural/racial mixing that resulted from the conquest the basis of a new national culture (see page 134) have enjoyed some success. Many Mexicans now take a certain pride in their mixed ancestry. *'¡Hijos de la chingada!'* – 'Children of the rape!' – they chorus during *el grito* (the shout), the ceremony that commemorates the birth of the movement for Mexican independence in 1816.

For many women, death, suicide, miscarriage or self-multilation seemed a

93

better option than the hell the Europeans preached about and then visited on them during the early years of the conquest. Diego de Landa records the story of a young married Maya called Bacalan who, after being captured by the Spaniards, took her own life rather than be defiled. According to Diego de Landa, she was 'thrown to the dogs', her incidental disposal inspiring the dedication of Bulgarian literary critic Tzvetan Todorov's book *The Conquest of America* (New York: Harper & Row, 1984) to 'the memory of a Maya woman devoured by dogs'.

As the conquest intensified, so did the apparent starkness of the choice facing indigenous people: compliance leading to servitude and loss of cultural identity, 'a living death' in one indigenous leader's words, or resistance leading to probable physical death. Outright resistance took many forms:

- The public, symbolic protest of leaders like Ajuricaba, the leader of the Manu nation who leapt, chained, into the river Pará in 1728 rather than face imprisonment and probable death.
- Political uprisings such as those of Tupaq Amaru in Peru who declared himself Inka in 1780 with the Quechua words, '*Mañanam kunanmanta wakchakayniykiwan wiraqocha mikhunqañachu!*' – 'From this day on, the Spaniard shall no longer feast on your poverty!'
- Intellectual protest by writers such as Felipe Guaman Poma, who toured the Andes to complete a 1,200-page treatise on conditions for the Spanish monarch, Phillip III.
- The cultural resistance of men like Sequoyah, a Cherokee often known by his English name George Guess, who in the 1820s devised a Cherokee alphabet of 86 characters which was quickly adopted for newspapers, books and letters.

But the most effective resistance was the everyday struggle of ordinary people to keep the conquerors and their works at bay. From the Arctic to the Antarctic, indigenous people have made use of what have been termed 'the weapons of the weak', the title of a major study by James Scott, Eugene Meyer Professor of Political Science at Yale University (listed in the bibliography to Chapter 1). Such 'weapons' include dissimulation, feigned ignorance, artificial compliance, manipulation, flight, theft, acquiescence and the occasional act of violence, including murder, passed off as a common crime.

But whatever the mixture, a key element in this strategy has been a conspiracy of silence, one reason outsiders know so little about it. This was a strategy for cultural survival, a guerrilla war by other means waged by most indigenous people for years after their supposed conquest. Direct confrontation cost lives, sometimes the lives of whole nations; this more subtle and amorphous resistance, perfectly matched to local needs and conditions, did not. It was and is fought on every front – economic, social, political – as indigenous cultural defiance insistently probing the weaknesses of different states at different times.

The strategy went back to the earliest days, a philosophy first publicly expounded in 1534 by Manku Inka Yupanki, the half-brother of Inka Atawallpa. According to his son Titu Kusi Yupanki, shortly after he retreated into the Vilcabamba mountains after launching a fightback, he told his followers:

> Give the outward appearance of complying with their demands. Give them a little tribute, whatever you can spare because if you don't give it to them they will take it from you by force ... I know that some day, by force or deceit, they will make you worship what they worship, and when that happens, when you can resist no longer, do it in front of them, but do not forget our ceremonies ... reveal just what you have to and keep the rest hidden. (Titu Kusi Yupanki, *Relación de la conquista del Peru*. Lima: Biblioteca Universitaria, 1973)

Revealing only what they have to and keeping the rest hidden, making the necessary compromises and minimal adaptations, feigning conversion or change, adapting European know-how or technology to their own ends – these have been the hallmarks of indigenous resistance ever since.

Resistance on the Reservations

The main arena for such resistance has been the indigenous community or reservation. Although often centres of poverty and all the other social problems associated with forced relocation, such communities, originally a symbol of abuse and control, have been subverted to become at least potential centres of ethnic pride and culture.

Today, the boundaries of an indigenous village or the lines on a map which designate a reservation or ethnic territory are the most obvious physical evidence of the cultural separateness of 'first nations'. In these cultural concentrations indigenous people could 'go back to the blanket', the North American white man's phrase for returning to tribal dress and manners.

The whole process began in the second half of the sixteenth century in Spanish America, after the War of Independence against Britain at the end of the eighteenth century in the United States, and in Brazil from 1850 onwards, when an independent government took the first tentative steps towards recognizing indigenous land. It took a variety of different forms: the creation of *congregaciones* in Mexico and Guatemala, *reducciones* in Peru, *resguardos* (reserves) in Colombia. Reservations followed in North America, often after treaty agreements or relocations. Indigenous territories in Amazonia and other forest regions continue to be demarcated to this day.

In Latin America, the move towards special territories took place during a period when the Spanish Crown began to assert itself over the hitherto somewhat autonomous settlers. By 1550, population collapse was seriously threatening the viability of the Spanish Indies. If the Crown's primary aim was the more efficient extraction of tribute and labour it was worth trying to protect what remained of the indigenous population so that it could be exploited more effectively.

The 'Republic of the Indians' which the Spanish Crown set up lent indigenous people important weapons for their resistance, most notably limited autonomy in the form of their own laws and political institutions. They were hybrid structures with the traditional Hispanic administration of a *cabecera* (head town) over *subjetos* (villages) overlain by indigenous *cabildos* (councils) in which tribal elders wielded traditional authority.

In the lowlands the Catholic Church was the most active agency, establishing similar structures but based on religion. As a result equally hybrid religious forms emerged, as ritual dances, pageants and traditional worship were incorporated, overlain by Christian practice. Traditional gods took on the form of individual saints, not least because the Catholic Church was usually built on a site of pre-conquest worship. The Hispanic *cofradías* (religious brotherhoods), imposed by the missionaries, became important social hierarchies which reinforced community life.

Throughout the Americas, such subversion has transformed what were imposed, colonial structures and their legacies, into mechanisms for survival. In the sixteenth century, Spaniards and *mestizos* were forbidden to live in indigenous communities; today they remain few or non-existent and are unwelcome.

In the seventeenth century, indigenous communities were allowed to use the special courts, *juzgados de indios*, to bring cases and to petition the Spanish Crown in defence of their interests. Today the special courts have gone but the tradition of lobbying governments and even taking legal action is still very much alive. Sometimes, as in contemporary Colombia, this involves reasserting rights which go back to the time of the Spanish Crown.

Indigenous towns or villages have been described as 'closed, corporate communities', but, as historian Jim Handy has pointed out, they are more like sealed cultural containers with self-regulating valves that can open or close to admit or expel the outside world as required. Their ability to incorporate alien influences and adapt them to their own purposes has been remarkable. Adapt, evolve and survive became the watchwords of indigenous resistance.

Historically, the *cofradías* have served to cement collective identity; today it may be the radio which performs the same task, a Western import which now brings news, literacy classes and traditional medical tips in indigenous languages. Its mechanisms vary, but the manner of the 'indigenization' of outside influences does not. Even enforced militarization, apparently so culturally intrusive, can be 'indigenized'.

Throughout the Americas the interaction between European and indigenous society intensified as the numbers of settlers increased during the first two centuries of colonial rule. Trade, labour, land encroachment and the need to pay tribute meant that indigenous people were inexorably sucked into the money economy and the invaders' society. Indigenous people moved to the Europeanized cities for work (Plate 36); creoles and *mestizos* settled, often illegally, in indigenous communities. As the interaction speeded up, the definition of an indigenous person changed. Initially it had been based on race; now it came to be based on culture, because many who were racially indigenous now became culturally *mestizos* or *ladinos*, de-ethnicized Indians.

The phenomenon of Europeanization has always been seen through Western eyes in terms of externals: the tendency of indigenous people to abandon their dress, language and most visible customs. In fact, this process is a two-way street, with indigenization, the impact of indigenous culture and values on peoples and governments in the Americas, as valid a phenomenon as

36. *Mexico: Us and Them. Indigenous woman sells produce on the street outside a* mestizo-*owned shop.*
© JULIO ETCHART/REPORTAGE

Westernization. The process which evolved was syncretism, a growing together of new beliefs and old, and should be seen as an important expression of indigenous resistance. Syncretism was the main way of introducing the values of the 'conquered' world into that of the 'conquerors'. It also reflects a sort of status quo which has ensued since shortly after the conquest, allowing Europeans to believe they have 'civilized' the indigenous population and the indigenous population to believe they have preserved their culture.

Disease, forced labour, institutionalized racism, conversion and militarization – by the end of the eighteenth century indigenous peoples in the Americas had survived the very worst that three hundred years of colonial rule could throw at them. Although weakened, Indian societies had survived, encoding their values and vision within those of their conquerors. Survival, however subtle and subterranean, was all. It would ensure that future generations could combat future repression with new, more potent forms of resistance.

Bibliography

The Americas: Human Rights Violations against Indigenous Peoples (London: Amnesty International, 1992).

Berkey, Curtis, G., 'International law and domestic courts: enhancing self-determination for indigenous peoples'. *Harvard Human Rights Journal* 5 (Spring 1992).

Brading, D. A., *The First America* (Cambridge: Cambridge University Press, 1991).

De las Casas, Bartolomé, *A Short Account of the Destruction of the Indies* (London: Penguin Books, 1992).

Indian Rights, Human Rights: Handbook for Indians on International Human Rights Complaint Procedures (Washington, DC: Indian Law Resource Center, 1988).

Morales, Patricia (ed.), *Indigenous Peoples, Human Rights and Global Interdependence* (Tilburg: International Centre for Human and Public Affairs, 1994).

Plenty-Coups (Crow), *Plenty-Coups, Chief of the Crows*. Edited by Frank Bird Linderman (Lincoln, NE: University of Nebraska Press, 1962).

The Rights of Indigenous Peoples, Fact Sheet no. 9 (Geneva: United Nations, 1992).

Stannard, David E., *American Holocaust: Columbus and the Conquest of the New World* (Oxford: Oxford University Press, 1992).

Stavenhagen, Rodolfo, *Derecho indígena y derechos humanos en América Latina* (Mexico, DF: Instituto Interamericano de Derechos Humanos y El Colegio de México, 1988).

Stern, Steve (ed.), *Resistance, Rebellion and Consciousness in the Andean World* (Madison: University of Wisconsin Press, 1987).

Wilson, Richard, *Maya Resurgence in Guatemala* (Norman: University of Oklahoma Press, 1995).

Wright, Ronald, *Stolen Continents: The Indian Story* (London: Pimlico Books, 1992).

4
Land and Environment

Some forty Quechua lean forward on their rough-hewn wooden stools. The classroom they fill smells of the potatoes and maize they grow and the sweat and earth with which they do it. They glare at the blackboard from under their brightly-coloured *chollos* (caps), some with the names of their villages knitted into the foreheads, the tassels on their long earflaps swinging as they strain to read the text. Lawyer Fernando Monge reads aloud as his black marker pen squeaks across the sheets of rough brown paper hanging over the blackboard:

> Title ten and eleven of the Peruvian constitution, 'Use of Communal Land', Article 46. 'Communal lands are the property of the community. They are inalienable, imprescriptible and unmortgageable in accordance with the constitution and its laws.' Article 47. This defines community residents' rights to use of the land and forbids its division into parcels. 'The legal definition of a community under Peru's agrarian reform law is a group of people living in a determined area with a common set of customs . . .'

Fernando Monge works on land issues with the Bartolomé de las Casas Centre in Qosqo, the ancient capital of the Inka empire. The audience are the 38 presidents of peasant communities (*comunidades campesinas*) which compose a nearby district. As the class breaks up for the day, Monge shouts over the growing Quechua hubbub: 'If anyone's got land titles they want me to look at, I'll be here at 7 a.m. tomorrow morning.'

Fernando Monge's class was being held against the backdrop of a constitutional referendum that threatened to eliminate indigenous communal land rights in Peru. Such rights, dating back to the Spanish Crown's 'Indian Republic' laws and, post-1968, the agrarian reform of the radical military government of General Juan Velasco Alvarado, have come under threat throughout the Americas in recent years. Mexico ended them in 1991–2 by amending Article 27 of the constitution drawn up at the end of the Mexican Revolution in 1917. The changes formally ended land redistribution, abolished the right to ancestral claims and allowed the sale of all land. 'There is only one logical consequence, a return to large *haciendas* and slavery', claims Margarito Ruiz, a Tojolab'al Maya who co-ordinates the Independent Indigenous Peoples' Front (FIPI) in Mexico.

Neo-liberal economics, fuelled by the debt crisis, has driven the 'modernization' of agriculture, in essence an acceleration of a post-war surge in mechanization and cash crop development. New technology, fertilizers and population pressure have made once-marginal lands, usually indigenous land, viable for such 'development'. Unprecedented population growth has made such land more attractive. Indigenous smallholders, desperate to extract more from an ever-shrinking land base, are increasingly growing cash crops, sometimes under contract to large agribusiness multinationals, abandoning the subsistence agriculture that has been their cultural umbilical chord.

The importance of land to the region's indigenous peoples, summarized in Chapter 1, cannot be over-emphasized. Most define themselves by where they live, be it village, forest, plain or tundra. It determines indigenous peoples' lifestyle and survival – feeding, nourishing, healing and sheltering by means of the animals, vegetation and foodstuffs it yields. If indigenous culture and identity have any such thing as a common root it is the land. 'Take our land and you destroy the opportunity for us to be real people,' explains Milton Born with a Tooth, a Peigan activist from Canada. Many indigenous people find it impossible to define themselves either individually or collectively away from their land – and not just any land, but each individual nation's particular land.

Many feel a deep spiritual obligation to die and be buried on their land, to hand over stewardship to their children. Being forced off their land is not just the beginning of a material, cultural demise, but is also the cause of a sort of spiritual destitution that many indigenous people describe as a fatal sickness. 'If we had to move, this would be like the sadness of death to us all,' complained the Akawaio of Guyana to their government in the face of a proposed dam project in 1977. To many indigenous peoples, the land possesses man rather than the reverse. 'Wars are fought to see who owns the land but in the end it possesses man. Who dares say he owns it – is he not buried beneath it?', asks Nino Cochise, a Chiricahua Apache.

Securing enough land to ensure survival, and the legal right to resources contained within that land, is the sole issue that connects peoples as diverse as the Inuit of the Arctic and the Tucano of the Amazon forest. Whether you are a hunter in the frozen North, a hunter-gatherer in the tropical forest of the equator or a subsistence farmer at 10,000 feet in the Andes, you need enough land to support your family and kinship group.

In forest, mountain, grassland or desert, land is life in a such a fundamental way for indigenous peoples that it is almost impossible for others to fathom. Securing it, having access to it, seeding it, harvesting it is a matter of life and death. 'Without the land and animals our spirits will die,' says Norma Kassi, a

Gwich'in from the Yukon, echoing sentiments expressed by indigenous peoples throughout the Americas.

Today the lack of a viable land base, the result of five centuries of theft, massacre and expulsion, is the single most important reason for the poverty and marginalization of indigenous communities. It has forced hundreds of thousands of indigenous people to migrate to the continents' cities. It is the most important cause of indigenous resistance to governments, be it grassroots organization, mass protest, international lobbying or even armed resistance. It is the most important factor in the changing perception and cultural evolution of indigenous peoples in the Americas today.

The centrality of land gives it a mystical importance (Plates 37 and 38). Its mountains, rivers, caves and forests are for many indigenous peoples the home of the spirit world that gives sense and meaning to their universe. Most indigenous Creation stories tell of emergence from the earth, the proverbial clay of Adam, or some substance derived from the land, such as wood, bark or maize flour.

Ancestors, buried in the earth, give new life to the generations that follow, through the earth. This is what one indigenous chief meant by being 'reborn to belong' and another by 'bodies being formed by the dust of our forefathers' bones'. The spiritual significance of land is reflected throughout indigenous language and expression.

Land is often linked to heart, soul and breath, the essence of being. Such expression often carries a striking resonance in the light of scientific environmental knowledge. Consider this from Kayapó leader, Paulinho Paiakan: 'We are fighting to defend the forest because the forest is what makes us and what makes our hearts beat. Without the forest we won't be able to breathe and our hearts will stop and we will die.'

Conquest and Colonization: 'We Cannot Sell'

The threat of further loss of their community lands is nothing new for the Quechua presidents attending their class in Qosqo. Literally and figuratively, land has been the main battleground ever since the first Europeans arrived. The conquest was rooted in colonization and occupation of territory, even though initially at least the Spanish and Portuguese conquistadores of South and Central America came to loot, while their English and French counterparts in the North came to settle.

Indigenous people have lost land at every stage of post-conquest history by every possible means, whether legal, pseudo-legal or illegal. They have been the victims of war, invasion, eviction, relocation, treaty violations (particularly in North America) and purchase, whether compulsory or private. They have also

37. *Peru: sowing maize in the Andes, seventeenth century.*

Illustrations by Felipe Guaman Poma, c. 1620, from his 1,200-page treatise on the Andes entitled The First New Chronicle and Good Government, *addressed to Philip III of Spain.*

COURTESY OF TONY MORRISON/SOUTH AMERICAN PICTURES

resisted by every means possible, including armed struggle, occupying claimed territory, vociferous lobbying for land rights, alliances with non-indigenous peoples, economic diversification and flight or relocation to other regions or countries.

In the wake of the conquest of Latin America, land grants were made in units of *peonías* (about 100 acres) and *caballerías* (about 500 acres) in Latin America. The most trusted conquistadores also received *encomiendas*, a title which fixed a set amount of indigenous tribute and labour due to them, the latter modelled on the *mit[']a* labour tribute of the Inka state. Initially, indigenous slavery was common in the extraction of gold and the development of sugar plantations in Brazil and elsewhere. However, from 1538 onwards, as the indigenous population declined sharply, imported African slaves began to take their place.

Labour shortages in mines and plantations in the latter half of the sixteenth century produced the first of the continents' endless resettlement programmes. *Congregaciones civiles*, towns and villages on the Hispanic gridiron pattern, were created. Into these, scattered populations living in tiny villages throughout Mexico, Peru, Colombia and Guatemala were concentrated. Each family was given a plot of land, and the community as a whole acquired the title to common lands for pasture, subsistence and commercial cultivation, the proceeds of which were spent on communal projects. Under the provisions of the 'Indian Republic' (the separate laws and land tenure system applying to indigenous communities), smallholding subsistence agriculture existed side by side with the emerging capitalist cultivation of the colonists. The latter took two forms.

The plantations grew mostly sugar at first, but later other commodity crops for export, using slave labour in northeastern Brazil, the Caribbean, coastal Peru and Colombia. The haciendas produced food and meat for the domestic market in areas of greatest indigenous population: Peru, Ecuador, Bolivia and Mexico. It was medieval Spain transplanted to the New World; the indigenous workforce renting small patches of land on which to grow food and living in the self-contained world of what were often vast estates.

The cheek-by-jowl co-existence of these types of landholding, the *latifundia* of the *haciendas* and plantations and the *minifundia* of indigenous smallholders, set in train processes whose ongoing consequences can still be seen today. The first was the ever-growing concentration of land. Plantations became bigger and bigger. Economies of scale, environmental degradation and expanding overseas markets were the impetus, but a ready supply of slaves and a contracting indigenous population vacating the land made it all possible.

The second process was the tendency of many landholders to under-use land or even leave their estates fallow. Hacienda owners, aping aristocrats at home, saw land ownership as a symbol of power and wealth as much as a means of

103

actual profit. As the size of the indigenous population began to grow again in the eighteenth and nineteenth centuries, land-hungry peasants were confronted by growing expanses of empty, fallow land, land which their ancestors had once farmed.

Land epitomized the cultural abyss separating the two societies now confronting each other. Enclosing, owning and selling land, the concept of private property, was a largely alien concept to all the indigenous peoples of the Americas. They had a sense of territory, but it was seen as communal and inalienable; land to them was on a renewable lease from a higher authority. 'We cannot sell the lives of men and animals; therefore we cannot sell this land. It was put here for us by the Great Spirit and we cannot sell it because it does not belong to us,' replied a Blackfoot chief on being asked for his signature on one of the first US land treaties. 'The land was never divided for it belongs to all for the use of each. It belongs to the first who sits down on his blanket or skins ... and until he leaves, no other has a right,' observed Tecumseh (Cougar Crouching for His Prey), the celebrated Shawnee chief, during land negotiations in 1810.

It was the absence of 'a fence around it', as one indigenous leader put it, that allowed Europeans to claim that the Americas were legally *terra nullus* or *vacuum domicilium*, an empty land, unclaimed and unsubdued. The claim was the greatest of all the myths of conquest: that indigenous people, farming, hunting and harvesting the land, did not really occupy the land, did not really exist, a myth that survives to this day.

Even when their existence was accepted, indigenous people were accused of under-using the land by practising their sustainable forms of slash-and-burn agriculture (Plate 39). International capitalism grew to abhor the concept of growing or extracting for need, not profit. This remains the basis of today's accusations that indigenous agriculture is 'primitive', 'inefficient' and 'unproductive'.

Nothing could be further from the truth. The accusation, often levelled by politicians or landholders who own thousands of acres of frequently fallow land, illustrates the ability of white capitalist landowners to project their own failings on to subsistence indigenous farmers. Study after study in the Americas has shown that the smaller your landholding, the more efficient you have to be, the more sustainable your methods have to be, the more essential your product has to be. 'No one here can afford to waste an inch of land, an ear of corn, or a drop of water,' one Mixtec farmer in Oaxaca, Mexico, explains.

Indigenous agriculture is generally efficient, environmentally sustainable and highly productive. When Ecuador's indigenous people decided to press their land claims by blocking roads in May 1990, the country's cities went hungry within days, graphically demonstrating that where they predominate in the Americas, indigenous farmers produce most of the food.

104

Guatemala: at the market, Joyabaj, Quiché
© PAUL SMITH

Guatemala: indigenous women on their way to the town fiesta,
celebrated under the eyes of the army
© PAUL SMITH

Brazil: Kayapó Indians, who have been at the forefront of resistance to the building of giant dams on indigenous lands
© STEVE COX/SURVIVAL INTERNATIONAL

Brazil: Kayapó Indians
© STEVE COX/SURVIVAL INTERNATIONAL

*Peru: Inti-Raymi, a traditional Inka sun festival,
at the ruins of the Inka fortress, Sacsaywamán, overlooking Qosqo*
© BERNARD REGENT/HUTCHISON

Mexico: Tarahumara woman and child
© JOHN RUNNING/SURVIVAL INTERNATIONAL

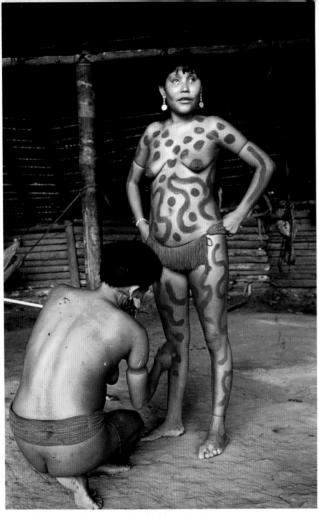

Brazil: Yanomami body painting, the Amazon
© VICTOR ENGELBERT 1980/SURVIVAL INTERNATIONAL

Ecuador: traditional midwife
© PAUL SMITH

Canada: teepee at suns
© LANGELLE/NFN/SURVIVAL
INTERNATIONAL

USA: child in a Miccosukee school. Bilingual education has played an important role in revitalizing indigenous culture

© JACQUIE SPECTOR/SURVIVAL INTERNATIONAL

UK: Paulinho Paiakan outside the Houses of Parliament, London. Indigenous leaders have become effective international lobbyists in recent years

© LUKE HOLLAND

Colombia: Páez women weaving. Traditional crafts provide an important source of income to many families

© PAUL SMITH

Colombia: Arhuaco farmers preparing the ground for planting
© YEZID CAMPOS/SURVIVAL INTERNATIONAL

French Guiana: Wayana schoolchildren playing football
© TONY MORRISON/SOUTH AMERICAN PICTURES

Panama: Kuna woman in traditional dress. The Kuna have successfully turned their
extraordinary textiles into a source of income from tourists

McIndian: Canadian indigenous child combines
traditional and modern ways at a cultural event
© SURVIVAL INTERNATIONAL

39. *Peru: working potato fields with simple hoes and digging-sticks. Contrary to prevailing stereotypes, indigenous agriculture is generally sustainable and highly productive.*
© H R DÖRIG/HUTCHISON

Amazon to Arctic: Dispossession, Dislocation, Deculturation

Beyond the clash between subsistence and capitalist agriculture lies an even more basic conflict of perception about the natural environment. Europeans, thousands of miles away from home and isolated in what many considered a hostile environment, came to conquer the natural world – the wilderness, dark forest, Wild West as it variously became known – as much as the indigenous people who populated it.

Indigenous people, who knew from experience that their survival in often precarious, delicately-balanced environments depended on harmonizing with the land, saw themselves as an integral part of it. These links led them to ascribe spiritual, mystical powers to the earth. Luther Standing Bear, a Lakota Sioux chief born in 1868, has perhaps best put this philosophy into words:

> The soil is soothing, strengthening, cleansing and healing. That is why the old Indian still sits upon the earth instead of propping himself up and away from its life-giving forces. The old Lakota was wise. He knew that away from nature man's heart becomes hard; he knew that lack of respect for growing, living things soon led to lack of respect for humans too. (Luther Standing Bear, *Land of the Spotted Eagle*, 1933)

105

Return of the Indian

The money economy and certainly the international capitalist agriculture that evolved from the sixteenth century onwards was alien to most indigenous people. Buying and selling land, land which contained the bones and spirits of their ancestors, was to many the literal equivalent of selling their grandmothers.

In North America colonization, although different, had just the same impact: dispossession. Initially, indigenous groups such as the Powhatan had kept the first European colonists, many themselves dispossessed back in England, alive with gifts of corn and game. But in the first settlements in Virginia and New England this attitude soon changed as the colonists' insatiable appetite for land and their refusal to recognize indigenous hunting territories became a major source of friction.

As the French moved down from their Canadian trading stations in the North and the Spanish moved up through what is today Florida and the southwest of the United States, the land squeeze intensified (Plate 40). Competition led to wars among the European powers but the victims were invariably the continents' indigenous people. Alternately courted as allies, then (usually) betrayed before being mercilessly repressed, European wars set Indian against Indian as shifting allegiances were forged with different colonizing powers.

As in the South, the sheer numbers of colonists, the impact of disease and the

40. *USA: Seminole settlement sandwiched between citrus groves and agricultural land in Florida's Everglades.*
© BRIAN MOSER/HUTCHISON

effectiveness of the white man's weapons took their toll in North America, but so did trade and the consequent absorption into a barter or money economy. Nowhere was this more evident than in Canada and the northern United States, where the soaring demand for fur, particularly beaver pelts, encouraged a system of barter for the settlers' iron traps, firearms and alcohol. It was a model of mercantile exploitation which created dependence and cultural change.

The large migratory bands needed to catch large game for food were replaced by smaller groups or individuals hunting smaller game for fur to trade. Demand led to over-hunting, pushing the Algonquians and Iroquoians farther inland where they clashed with others who in turn soon needed the white man's guns to defend themselves. Indigenous people began to subdue each other; the settlers did not even have to leave their trading posts in Canada to have the same impact as the 'Indian wars' farther south.

Trade or, more frequently, direct economic exploitation, land seizures and the resettlement that such processes involved had a predictable effect: dispossession, dislocation and deculturation. Anyone who doubts that such processes continue today need only consider those peoples of the Amazon basin or the Arctic North who have felt the full impact of the continuing conquest in the last generation. Two testimonies express their outrage:

> In a few short years we have been completely robbed of our land and freedom. To keep us in one place the Canadian government have tried to separate us from everything that gives our life as a people meaning. It has meant that we have been changed in only a few years from one of the most self-reliant and independent peoples in the world to one of the most dependent. You need not ask me if I feel betrayed.
>
> (Rose Gregoire, Innu woman, Canada, 1989)

> Look! I don't like this here. This is where I lived, it was beautiful then ... there was a good forest, good land. Now the land is destroyed. Now they've consumed the trees! What I am showing you is awful ... we lived here without bothering anyone and you destroyed it. We need land where there are no white people.
>
> (Aka, Panara elder and leader, Brazil, 1991)

The Innu of Labrador, Newfoundland and northern Quebec in Canada, a nomadic hunting people, were subject to several government relocation schemes from the 1950s onwards. The social collapse that followed was spectacular. Between 1973 and 1992 there were 47 alcohol-related deaths among the Mushuau Innu settled at Utshimassits (Davis Inlet) alone. In two and a half years from July 1991, there were 203 attempted suicides among a population numbering less than 500.

In 1993, film of Innu children barricaded inside an unheated shack in temperatures of 40 degrees Celsius below zero, sniffing gasoline and screaming that they wanted to die, created an international scandal. In August 1993 the Canadian Commission on Human Rights issued an unequivocal report concluding that 'It is clear that the Mushuau Innu are the victims of ethnocide or cultural genocide.' The report blamed the Canadian and Newfoundland governments.

By the time the Panara were relocated to the Xingu National Park from their native Peixoto forest in 1975 they were already on the verge of extinction. Between 1976 and 1991 their numbers rose from 67 to 130 but their future remains precarious. White farmers and gold prospectors are encroaching on to their land even within the Xingu.

When a delegation led by Aka made a return visit to the Peixoto, their pain and anger was obvious. The road that had reduced their numbers in the first place ran like a sword through their forest, bringing in 80,000 gold prospectors to a newly-established town. Virtually all the trees had been cut down for miles on either side of the road while much of the earth resembled a white moonscape – the craters and bleaching effect of mercury testimony to the lust for gold that had driven the continents' first settlers.

Independence and the Nation-State: A New Offensive

If things were bad in the first three hundred years of settlement in the Americas, they took a turn for the worse during the nineteenth century. Independence for the United States in 1776, and for the Spanish and Portuguese colonies in the 1820s, swept aside the limited protection which surviving indigenous peoples had enjoyed from some relatively enlightened European monarchs in the seventeenth and eighteenth centuries. Nationhood brought a new preoccupation with integration, incorporation and the integrity of borders. The word 'nation', which had previously applied to indigenous people, was now gradually expropriated by the 'patriots', the European settlers or *mestizos* who had fought for independence. During the nineteenth century much of the continents' remaining indigenous land was usurped along with its occupiers' identity.

The struggle to define borders in the new fragmented continent pushed the conquest deeper into the jungles and mountains of the most marginal indigenous areas. Massive emigration from Europe heightened the pressure on land as the indigenous population continued to recover from its post-conquest low. These developments spurred political and economic changes.

The European or Creole élites in the Americas had fought for independence in order to seize power for themselves and to gain direct access to international trade by breaking the monopoly of their respective colonial powers. The new

108

rulers set about both with a vengeance, the victims being the ruled, largely Indian, peoples, who yielded the land and labour which in turn provided the new cash crops for export, in particular grain, sugar and coffee.

The most dramatic change was the wholesale conversion of community land into private property to be divided up among individuals. In many areas, this extension of the European concept of private property was the most significant cultural onslaught since the first years of the conquest. Individual indigenous land-holdings could now be bought, and in many cases were, as a result of debt, migration or sheer ignorance of the workings of a market economy. More frequently however, indigenous land was occupied or expropriated, as *haciendas* and plantations evolved into fully capitalist agro-export businesses. Legislation, often couched in terms of agrarian reform, declared millions of acres farmed by subsistence agriculture empty on the basis of 'under-utilization'. Those who resisted now found themselves appealing directly to their oppressors, rather than to the Crown.

Even those who had land titles were disregarded; in some courts in Latin America it became common practice to demand titles as evidence simply in order to tear them up. In some areas resistance was fierce. In Colombia, where communal land ownership was formally abolished in 1850, indigenous groups achieved some measure of protection for the *resguardos*, the Indian reserves created by the Spanish. In many countries, however, this took nearly a century. Legal and constitutional changes once again recognizing the legality of the Indian community were not reintroduced until 1920 in Peru, 1937 in Ecuador and 1938 in Bolivia.

There was another side to this 'agricultural modernization'. The crops that replaced the staple maize and potatoes indigenous people had always grown varied, but they were all labour-intensive and destined for export. Dispossession by whatever means not only released swathes of land for cash crop production, but also created the landless or semi-landless rural workforce that was essential to produce them. Indigenous people became prisoners on their own land – prisoners with a life sentence of hard labour (Plate 41).

The whole process gathered even more pace in the latter half of the nineteenth century, as a whole series of 'Indian wars' were waged against the *indios bárbaros*, the nomadic or unpacified ethnic groups who had until then existed relatively undisturbed on the margins of the new states. Northern Mexico and what is now the southwestern United States, the land of Apaches, Comanches and Navahos, were settled by creoles and *mestizos* in military colonies.

Armies from Argentina and Chile were sent into the pampas and Patagonia to secure the 'frontiers' of land still occupied by groups like the Mapuche. In the new states of Peru, Brazil, Colombia, Ecuador, Venezuela and the Central American republics, so-called liberal governments redoubled their efforts to push back or settle 'barbarians' in *congregaciones* in the name of civilization. This duly arrived

41. *Amazon: Indian rubber collectors with overseer, c. 1900. Thousands of Indians were made to work in conditions of near-slavery during the rubber boom.*
© KIMBALL MORRISON/SOUTH AMERICAN PICTURES

in the form of ranchers, immigrants and what Mahpiua Luta (Red Cloud), the Oglala Sioux chief, referred to as 'the dangerous snake': the railroad.

None of this went unresisted. In 1847, a Maya rebellion against a small white élite of *henequen* plantation owners in Yucatán was just one of several revolts that rocked Mexico in the nineteenth century. But the war of the castes, as it became known, led by Cecilio Chi and Jacinto Pat, went further than most, producing something close to an independent Maya state. It was to last fifty years and pave the way for the continents' largest armed uprising, the Mexican Revolution, a struggle for land which claimed the lives of a million peasants between 1910 and 1917.

Land lay at the centre of the caste war in Yucatán. The Maya were particularly outraged when whites burned their maize fields. Burning maize, referred to as 'the Grace of God' and the raw material from which the first men were moulded, was tantamount to blasphemy. But in the summer of 1848, when the Maya army had taken the whole Yucatán peninsula and had the whites at their

110

mercy in the two largest towns, Mérida and Campeche, the advance suddenly faltered. Years later, Leandro Poot, a son of one of the commanders, explained that during the preparations for the attack on Mérida, swarms of *sh'matanheeles*, the winged ants which presage rain, had appeared on the horizon. 'When my father's people saw this they said to themselves: "Ehen! The time has come for us to plant, if we do not we shall have no Grace of God to fill the bellies of our children."' Despite opposition from their chiefs, Poot said, his father's men refused to stay, and 'in the morning each man rolled up his blanket ... tightened the thongs of his sandals and started for home and his cornfield'. Six generations later in the 1980s, history repeated itself when, as part of a counter-insurgency campaign against several guerrilla groups, the Guatemalan army burned Maya Indians' maize as a means of waging a cultural war. Meanwhile, the mainly *ladino* guerrilla leaders complained about Maya recruits deserting their ranks as soon as the planting season arrived.

Treaties and Treachery: Legalized Theft

Battles often ended in treaties, and indigenous peoples in the Americas signed away far more land on paper than they ever lost shedding blood on the battlefield. In the United States alone, 374 treaties were signed in the 90 years up to 1868. In many cases these treaties lie at the heart of indigenous peoples' current campaigns.

The legal basis for treaties between indigenous peoples and settlers was established in the sixteenth century by a Spanish court, reflecting the colonial governments' desire to have some pseudo-legal claim to the 'discovered' territories. Initially treaties formalized trading relationships, recruited Indian army auxiliaries or guaranteed passage through Indian land, but after independence they became little more than bills of sale.

The concept of written agreements over land was completely alien to indigenous peoples in the Americas. As a result, misrepresentation, duplicity and corruption riddled the process. As Mahpiua Luta (Red Cloud) recalled, 'In 1868 men came out and brought papers. We could not read them and they did not tell us truly what was in them ... When I reached Washington the Great Father [President] explained to me what the treaty was and showed me that the interpreters had deceived me.' That experience was almost universal. Even if they were aware of what they were signing, Indian leaders found the provisions of such treaties ignored. As Tatanka Yotanka (Sitting Bull) asked in 1885, 'What treaty that the whites have kept has the Red Man broken? Not one. What treaty that the white man ever made with us have they kept? Not one.'

In March 1871, Congress halted the process of making treaties with indige-

111

nous groups on the grounds that 'none of them have organized governments'. As the Indian Appropriation Act of the same year explained, 'No Indian nation or tribe within the territory of the United States shall be acknowledged and recognized as an independent nation, tribe or power with whom the United States may contract by treaty.' The law now considered indigenous peoples wards of the government, rejecting any suggestion that they were sovereign nations. In Canada, where seven treaties were signed between 1871 and 1877 to give the government all the southern part of the prairie provinces, the Indian Act of 1880 amounted to the same thing.

Weakening, ignoring or abrogating the legal import of the treaties, with their acknowledgement of sovereignty, collective rights and 'in perpetuity' clauses, has been the purpose of both North American governments ever since. 'Agreements' and a raft of legislation have followed, much of which has legalized the seizure of indigenous land that would be totally illegal were it to happen to non-Indians.

The 'plenary powers doctrine' of 1899, the principle that applies to powers unrestricted by the Bill of Rights, has been used to argue that the US Congress has, effectively, unlimited powers over Indian peoples. A second legal principle, derived from the 1955 case of the Tee-hit-ton Indians of Alaska, states that the US government may encroach on Indian lands in the absence of a treaty.

In the same year, the US Supreme Court extended this principle to land protected by treaty but already encroached on by a federal agency. The case, which orginally referred to the Department of the Interior's encroachment on Western Shoshone land in Nevada, set a precedent for financial compensation of the value at the time of seizure, but no right to regain land, however blatant the expropriation.

Since then, indigenous people have hit back as the outrage over the treaties and the legal ploys have become central to their campaigning. They have pursued cases through the courts as well as in international fora determined to show, in the words of Harold Cardinal, a Canadian Cree, that 'for us the treaties represent a Magna Carta'.

Rather than accept pennies per acre, an increasing number of indigenous groups have refused to accept the retroactive market values for their land awarded by the US Indian Claims Commission. The Western Shoshone have refused to accept US$26 million for the loss of their land, while the Lakota Sioux have rejected US$105 million in compensation for the loss of the Black Hills of South Dakota, claiming that just one of the mines that now litter their sacred site has yielded US$250 billion in gold since 1876.

While the fight to right past wrongs continues, the wrongs themselves continue by different means. In 1971 the US Congress passed the Alaska Native Claims Settlement Act (ANCSA), 'settling' indigenous claims to Alaska in

112

42. *USA 1881: a reception for Indian leaders in the White House at the height of white settler expansion onto Indian lands.*
COURTESY OF THE MARY EVANS PICTURE LIBRARY

exchange for recognition of the rights of 86,000 Inuit, Indian and Aleuts to 44 million acres, about 11 per cent of the state, and US$1 billion. The key as ever was Alaska's wealth of oil, minerals, timber and seafood, the settlement amounting to 'an assimilationist effort to solve territorial rights issues by cutting indigenous people in on capitalist development', in one anthropologist's words.

It soon became clear it was a meagre cut. The land and money granted to the state's indigenous people were controlled by 13 regional corporations and more than 200 village corporations. These were not primarily concerned with indigenous people's economic benefit, according to most native Alaskans who complained about unresolved issues on stock-holding, taxation and land protection.

Oil spills such as that from the tanker *Exxon Valdez* illustrated just what price Alaska's indigenous people could pay for such development. However, vociferous lobbying forced potentially significant changes in ANCSA in 1991 when the original 20-year transitional period of the Act was completed. To date, the jury is still out; the threat of development on other people's terms remains, as does the legacy of years of damage.

In 1994 a comprehensive study by the Alaska Native Commission concluded that Alaska's entire native population was 'at risk of becoming permanently imprisoned in America's underclass ... at risk of leading lives, generation to generation, characterized by violence, alcohol abuse and cycles of personal and social destruction ... at risk of losing, irretrievably, cultural strengths ... at risk, inevitably, of losing the capacity to self-govern'. The report argued for a complete break with previous policy which has only created dependency. In the words of one indigenous Alaskan, Pete Schaeffer, 'I think it's clear to us that if we as native people are to be saved, we're going to have to do it ourselves.' The outstanding question remains, will they get the chance?

Removal and Relocation: The 'Trail of Tears'

Nowhere in the Americas was the process of expansion on to indigenous land more rapid and disastrous in the nineteenth century than in North America. An inexorable push westwards saw Kentucky, Tennessee, Ohio, Indiana, Mississippi, Illinois, Louisiana and Alabama added to the Union in the first 20 years of the century. Settlers poured into the lands of the Creeks, Choctaws, Cherokees and others.

Congress, even if it had wanted to, could no more restrain the frontiersmen, the 'Long Knives' as indigenous people knew them, than could the British. Tribes fragmented as some moved westwards, while others decided to stay and fight. One such was Tecumseh (Cougar Crouching for His Prey), a remarkable Shawnee leader who travelled from the Gulf of Mexico to the Great Lakes in an effort to unite indigenous peoples to resist the encroachment. A fiery orator, he was capable of stirring Indians to a frenzy:

> The way, the only way, to check and stop this evil, is for all Redmen to unite in claiming a common and equal right in the land, as it was at first and should yet be ... Where today is the Pequot? Where are the Narragansetts, the Mohawks, the Pokanoket and many other once-powerful tribes of our people? They have vanished before the avarice and the oppression of the White Man, as snow before a summer sun.

Tecumseh's grand coalition of peoples never materialized. He died in October 1813 as he had advocated living, in battle, fighting for the British in Canada against the US forces who had driven him out of his Ohio River valley home. As he lay dying he shed his British army jacket for an Indian buckskin, perhaps recalling his own words: 'The white people are like poisonous serpents; when chilled they are feeble and harmless, but invigorate them with warmth and they sting their benefactors to death.'

The nature of the United States and its leaders shifted along with its border. The passing of the patrician Europeans who had won independence was symbolized by the election of Andrew Jackson, 'Old Hickory', as President of the United States in 1828. A frontiersman and dedicated 'Indian fighter' ('Sharp Knife', as Indians nicknamed him), he stood for election on the platform that all tribes currently east of the Mississippi River should be moved west of it, by force if necessary. As most of the new states extended their jurisdiction over indigenous land within their boundaries, Congress kept Jackson's election promise, passing the 'Indian Removal Bill' in May 1830. The Act provided for the forcible removal to present-day Oklahoma (from the Choctaw meaning 'Red People') of five tribes. The barren land here was promised to them 'in perpetuity' just as the land they were now losing had been under previous treaties.

But John Ross, Principal Chief of the Cherokees of Georgia, chose to fight, taking his nation's case as far as the Supreme Court in Washington. In two separate rulings, Chief Justice Marshall vindicated the Cherokees, ruling that the government in Washington was the legal heir to the British government's Royal Proclamation of 1763. The Proclamation had recognized that Indian nations were sovereign and independent with unquestionable legal title to their lands, a legal title that could be extinguished only by a treaty with the Crown. In theory, Marshall's rulings, confirming indigenous peoples as distinct independent communities retaining their natural rights, remain the foundation of indigenous policy in the United States today. In practice, their execution has been closer to President Jackson's reported reaction on hearing of the rulings. 'Marshall has rendered his decision,' he scoffed. 'Now let him enforce it.'

Eventually a group of Cherokee leaders, harassed and arrested by the Georgia Guard, signed a treaty, exchanging the last 20,000 square miles of the Cherokee nation for US$5 million and the promise that they could continue to be a nation in Oklahoma. Jackson pushed the treaty through the US Congress where it passed by one vote. In 1838 the US army rounded up all 16,000 remaining Cherokees and marched them at bayonet point through the frozen winter prairie. Some 4,000 died on what has been known ever since as the 'Trail of Tears'.

In the fifty years that followed, dozens of other trails of tears converged on Oklahoma as other indigenous nations – the Nez Percé from the far northwest, the Modoc from California, the Pawnee from Nebraska – were forcibly resettled and European colonization west of the Mississippi proceeded even faster than it had done to the east. 'I think you had better put the Indians on wheels. Then you can run them about whenever you wish,' a Sioux named Red Dog complained bitterly to Treaty Commissioners in 1876.

Encroachment and theft provoked constant complaints from indigenous peoples. 'We have scarcely a place left to spread our blankets,' complained one; 'hardly enough ground to stand on,' lamented another. 'We are rolled back, nation upon nation until we find ourselves fugitives, vagrants and strangers in our own country,' declared John Ross, during the Cherokees' case at the US Supreme Court in 1830.

By the latter half of the nineteenth century white immigrants were settling anywhere there was land, arriving 'thick as grass', in one Indian phrase (Plate 43). To accommodate them, Washington began to undermine its own reservation system. As described above, in 1871 the US government stopped making treaties with indigenous groups, turning them instead into wards of the

43. *USA: land rush in Oklahoma. The passing of the Dawes Act in 1887 started a free-for-all, as Washington seized territory from the indigenous nations and gave it to settlers moving West.*
COURTESY OF THE MARY EVANS PICTURE LIBRARY

government, their land not their own, but public property set aside for use by the government.

In 1887 Congress passed the General Allotment Act, known as the Dawes Act after its sponsor, Senator Henry Dawes. It introduced the same process as in Latin America, parcelling out individual landholdings; what the Osage Indians aptly termed 'Can't Go Beyond'. Every male head of family was awarded 160 acres of reservation land, to be held under a form of trust. Then any 'surplus' was bought up at bargain prices by the government for distribution to settlers under the Homestead Act.

There was plenty of surplus. In 1890 the government's Commissioner for Indian Affairs reported proudly that in just one year, 17.4 million acres, almost one-seventh of total indigenous land, had been 'restored to the public domain'. By the time the Dawes Act was repealed in 1934 it had been spectacularly successful: indigenous people had lost 90 million of the 138 million acres they had legally held in 1887. 'Egypt had its locusts, Asiatic countries their cholera … England its black plague, Memphis had the yellow fever but it was left for the unfortunate Indian territory to be afflicted with the Dawes Commission,' complained one Oklahoma Creek. Dawes himself justified his act by explaining that 'Indians need to learn selfishness which is at the bottom of civilization.'

The Dawes Act opened up what remained of Indian land to the forces of the free market, and unprecedented corruption, mismanagement and theft by agents and officials followed. Yet against all expectation (by 1900 numbers in the United States were down to 237,000), the Indians did not disappear. Instead, their numbers began to rise, in part because of the reservation system, where something of the old ways could be retained despite the abject poverty. Here, in cultural terms, at least, Indian blankets could be worn again and 'buttock bags' (trousers) discarded.

Armed Revolution and Land Reform: Mexico Leads the Way

Wherever indigenous people were still a majority or significant minority, changes in land ownership in the second half of the nineteenth century created a major social crisis. This was especially the case in Mexico, which in November 1910 erupted into seven years of political turbulence that became known as the Mexican Revolution. During this time more than a million peasants, mostly Indians, died in what was for them, at least, a fight to recover their land from the *hacendados*, the hacienda owners.

No one embodied the revolutionary demand for 'Land and Liberty' more completely than Emiliano Zapata (Plate 44), a Nahuatl-speaking muleteer from the mountains of Morelos, south of Mexico City, who became a fearsome

117

44. *Mexico: Emiliano Zapata, a Nahuatl-speaking muleteer from the mountains of Morelos, south of Mexico City, who became a leader of the Mexican revolution. He was betrayed and assassinated in 1919.*
© PEDRO MARTINEZ/SOUTH AMERICAN PICTURES

guerrilla leader. The 1917 constitution secured by the Revolution empowered the federal government to restore lost land to peasant communities, placed ceilings on the size of individual holdings and redistributed expropriated holdings in the form of inalienable common lands, known as *ejidos*. The *ejido* was a modern version of the traditional indigenous community holding, where title was held by the community, which then leased plots to individual heads of families.

As ever, the real issue was whether the constitutional provisions would ever be enacted. Zapata was murdered in April 1919 when the ceremonial guard at a conference to which he had been summoned turned their rifles on him. His betrayal seemed to symbolize that of his indigenous footsoldiers. Just days before he was gunned down, he had written to President Venustiano Carranza, protesting, 'The old landholdings have been taken over by new landlords . . . and the people mocked in their hopes.'

But his war cry, 'Better to die on your feet than live on your knees', has echoed throughout the continent for the rest of the twentieth century. In the early hours of New Year's Day 1994, an army of several thousand Maya from the southernmost Mexican state of Chiapas seized four towns to protest against exactly the same erosion of land rights. They even called themselves the Zapatista National Liberation Army.

The largely indigenous sacrifice of the Mexican Revolution was not entirely in vain. Continued peasant militancy ensured that nearly 57 million hectares of land was distributed by 1934, when the Revolution's goals were given a new impetus by President Lázaro Cárdenas, who redistributed a further 109 million acres in the six years to 1940.

Across Latin America, land reform was now on national agendas, sometimes after a revolution as in Bolivia (1952), Cuba (1959) or Nicaragua (1979), sometimes after the election of left-wing governments as in Chile (1970) or Guatemala (1950) or after the continent's one left-wing military coup in Peru in 1968. Other governments with significant indigenous populations such as Ecuador and Colombia began their own land reforms after the launch of Washington's Alliance for Progress initiative in 1961. This programme made US funds available to encourage reforms in order to ward off the possibility of further revolutions like that in Cuba. Unfortunately, many programmes continued the pattern of breaking up community holdings to create individual plots, and others became quasi-legal means of giving land to large landowners rather than peasants. Most programmes were, however, short-lived and half-hearted, short-term or token responses to what at the time were seen as short-term political pressures.

Many programmes were abandoned after coups or changes of government; even the best benefited only a fraction of the growing number of landless peasants. Many involved transmigration, settling landless indigenous people from highland regions in lowland tropical forest zones on the false assumption that such land was both empty and suitable for subsistence agriculture. In Peru, Bolivia, Guatemala and Mexico such programmes often sent one dispossessed highland indigenous group to dispossess another lowland group.

However, some highland communities benefited from agrarian reform programmes. The formal land titles now handed out by the state often proved a lifeline in future battles; agrarian reform offices or legislation provided a new focus for campaigns and lobbying; a commitment to land reform, however superficial, allowed indigenous organizations to highlight government hypocrisy – the ever-present gap between rhetoric and reality (Plate 45).

Most agrarian reform programmes got under way just as the 'green revolution' started in the 1960s, with a new wave of state and foreign investment developing the sort of capital-intensive farms that had emerged in North America. The grandiose schemes which brought dams for irrigation or minimum prices for key export crops spelt disaster for indigenous communities practising sub-

45. *Peru: signing land agreements. According to the indigenous photographer, 'The possibility of community development depends on the ability of our leaders to confront endless paperwork.'*
© JUAN DE DIOS CHOQUEPUMA/TAFOS/PANOS

120

sistence agriculture. Such schemes meant another round of land concentration and increased malnutrition as communities were dispossessed, higher prices for imported staple foods as domestic production slumped, and further cuts in bank loans to small farmers for anything other than export crops. 'They came to take our land. They are certainly taking it,' noted Davi Yanomami with frightening finality.

Guatemala is one of only two countries in the Americas with a majority indigenous population, and not coincidentally has one of the most unequal systems of land distribution in the Americas. Farms have become smaller and smaller as the rural population has grown, while under the imposed system of individual ownership, heads of household have divided smaller and smaller plots among increasing numbers of offspring. By 1979, the date of the last agrarian census, 89.9 per cent of Guatemala's farms were smaller than the 7 hectares considered the minimum necessary to support an average-sized rural family. This was more than double the proportion recorded three decades earlier in the 1950 census. In 1950 there were 74,269 plots under 1.7 acres, the smallest category registered in Guatemala. By 1979 this process of 'parcellization', as it was known, had trebled the number to 250,918. By 1988, the Guatemalan Bishops' Conference estimated that 98 per cent of the country's indigenous families were landless or did not own sufficient land to support themselves.

For Guatemala, read Mexico, Peru, Bolivia, Ecuador, Colombia or any substantially indigenous country in the Americas. The detail may vary but the trends and tendencies do not. Eviction, often enforced by hired gunmen, was one factor; lack of title and a corrupt and inadequate national land registry were others. But the biggest single cause was the unfettered impact of the 'free market' and agricultural 'modernization', with new technology, capital and export crops making once-marginal indigenous land viable, if only for short periods.

Rigoberta Menchú, the Maya Nobel Peace Prize Laureate of 1992, has described something of the process in her book, *I, Rigoberta Menchú* (London: Verso, 1984). 'My parents weren't exactly evicted but the *ladinos* just gradually took over. My parents spent everything they earned and they incurred so many debts with these people that they had to leave the house to pay them.' The Menchú family's story was that of millions of other indigenous families throughout the Americas.

Endangered Environment: The Culture Clash

Indigenous land has also been disappearing in a very different way, as Hobart Keith, an Oglala Sioux, has pointed out: 'Why are there only 8 inches of topsoil left in America, when there were some 18 inches at the time of the Declaration

121

of Independence in 1776? Where goes our sacred earth?' The answer is into the sea, rivers and air. Deforestation, over-use and chemical fertilizers have broken down soils and reduced yields. No one is more exposed to the consequences than the continents' indigenous people living for the most part in the forests, mountains and tundra that make up the region's most fragile environments. 'Everywhere the white man has touched the earth it is sore,' noted one Wintu Indian woman from California as she contemplated the hydraulic gold mining and intensive logging that had changed her home beyond recognition.

Like land ownership, the environmental question goes back to the clash of philosophies thrown up by the conquest. Indigenous societies believed their gods were to be found in nature, creating a symbiotic relationship between the social and natural orders that pre-Columbian peoples observed with religious reverence. The Christian God, by contrast, assumed the form of man who was put at the centre of the universe. The Roman Catholic Church rejected the deification of nature as heresy.

Tropical forest and the 'howling wilderness' of the prairie was seen by many, Catholic and Protestant alike, as 'the Devil's Den'. Subduing it was as much God's work as converting the heathen. This paved the way for the unbridled exploitation of natural resources and the subjugation of nature, of which the peoples of the Americas, the 'unnatural naturals', as one European labelled them, were just a part. The conquest has been as much environmental as human. 'If Nature opposes us, we will struggle against her and make her obey,' warned Simón Bolívar, who led the fight for independence in much of South America.

The environmental and biological consequences of the arrival of the Europeans were in some ways even more devastating than the physical and cultural consequences. Despite the impact of the diseases brought by the Europeans, the flora and fauna which accompanied them may have been even more catastrophic.

A central objective of the conquest was to provide the *conquistadores* and the settlers who followed them with the foods and animals they were accustomed to and to supply Europe with the natural resources and agricultural crops it coveted. Such new crops and animals tended to muscle native flora and fauna aside in an ecological war on everything and everyone indigenous to the Americas.

The plantation and *hacienda* were the shock troops in the environmental onslaught. Land was cleared, foreign species without natural predators introduced, and other natural species not conducive to the new crop suppressed. Today, the most environmentally degraded parts of the continent, such as Haiti, the Dominican Republic and northeastern Brazil, are those which were first deforested and irrigated for sugar, the region's first cash crop. Later the piedmont forests of Mexico, Central America, Colombia, Venezuela and southern Brazil fell prey to coffee plantations. Cotton swept away the coastal forests of Central America.

Satellite technology has allowed scientists to calculate that about 18 per cent of the total landmass of South America has been degraded or converted for direct human use over the past five hundred years, and the pace is quickening. Some 3 per cent of this total has been lost in the past decade. Closed canopy forest has fared worst, losing a total of 22 per cent or 696,000 square miles, of which 217,000 square miles or 31 per cent of the total has been lost in the past decade alone. 'Even the Spanish conquest was not as direct or devastating as this,' observes Rafael Pandam, leader of the Confederation of Indigenous Nationalities of Ecuador (CONAIE).

The biggest losses have been along the Brazilian coast (where just 5 per cent of the tropical moist forest remains), in the Amazon basin (Plate 46) and in the once vast araucaria pine forest of southern Brazil, where just 1 per cent of the original 400,000 square miles remains undisturbed. Here, unsurprisingly, no indigenous people remain.

In the United States less than 5 per cent of primary forest remains intact. Grasslands and woodlands have fared little better. Some 23 per cent or 300,000

46. *Brazil: environmental destruction in the Kayapó Indians' area of the Amazon.*
© MIKE BECKHAM/SURVIVAL INTERNATIONAL

square miles of the former has been converted or turned into wasteland in South America; about 18 per cent or 270,000 square miles of the latter has been destroyed.

Deforestation set off a chain reaction in tropical environments where most nutrients are stored in plant life. Wildlife was soon deprived of food and protection, soil of nutrients, and eventually the region was starved of rainfall. Rapidly contaminated water supplies and exhausted soils meant that the plantation economy was sustainable only through constant expansion into virgin territory and the addition of environmentally destructive inputs such as fertilizers and pesticides.

Ranching had similar environmental consequences in the grasslands of North America, the pampas of Argentina and the llanos of Venezuela. Today cattle ranching, and the cheap beef for export it yields, accounts for much of the destruction of Amazonia where an area the size of Belgium was felled in just a few months as recently as 1988. 'Why do white men burn all of this and then not plant anything to feed their children? I am too old to understand any of this,' complained Beptopoop, a Kayapó shaman returning to his abandoned village of Gorotire that same year.

Clearing forest for cattle is nothing new, although the scale of the clearing certainly is. Cattle have thrived from the earliest days in the Americas with herds of 150,000 reported in northern Mexico as early as 1579, when the largest herds in Spain numbered a mere 1,000. Cattle were only one species among many. Pigs, goats, sheep, horses and chickens, all unknown in the Americas until they came ashore from European ships, underwent a biological explosion. Breeding rapidly with few predators, they penetrated all corners of the Americas much more rapidly than the people who brought them. These animals played a key part in the indigenous holocaust, eating and trampling food crops and transmitting disease to the only native draught animals, the alpaca and llama, South America's camels. Eventually, however, these European imports became an essential part of indigenous peoples' survival. Peoples who had been terrified by *conquistadores* on horseback became expert horsemen, hunting the buffalo and wild cattle that strayed on to the grasslands from Alberta in the north to Patagonia in the south and resisting the European advance in the process. Today, few indigenous families in the Americas could survive without a few of the goats, chicken, pigs or even sheep and cattle that the colonists introduced.

That adaptation reflected an indigenous tradition. A growing body of research by scientists and anthropologists shows how forest peoples have not only adapted to their environment but moulded it. Farming by means of 'gardens' in different clearings, they transplant food or fruit plants from one part of the forest to another, managing soils and genetically improving plants in the process. They use nests of termites to control more predatory insects, grow weeds amid their crops to shade the soil from sun and rain while trapping nutrients, and

124

even manage the re-encroachment of the forest after a few years by favouring those trees and plants that will provide useful barks, leaves or vines.

Throughout the 1980s, Darrell Posey, a North American anthropologist, co-ordinated a team of more than 20 ethnobiologists researching the knowledge of just one group in the Amazon basin, the Kayapó. 'We were each humbled by the detail and richness of Kayapó scientific knowledge,' he commented in 1989. 'Kayapó specialists who have never been in a classroom in their lives guided PhDs in the development of new hypotheses to test or expand existing Western scientific knowledge.'

It all begged the question posed by Stephen Corry of Survival International when he asked what the world was missing in failing to prevent the physical annihilation of such peoples. Western academics have begun a race against time and are now inviting indigenous specialists to scientific conferences as environmental scientists rather than anthropological exhibits. In 1988, the strength of a growing grassroots ethnobiology movement was demonstrated in Belém, Brazil, when 600 delegates from 35 countries participated in the First International Congress of Ethnobiology.

The whole experience seemed to bear out the words of Sioux author Vine Deloria Jr.: 'The common knowledge of Indian tribes, when discovered by non-Indian scientists, is seen as an exciting breakthrough. But from the Indian perspective it is mere child's play. It is information which traditional people expect youngsters to acquire as a matter of course.'

Mines and Minerals: The Curse of Wealth

There was one other major source of environmental degradation: mining and the extraction of minerals. The human cost was examined in Chapter 3, but the environmental cost was almost as great. Elizabeth Dore, a lecturer in Latin American history at the University of Portsmouth in Britain, has divided the environmental impact of mining in the Americas into three distinct periods: 1492–1900, 1900–1960, and 1960 to the present. Each has been far more destructive than the last, highlighting the growing environmental crisis caused by mining.

In the first period, large-scale silver mining was confined to Mexico, in particular Guanajuato and Zacatecas and Potosí in Bolivia. The discovery in the 1570s of mercury at Huancavelica in the Peruvian central Andes saw the development of new extraction processes and a surge in the industry's environmental damage. Rivers were contaminated, setting off a chain reaction as fish, plants and animals with mercury-laden tissue were consumed.

Today mercury is still poisoning water and the food chain in the Amazon basin as a result of massive incursions mostly by wildcat prospectors, known as

125

garimpeiros in Portuguese, panning for gold in indigenous areas. By 1995 the diseases they had brought, such as malaria, tuberculosis and measles, had killed an estimated 21 per cent of the region's largest forest tribe, the Yanomami, according to the International Work Group on Indigenous Affairs (IWGIA).

'What we are seeing in the Americas today is the sort of gold rush we saw in the earliest days of the conquest,' says Roger Moody, editor of *The Indigenous Voice*, an anthology of indigenous writing, statements and speeches. 'The myth of El Dorado, the golden kingdom, the holy grail, is alive and well among the prospectors.'

Gold production in Brazil, Ecuador, Bolivia, Peru, Colombia, Guyana and French Guiana has soared but indigenous people have paid the price. By 1989, one-third of the 518 Indian areas recognized by the Brazilian state had been invaded. For most groups, such invasions brought swift disaster. 'Malaria, mercury, guns, alcohol, divisions in the community – it's hard to say what is going to happen,' said Davi Yanomami on a tour of Europe in 1989.

One old Yanomami medicine man or *paje* had his own explanation, not unlike some of the rationales developed in the mines of the Andes in the sixteenth century:

> When the gold stays deep down in the cold earth, it is not dangerous. When the white man brings it up and burns it, stirring it like flour, smoke comes out of it. Thus the *xawara*, the smoke of gold, is created ... spreading throughout the forest. It becomes very aggressive and when this happens it wipes out the Yanomami. That is what the old people say.

The twentieth century has seen the environmental toll rise as a result of the industrialized world's increased demand first for 'base' metals such as zinc, copper and lead, then for nitrates and oil. Transport, refining and exhaust fumes added a new level of environmental threat with the scale of the risk increasing as the scope of the projects grew steadily larger. Recent economic liberalization, opening up mining along with agriculture to foreign investors, has only accelerated the process.

From the 1960s onwards, huge open-cast copper, iron and bauxite mines along with a massive increase in oil extraction intensified the pace of environmental damage. Many of the new developments were in predominantly indigenous areas: the oilfields of northern Canada, the southern Mexican states of Chiapas and Tabasco, the western Amazonian regions of Peru, Ecuador and Colombia; the oil wells and iron–bauxite mines of the Orinoco River basin in Venezuela; the Carajas iron ore project in the Brazilian Amazon, the world's largest mining project.

The despoliation in the second half of the twentieth century exemplifies what indigenous people have suffered throughout the history of the Americas; what the Uruguayan writer Eduardo Galeano has labelled 'the curse of their own wealth'. Not only has their own wealth been stolen, but their environment is often made uninhabitable in the process. Worse still, their wealth has funded further theft and destruction in a vicious cycle not unlike the unsustainable plantation agriculture they were obliged to work in after losing their lands.

It has been calculated that mining and the extraction of mineral resources in the Americas have caused more environmental damage in the past 30 years than in the previous 470. Nothing demonstrates this better than the Carajas project. The iron ore deposit lies at the centre of a web of open-cast bauxite, copper, chrome, nickel, tungsten and gold mines. Infrastructural support includes processing plants, steel and aluminium factories, agro-livestock industries, hydroelectric dams, railways, roads and deep-water ports.

All such projects act like magnets, sucking farmers, prospectors and workers into indigenous territory. Carajas uprooted 12 indigenous communities and displaced 10,000 people. 'One day in 1980 I was hunting in the woods when I saw people doing a survey for the construction of railways and roads. We were not consulted, not even informed,' says Tiure, a local activist who became the first Brazilian Indian to secure political asylum abroad.

Around Carajas today 1.6 million acres of timber are cut annually just to stoke the pig-iron smelters and provide timber for construction. The figure demonstrates how deforestation is often driven by other environmentally destructive activities and how it has increased exponentially in the Americas.

In Barbados, cane planters deforested the whole island in just 20 years to build and fuel their sugar mills. More than 75 per cent of deforestation in the Brazilian Amazon has taken place in the past 20 years, a period in which, ironically, environmental awareness in the industrialized world has reached unprecedented heights. The nature of that awareness and indigenous relations with environmentalists have been the subject of fierce debate in recent years. By the 1980s, many indigenous leaders felt that environmentalists with whom they had forged alliances were speaking for them, superimposing their own conservationist agendas on to living cultures. 'Who is the conservation for? For other people?', asks Nicanor González, a Kuna involved in managing a forestry project in the group's homeland in Panama. 'You can't say to indigenous peoples, "Don't fish in this area, or hunt this animal or go into what they call national parks or protected areas."'

Indigenous people want sustainable development and international solidarity on their own terms, not paternalism or colonialism by other means. However Indian autonomy and self-determination also includes an ethnic group's right to degrade or pollute its own environment. Today the Kayapó have been logging their hardwood trees at what is probably an unsustainable rate; Quechua and Maya are using destructive chemical fertilizers on their strips of land in a desperate effort to boost yields; North American peoples are considering allowing the burying of nuclear waste on their reservations. Such 'choices' are usually forced by external factors such as poverty, corruption or de-ethnicization of leaders or whole peoples.

Most would accept the views of Guajiro writer José Barreiro that indigenous peoples are 'the miner's canary of the human family'. Their direct dependence on the natural realm means that when their land and environment are destroyed, so are they. It is a sentiment for which many indigenous peoples have proverbs based on the observation of the natural world around them. As the Teton Sioux axiom puts it, 'The frog does not drink up the pond in which he lives.'

In the words of Guaraní holy man Pae Antonio, whose Argentine village was burnt to the ground in 1991, 'When the Indians vanish, the rest follow.' Environmental awareness also permits indigenous groups to take a longer-term view of events: 'The whites too shall pass – perhaps sooner than other tribes,' noted one Californian Indian. 'Continue to contaminate your bed and you will one night suffocate in your own waste.'

Bibliography

The Conquest of Nature, 1492–1992. NACLA Report on the Americas (New York: North American Congress on Latin America) vol. 25, no. 2 (Sept. 1991).

Crosby, Alfred, *The Columbian Exchange* (Westport, CT.: Greenwood Press, 1972).

Dorner, Peter, *Latin American Land Reforms in Theory and Practice: A Retrospective Analysis* (Madison: University of Wisconsin Press, 1992).

Durning, Alan Thein, *Guardians of the Land: Indigenous Peoples and the Health of the Earth*, Worldwatch Paper 112 (Washington, DC: Worldwatch Institute, December 1992).

Indigenous Affairs (Copenhagen: International Work Group for Indigenous Affairs, Oct./Nov./Dec. 1994).

Johnson, W. F., *Life of Sitting Bull and History of the Indian War 1890–91* (Edgewood Publishing Company, 1891).

Plant, Roger, *Land Rights and Minorities* (London: Minority Rights Group, 1994).

Posey, Darrell A., 'From warclubs to words'. *NACLA Report on the Americas*, (New York: North American Congress on Latin America) vol. 13, no. 1 (May 1989).

Weatherford, Jack, *Indian Givers: How the Indians of the Americas Transformed the World* (New York: Crown, 1988).

Wilson, Richard, *Before Columbus* (Birmingham: External Affairs, Central Television, 1992). (Booklet to accompany a television series.)

5
Assimilation and Development

War, massacres, expropriation, relocation ... When the dust settled at the end of the nineteenth century, the indigenous population of the Americas, far from disappearing as 'the natural effect of one race replacing another', in the words of one US senator, was once more on the increase. It still is.

As dispossession and industrialization sucked more indigenous people into the cities and more settlers into the countryside, the 'Indian problem' (North America) and *la mancha india* ('the Indian stain', as it was known in the Andes) became more pressing than ever. For indigenous peoples, their 'white problem' was also growing as more and more of them were subjected to the effects of rapid changes and integrationist state policies.

Annihilation had been tried by colonists and independent governments alike, yet the Indian clung on. Confinement on reservations, in special communities or in reserves – managed decline – had followed, but had backfired, consolidating indigenous peoples' sense of their own distinctiveness. In the twentieth century, assimilation became the third option. It brought the budding indigenous revival into full bloom.

Right from the beginning, whenever they were consulted, indigenous leaders have always said that some form of coexistence, even mixing, was not only possible but inevitable. 'If my people are to fight they are too few; if they are to die they are too many,' a Mohawk leader concluded, assessing the odds in the eighteenth century. The only real issue was on whose terms coexistence would take place, a question that remains at the heart of the struggle for self-determination today.

The dramatic consequences of the war on indigenous peoples' economic base in the nineteenth century meant that initially, at least, assimilation appeared to be occurring on governments' terms. As governments desperate to boost exports, settle immigrants and feed growing populations saw it, assimilation was their only option. The swelling ranks of their own migrants now wanted to be everywhere from Prudhoe Bay in the north to Patagonia in the south. Removal and relocation served no further purpose once there was no unwanted land left to which the remaining Indians could be sent.

The attempt to assert the dominance of the *mestizo*, the Hispanicized Indian, started in Mexico with the end of the Revolution in 1917. *Mestizaje*, the mixing of the races and cultures, became state policy and the basis of a new nationalism. Incorporating the landless, impoverished indigenous masses into the state was seen as a guarantee against further uprisings; distribution of some land and minimal welfare was the price of stability.

Not long afterwards a similar philosophy sprang up in the Andes, finally emerging as official government policy after a revolution in Bolivia (1952) and a military coup in Peru (1968). The highland Aymara and Quechua were redefined out of existence, rechristened *campesinos*, or peasants, the new term being both a symbol and an aspiration for the new governments. Political parties, trade unions and co-operatives were organized in the mines and villages of the *campesino* masses as governments sought to shore up their support by incorporating their 'non-national' elements.

In Canada and the United States similar redefinitions saw 'civilized' Indians offered full citizenship as a means of escaping the poverty and corruption of the reservations. Complete control of Indian life and reservations through the system of agents was, in the United States, followed by 'termination' of peoples' legal status and 'relocation' of their remaining members to the cities.

These changes were implemented by government departments, state-funded indigenous institutes, cultural offices and Indian bureaux (Plate 47). One by one these new agencies sprang up, their names often betraying their objectives: the Bureau of Indian Affairs (United States, 1871); the Indian Protection Service (Brazil, 1910); the Department of Rural Schools for the Incorporation of Indigenous Culture (Mexico, 1925); the National Indigenist Institute (Guatemala, 1945).

As time wore on it became clear that what governments defined as assimilation was in fact as much a myth as the conquest. More often than not, 'acculturation', the process of accommodation and change as a result of cultural contact, and 'assimilation', the complete cultural absorption of one group by another, proved a two-way process, producing a syncretic blend of two or more cultures. Partly because of the inequitable political terms under which such interchange took place and partly because of indigenous peoples' lack of access to the means to define or interpret this process, however, there was a general perception that assimilation was a one-way street, a perception reinforced by the rhetoric of its proponents.

Try something very Indian for a moment: turn the tables. Were Spanish, English, French or Portuguese settlers or their descendants thought to be 'assimilating' when they smoked tobacco, ate potatoes or used a canoe? They adopted the indigenous words for such 'New World' products, absorbing them into their own languages, but were their languages now tainted or indigenized

130

47. *Peru: worlds apart. Officials from the government agency for Indian affairs in Qosqo, c. 1920.*

as a result? Definitions are in the hands of the definer, and the absence, until relatively recently, of indigenous anthropologists to interpet cultural changes has been a persistent complaint of Indian activists.

There is no such thing as complete cultural purity; anthropological ring fences cannot be put up around one culture or another. As David Courchene, President of the Manitoba Indian Brotherhood, has pointed out, 'Your culture is not the culture of your ancestors, of five hundred years ago. Nor is ours. We are developing a twentieth- and twenty-first-century culture, and it will be an Indian culture.'

That said, there is no doubt that many individuals and whole peoples have been assimilated with increasing speed in the twentieth century. They have lost all or virtually all their indigenous traits, adopting Hispanic or Anglo cultural norms and becoming *mestizos*, *ladinos* or *misti*, racially mixed but culturally non-indigenous. They have adopted the language, value system and cultural norms of the dominant society, which often includes openly despising indigenous culture and peoples.

Why? For many, imitating white ways by crossing the cultural border was the only way to secure the social rights previously denied them over work, land or

131

education. For others it was never a conscious process but the inevitable consequence of cultural dislocation, being driven off their land and/or obliged to move to the city. 'If no one around you speaks your language how can you speak it?', asked one Chuj Indian, forced to relocate to Guatemala City.

Ana María Condori, an Aymara Indian from Bolivia, has described some of these pressures in her book *Nayan Uñatatawi – Mi Despertar* (My Awakening). She describes how, as she worked as a domestic servant in the city, the values and attitudes of her employer rubbed off on her: 'Little by little she made me aware of my class, using words like "Indians" and "peasants", saying, "You shouldn't be like that, you're going to get civilized here.". . . You look after her things as though they were your own and after a while you start identifying totally with her mentality.'

For others, it was simply increased contact with the officials or agents representing an ever more centralized and intrusive state in villages or on reservations as they taxed, conscripted and registered. With indigenous peoples' economic base destroyed or steadily eroding, their increased dependency on the state in whatever form was inevitable. Cultural dependency often followed. 'Assimilation' as a policy took a variety of forms but sprang from a common delusion, namely that indigenous people could survive only by ceasing to be culturally distinct peoples. An even greater delusion, namely that such a transformation could be effected in an orderly, structured way by means of government policy, persists to this day in many quarters. The plan was, and still is in many countries, that Indians should lose their 'Indianness' and become 'brown' or 'red' whites; should become Christians who were literate in the colonizers' language; should become smallholders or tax-paying workers. They were to be freed from the collective constraints of tribal or community life that were deemed to prevent them from developing into free-thinking citizens.

North American Assimilation: Redefining the Indian

In North America this philosophy was accompanied by a raft of legislation defining indigenous people in law and eventually, once they were deemed sufficiently 'civilized', offering full citizenship. The Canadian Indian Act of 1880 subdivided the country's indigenous people into Inuit, 'status Indians' and 'non-status Indians'. The status group were afforded some special privileges such as exemption from certain taxes but found their land, education, housing and economic activity under the direct control of the new Ministry of Indian Affairs in Ottawa.

Being a 'non-status' Indian was the only way to escape what often amounted to dictatorial day-to-day control by government agents on the reservations. An individual could renounce 'status', take his or her share of the group's resources and move towards 'enfranchisement' as a Canadian citizen. All this was subject to approval by an agent of the Superintendent General and three years' probation to test the individual's 'degree of civilization' and 'integrity, morality and sobriety'.

In the United States, the Bureau of Indian Affairs performed a similar role in conjunction with the Dawes Act or General Allotment Act of 1887. Even white well-wishers, many of them anthropologists and sociologists, believed that the future for indigenous people had to be integration, the same future as that of the millions of Irish, Italians, Russians and Poles arriving in the Americas at this time. The land-grabbers and mineral prospecters formed an unlikely alliance with such liberal assimilators. Anthropologists rushed to reservations to study the ways and languages of indigenous nations whose own demise they were advocating by means of integration.

In 1881 Helen Hunt Jackson published a seminal work on Indian–settler confrontation in the United States, *A Century of Dishonor* (New York: Harper and Bros.). She concluded: 'Every human being born in this country or arriving here from any quarter of the globe can find protection in our courts, everyone, that is, except those to whom the country once belonged.' Yet even she saw the solution as assimilation into European systems of education, religion and land ownership.

The new policy repeated all the old hypocrisy, distrusts and ambiguities. In 1950 Dillon Miller became Commissioner of Indian Affairs, determined to 'free' his charges from reservations and federal support in a policy known to everyone but himself as 'termination' (of indigenous status). Between 1954 and 1962 61 Indian groups were terminated, the loss of federal funds eventually proving so disastrous that subsequently many successfully campaigned for the restoration of their former status. Indian leaders noted Dillon's previous government job, in charge of wartime detention of Japanese-Americans. His underlying aim was complete assimilation, epitomizing government policy at the time. 'What can we do to Americanize the Indian?', he asked one Indian delegation, to which one chief retorted, 'We ask, how can we Americanize you? And the first thing we want to teach you is that, in the American way of life, you have respect for your brother's vision.'

In Mexico there was a different emphasis, although the outcome and objectives of what was labelled *mestizaje* or cultural mixing were the same. Mexico has always been a unique case in the Americas. The size of the indigenous population in the Valley of Mexico when Cortés arrived, the relative development of the Aztecs' urbanized trade economy and the founding of the capital of New Spain on the ruins of the old Tenochtitlán have meant that syncretism, the fusing of the new and old, has always been a feature of Mexican culture.

Indeed, Mexico has produced the only Indian to lead an American country since precolonial times. In March 1861 Benito Juárez, a Zapotec lawyer from Oaxaca who spoke no Spanish until he was 12 years old, became Mexico's first elected civilian president. Juárez laid the foundations for the modern Mexican state by cutting the size of the army, adding a bill of rights to the constitution, expanding education and abolishing ecclesiastical and military immunity to civil courts. By 1872, when he became one of the few Mexican leaders that century to die in office of natural causes, Juárez had emerged as one of the greatest products and examples of syncretism: a pure-blooded Indian who had made it to the National Palace by means of a Spanish seminary, European law qualifications and a *criollo* political system. But like so many others, in imitating the white man, he had changed, in the eyes of his indigenous critics. He had lost touch with the Zapotec and Mixtec villagers whose cases he had pleaded in court in his twenties. The life of Benito Juárez, whose reforms paved the way for many of the changes subsequently wrought by the Mexican revolution, raised a crucial question still relevant today: how indigenous could an Indian remain while succeeding in the settler society? When did an Indian become a 'white Indian'?

Mexico was the laboratory for assimilation. As Minister of Culture in the post-revolutionary government of the 1920s, José Vasconcelos initiated a government campaign to fuse Mexico's *mestizos* and indigenous people into a national culture. In his book *La Raza Cósmica* (1925), Vasconcelos argued that conquest and its aftermath had produced a third race in its own right. This doctrine became known as *la raza* nationalism and in Mexico, Columbus Day, 12 October, was redesignated as the birthday of this new race, *el día de la raza*, the Day of the Race.

The shift of power away from the creole élite to the *mestizo* mass, hastened by the Revolution, now had philosophical as well as political roots. Organizations with memberships or constitutions based on ethnicity, reflecting the on-the-ground reality of dozens of distinct Indian languages and cultures, were banned. The Indian, it seemed, was to be legislated out of existence; a new definition of nationalism was born, a definition that excluded the Indian as much as the old one.

By 1940, when something calling itself the First Inter-American Indigenist Congress was held in Pátzcuaro, Mexico, to discuss the co-ordination of integrationist policies, indigenous culture seemed to have gone from being denigrated to being usurped. It said more about the *mestizo*, *criollo* or *misti* search for an identity than it did about indigenous consciousness. As one Mapuche from Chile put it, 'We know who we are because we have always lived here. They don't, because they don't know where they've come from and they've yet to find out where they are now.'

134

Indigenism in Peru: Growing from the Head Down

In Peru similar ideas took a slightly different form as *indigenismo*, a general revaluation and rediscovery of indigenous culture. The movement called for the recognition of indigenous peoples as a fundamental part of the nation and demanded an end to their marginalization. In Mexico, the catalyst had been the Revolution; in Peru it was the shock defeat by Chile in the War of the Pacific (1879–83). As the creole élite encouraged mass migration from Europe to counter the *mancha india*, some of its members noted that Peru's few successes in the war with Chile had been won by indigenous troops who had fought heroically to defend their territory.

Indigenismo was refined into a political expression in Peru by Víctor Raúl Haya de la Torre and José Carlos Mariátegui, both of whom founded left-wing parties as socialism and Marxism gained currency in the early twentieth century. Neither was indigenous, had first-hand knowledge of Andean culture, or spoke Quechua or any other indigenous language, but both saw in the social organization of the Inka state, in particular its communal solidarity, what they thought could become the basis for a uniquely Peruvian brand of socialism.

No one gave expression to Peru's split identity better than the man who took *indigenismo* to new heights of literary expression. José María Arguedas belonged to both Peru's worlds, Hispanic and Quechua. Others, most notably Miguel Angel Asturias, the Guatemalan Nobel laureate for Literature, steeped their literature in a deep understanding of the myths and reality of the Indian people of their countries, but none were insiders like Arguedas. The son of a provincial judge, Arguedas was rejected by his stepmother, who decided, according to the novelist, that 'since I was the object of as much of her scorn and rancour as the Indians, I was to live with them in the kitchen, eating and sleeping there on a wooden trough of the kind used to knead bread.' From then on Arguedas decided to 'stay with my people, the dispossessed, the deceived, the persecuted . . .' The language of the Inkas became his mother tongue and after study in Lima he returned to the Andes to teach, write and study indigenous culture. Quechua myths and rituals were the basis of his novels (in Spanish), most famously *Los Ríos Profundos* (1958, published in English as *Deep Rivers*, 1978), *Todas las Sangres* (Everyone's Blood, 1964) and *El Zorro de Arriba, el Zorro de Abajo* (The Fox Above and the Fox Below, 1970) and his poems (in Quechua), most notably his collected works, *Katatay*. Along with those of Miguel Angel Asturias, such works formed the basis of magic realism, a literary genre for which the continent later became famous.

To Arguedas, the first writer to hear and record the Inkarí legend cycle, the magic of his novels was a very real part of him. The tales told how Inkarí founded Qosqo, rounding up the stones with a whip, enclosing the wind and

135

tethering the sun so that he could lengthen the day to complete his task. The legend cycle was permeated by a strong messianic sense of return, based on a traditional cyclical sense of time. In the legends Inkarí, having been beheaded and buried, is believed to be growing again from the head down. When his body is complete, he will return to avenge the conquest, launch the *pachakut'i*, the overturning of worlds, and reunite the two halves of the Andean world, the *hanan* (upper) and *hurin* (lower), in the process restoring the complementarity that was rent asunder by the conquest.

Arguedas spent his whole life exploring and suffering this divide, labouring to bring the two halves of the conquest, European and indigenous, together, unravelling the indigenous consciousness of the highlands for consumption by the *misti* intellectuals of the coast. He personified his aim: a bilingual, bicultural Peru in which Inka culture was revered. However, his failure to match the two halves and make the body whole led to his suicide in 1969, ironically the very year in which Quechua became an official language in Peru. Arguedas' death can be seen as a metaphor for his whole life, both of which raised profound questions. Was it possible to have two identities without killing off one of them or indeed the body in which they struggled for supremacy? Was Andean duality, even in a bastardized form, possible in the aftermath of the conquest? He once asked in a poem, *Huk Docturkunaman* (A Call upon Some Doctors), written after a public attack by some intellectuals, who often ridiculed him as a romantic antiquarian:

> Imamantam ruwasqa ñutquy? Imamantapunim
> ruwasqa sunquypa waqaq aychan, taytallay ducturkuna?
>
> What are my brains made of? Of what the flesh
> of my heart?

Pachakut'i: Burying Themselves to Rediscover Themselves

Indigenous peoples in the Americas responded to the assimilationist onslaught of the early twentieth century in the same way as their ancestors had to similar threats. They adapted and kept their heads down, a strategy perfectly reflected in the metaphor that recurs throughout Andean literature and oral tradition: 'the people buried themselves'. After all, many of the people who lived under the Inkas, Aztecs and Maya had belonged to other, half-absorbed ethno-linguistic groups. The Cherokee and Iroquois in North America were loose confederations of nations; multicultural, plural and multiethnic. Such empires or confederations included people of different cultures and lifestyles, prototypes for the kind of multinational, diverse, decentralized entities indigenous leaders have argued for since they first came into contact with Europeans in the sixteenth century.

But just as their temples and gods were buried in the foundations of the new churches the Spaniards made them build (Plate 48), so much of indigenous identity over the past five centuries in the Americas has never been far from the surface. 'We hid our gods beneath the purple robes of their saints,' wrote Nicaraguan poet Gioconda Belli. Just as each earthquake, each *pachakut'i*, in Qosqo or Mexico City demolishes a little more of the Spanish architecture to reveal a little more of the Inka or Aztec foundations that lie below, so each land occupation, each indigenous school, each public protest, each election victory is stripping away a little more of the colonial body paint that covers the indigenous heart of the Americas.

Indigenous–state relations in the Americas this century have always been seen as the inexorable victory of a dominant, centralizing state over its weak and subjugated indigenous people. In fact this image, like much else in Indian–state relations in the Americas, is as mythical as El Dorado. Many Latin America states in particular are weak, with little more than the army and Church qualifying as genuinely national institutions. As loosely knit federations with numerous ethnic groups and a wide range of geographies, Canada and the United States have some similar characteristics.

But five hundred years after the conquest, the weakness of many Latin American states contrasts vividly with the strength and vitality of the indigenous nations they claim to rule. Some of the weakest states are those with the highest proportions of indigenous people (Bolivia, Peru, Guatemala). This points to another buried truth: far from being moulded by these states, indigenous peoples have played a crucial role in frustrating and weakening the centralizing tendencies of the nations in which they live.

One reason for the failure of states to exercise control lies at the heart of the cultural divide between settler and Indian. While communities, groups or nations have always acted as separate units in struggles with the state, the state has always treated indigenous people as a single entity. Generic 'Indianness', a post-conquest concept that survives in government policy throughout the Americas to this day, precludes seeing indigenous America as a range of peoples as diverse as Turks and Japanese, and thus devising policies to match. Self-deception has filled the vacuum, as government officials have convinced themselves that they are assimilating the indigenous population by means of education, religion or work in just the same way as their precedessors convinced themselves that they had conquered them.

Governments see the control of indigenous people as essential, yet the policies designed to exercise this control fuel the hostility of indigenous peoples and make control impossible. It is no coincidence that worldwide indigenous resistance to the nation-state has grown in direct proportion to the numbers and strength of those same nation-states. Before 1945 there were only 50

137

48. *Peru: Spanish church of Santo Domingo, built on top of the ruins of the Inka Temple of the Sun in Qosqo. Periodic earthquakes damage the Spanish construction but make no impact on the quake-proof Inka masonry.*
© TONY MORRISON/SOUTH AMERICAN PICTURES

nation-states worldwide; by 1989 there were 170; by the year 2000 there will be more than 200. Indigenous resistance this century has grown proportionately.

For indigenous people, what was a weakness during the invasion and conquest, namely the disunity and even enmity of different ethnic groups, has since become a strength. Plural and local, with communities just a few miles apart speaking different languages, following different customs and living different lifestyles, indigenous society in the Americas cannot be absorbed by any monolithic master plan. Assimilation village by village, people by people, and, as collective identity broke down in the twentieth century, individual by individual, has proved impossible. Indigenous survival has become more, not less, assured as the twentieth century has worn on.

The scope of indigenous resistance has had to broaden with the scale of the attack during the past 150 years. In particular, the onslaught on their economic base and Indians' steady migration into the cities have led to a new form of resistance: economic diversification. Indigenous migrants have become artisans, factory workers, small-scale entrepreneurs; Western education has produced an increasingly bicultural, bilingual class pushing into the burgeoning state bureaucracies. Increasingly, indigenous people have had to define themselves in terms of a broader, usually hostile, outside world to which more of them now have to relate. Many have begun to practise a new and different kind of multicultural diversity, assuming different identities at different times. Speaking their own language and perhaps wearing their own dress in their native villages, many switch to Western dress and Spanish, Portuguese, English or French when they travel to the city or plantation to sell their labour or produce.

Although most indigenous people see this as 'another way of expressing ourselves', in Rigoberta Menchú's words, the process is seen by others as a transitory phase in the 'assimilation' process. For some it certainly is, for while the number of indigenous peoples has grown steadily in the twentieth century, so has the numbers of *mestizos*. But for many indigenous people, this cultural camouflage has been another subtle means of resistance to the imposed identity of others, be they anthropologists, left-wing *mestizo* indigenists or right-wing assimilationists. Diversity of identity mirrors the diversity of culture that makes assimilation or political control of ethnic groups or indigenous communities so difficult for governments in the Americas. This multiplication of identities means that assimilating governments are always chasing a moving target; something as elusive as indigenous culture itself. 'In reclaiming our identity we are creating new ones. Think about who you are and you might get some interesting answers,' advises Alberto Esquit, a Maya archivist.

Schools of Resistance: 'Where Are Our Books?'

The key to government assimilation efforts was education (Plate 49), often subcontracted to the Church. In North America, reserve schools established under the treaties were followed by residential or boarding schools where, in the words of Sharon Venne, a one-time pupil who later became a Cree lawyer, the missionaries complained that 'we kept up our old ways, spoke our own language, practised our own religion'.

Integrated education amounted to a de-ethnicization programme, 'beating the Indian out of the young,' as one teacher put it. Indigenous children were taught the white man's history and curriculum in an alien European language, in an atmosphere of bullying and discrimination that for most served as an appropriate introduction to the adult white world beyond the classroom. For many, the schizophrenia of this cultural conflict proved too much. Laurence Bouche was just one who felt completely alienated on returning home after 12 years in a white boarding school: 'My parents were afraid of me because I represented everything they feared and the thing they feared most was anything

49. *USA: Chiricahua Apache children before and after being taken from their families and sent to a white-run school in Carlisle, Florida. Photos taken in November 1886 and March 1887.*
COURTESY OF JOHN N. COATE

that was white. So I was rejected. I had no identity, no language, no parents, no god.' Bouche became one of what the Stoney Indians of Canada term the *aintsikn ustombe* – the lost people – a label frequently applied to returned students. In February 1992, he was found dead on the streets of Edmonton, Alberta. He had taken his own life by slashing his wrists.

In Latin America, access to education, however dubious, was more varied but the principles of its purpose – assimilation, de-ethnicization – remained the same. 'The education of the white man is designed to convince us of the superiority of his culture, to accustom us to a feeling of inferiority, to devalue us and destroy us as a group,' complained Saúl Rojas Panduro on behalf of Shipibo and Conibo communities in Peru in 1978.

School in almost all cases meant an urban-oriented, Eurocentric curriculum, the course preceded by a culturally brutal 'Castilianization' programme, during which Spanish was taught in order to teach literacy. 'The school itself became the source of illiteracy, a place of cultural confrontation,' concluded Mario Leyton, a United Nations educational consultant working on indigenous programmes in Guatemala.

The evolution of limited bilingual education programmes in the Americas in the past twenty years has changed the situation little, according to the growing number of indigenous graduates. Indeed, many see bilingual programmes as being designed to achieve assimilationist objectives more effectively. 'They now use indigenous languages to teach Spanish, halting Maya language teaching as soon as the child has learned Spanish,' claims Demetrio Cotjí, a Maya with a doctorate in sociology. 'It is a government-financed programme of ethnocide and destruction.'

The situation has been complicated by a steadily growing demand for education and the fact that many indigenous people see it as more important to be literate in Spanish, French, English or Portuguese than to be able to read and write in their own language, even if they have a choice. One woman attending literacy classes in El Alto, the huge indigenous city that sprawls above the Bolivian capital, La Paz, summarized the dilemma: 'What is the point of learning to read and write Aymara? There is nothing to read and write in Aymara. It will not help us get a job or make money.'

Indians' desire for literacy in the official language of the country in which they found themselves showed the ambiguity of cultural change. For some it was part of acculturation, the acquisition of new cultural traits. But for others it was a tool of resistance, the only language in which to assert indigenous cultural rights. 'They've always said that poor Indians can't speak Spanish, so many people speak for them. That's why I decided to learn Spanish,' explains Rigoberta Menchú.

Literacy and education empowered new generations to seek economic, social and political change. Education itself became one of the first sectors to feel the effects, as increasing numbers of indigenous children were taught by indigenous teachers and in turn became teachers themselves. Ironically, it was the inability of government education to keep up with the demand that encouraged indigenous communities in many areas to set up their own schools. From the early 1970s Indian schools for groups as varied as the Mohawk, Maya, Mapuche and Makuxí sprang up throughout the continents. For many communities, the process of defying governments by establishing such schools or the sacrifices involved in raising the money to pay for teachers were in themselves a radicalizing process. These schools were truly indigenous, teaching an indigenous curriculum in an indigenous language. Setting up such a school was often a defining moment for a village, a reservation or a settlement.

'The battle for Indian children will be won in the classroom, not on the streets or on horses. The students of today are our warriors of tomorrow,' believes Eddie Box, a Southern Ute. 'Whoever controls the education of our children controls our future, the future of the Cherokee people and the Cherokee nation,' says Wilma Mankiller, Principal Chief of the Cherokee Nation of Oklahoma.

Many indigenous nations have had to agree alphabets for their languages before they can begin to make the transition from oral to literate culture. This in itself often involves wresting control from the anthropologists or missionaries who have previously monopolized the transposition of indigenous languages to the written page. Such efforts bring different nations together. An agreed alphabet makes the exchange of written material possible and cements links. 'Often people question the use of literacy classes when they start. But by the time they finish they are asking, "Where are our books? Where are our libraries?",' observes Andrés Cuz, the Cultural-Linguistic Director of the Academy of Maya Languages in Guatemala.

This process of educational empowerment is dramatically evident in the Ecuadorean Amazon. At 7.30 in the morning, as adults set off to tend their plots or pastures in a small river community in southeastern Ecuador, barefoot children head for a palm-thatched hut in the middle of the village. There, sitting on wooden benches, they begin their lessons. The teacher, at the front of the class, is a bright-red portable radio. Beside the receiver is a *teleauxiliar*, a local person with primary education and some basic training who supervises lessons in reading, writing, maths and history. Morning lessons have been supplemented by adult evening classes. As a direct result of the radio school, literacy now stands at 90 per cent. Every child in more than 400 communities, some with as few as 15 residents and more than a day's river trip from their nearest neighbour, attends five and a half hours of primary school a day. The lessons are broadcast from the Shuar–Achuar Federation's headquarters in the small town

142

of Sucúa. From separate studios on the first floor, four *telemaestros* (radio teachers) broadcast primary and secondary classes on up to four frequencies simultaneously (Plate 50). The radio school project, launched in 1972, replaced the schools established by Salesian missionaries in 13 education centres throughout the Shuar territory. Backed by the Ministry of Education in Quito, the scheme has become the most successful radio school in the world, playing a crucial role in making the Shuar one of the most effective defenders of indigenous territory in the Americas. 'The biggest disappointment is that others haven't managed to follow suit,' says Manuel Vinza Chacucuy, head of communication at the Federation. 'Many colleagues have come to study it, but it still has no equals.'

The Village in the City: Keeping Rural Traditions

In the twentieth century, the demand for education and other means of self-improvement has been the major factor driving migration to the swelling cities. In the past 75 years, countries throughout the Americas have been transformed from largely rural, agricultural societies into urban melting-pots, and Indians, by 'getting urbanized', in one US phrase, have been a key part of the transformation. As many as half the estimated 40 million indigenous people in the Americas may now live in large towns or huge conurbations such as Lima, Quito, La Paz, Mexico City, Montreal or Chicago. Neglect of the countryside, the loss of community lands, social changes that have freed many from debt peonage, natural disasters, government 'relocation' schemes and civil wars in countries such as Peru and Guatemala have all played their part.

Whole new streets and neighbourhoods have taken the names of the villages or reservations from which the new residents migrated, turning the cities, or more commonly slums, in which indigenous people settle into a test-tube of cultural mixing. In some cases, such as the migration of Zapotecs, Mixtecs or Chinantecs from Mexico to Texas or California, the process has become international as indigenous people cross frontiers seeking work, trade or refuge.

Migration is as complex a process as cultural mixing itself. Many first-generation migrants only 'half move' to the cities, retaining some link with their home village (Plate 51). Almost three-quarters of those settling in La Paz, Bolivia, for instance, return to their native village at least once a year. Many retain land there; others support families or relatives with occasional remittances from jobs as tradesmen, casual labourers, domestic servants or, most commonly, street vendors – all part of what has become known as the 'informal economy'.

In some instances, remittances from the capital or North America have reinforced indigenous society back in the villages. The Q'anjob'al, a small ethnic group living in Guatemala near the Mexican border, are a case in point.

50. *Ecuador: the Shuar Community Radio Project, which has raised literacy to 90 per cent. Every child in more than 400 communities, some with as few as 15 residents and more than a day's river trip from their nearest neighbour, attends five and a half hours of primary school a day.*
© LUKE HOLLAND

144

51. *Guatemala: Indian youth on his way to the Day of the Dead celebrations on All Souls Day (2 November). Young migrant workers return home for important festivals.*
© PAUL SMITH

Remittances of US dollars have allowed the relatives of migrants to buy out non-indigenous businesses and land, a trend now as noticeable in some highland communities in the Americas as its opposite, the settlement of outsiders in the forest territories of their lowland cousins.

Many migrants retain or even strengthen their native culture in their new city homes, often reviving previously neglected indigenous festivals. Whereas communities use them to assert their cultural identity, indigenous merchants promote their observance because of the opportunities they provide to sell the alcohol, material or special foods that are essential props for such events.

Urban activists claim that offerings made to the Pacha Mama in ceremonies marking the sinking of the four cornerposts or stones of a new home in La Paz are observed more religiously by Quechua or Aymara migrants than they are by their counterparts back in the countryside. 'It has become an affirmation of identity that the migrant community now needs more than ever,' asserts one Aymara academic.

The main agents of cultural cohesion are a variety of mutual aid societies, or associations, in which people from one district, village or reservation pool resources. These groups organize celebrations of important festivals and form pressure groups to demand running water, electricity and title for the land on which they have settled.

Lima has more than 6,000 district, departmental or provincial associations and thousands more representing individual towns, villages or neighbourhoods. Such organizations are a modern evolution of the traditional extended kinship groups, the Andean *ayllus* or the *calpulli* of Mesoamerica. They make use of *minga* or *tequio*, the co-operative community labour that formed the basis of such ties in pre-conquest times.

From the early 1980s in particular, such organization has thrived as the neo-liberal economic agenda of the governments of the region's states has imposed deep cuts in social services and slashed subsidies on basics such as food and transport. *Comedores populares* (soup kitchens) and Glass of Milk Committees, ensuring milk supplies for children, have thrived as migration continues to accelerate.

Some migrants keep their dual identity, whereas others forge a new one, an indigenous lifestyle which assumes a name and definition of its own, such as *chicha* culture in Peru. Such mixing consists of a syncretic language, Spanish using, for example, Maya, Nahuatl or Quechua grammatical structures; a syncretic religion, indigenous spirituality in a Christian church; syncretic medicine, as aspirins and antibiotics are sold from the same market stall as traditional herbs, bark and seeds; and syncretic music, blending for example the haunting melodies of the Andean *huayno* with the vitality of the Colombian *cumbia*.

But for some it has all been too much. Without family or traditional indigenous support structures to fall back on, many who move to the cities slump into a cultural abyss. Loss of self-esteem, meaning and a sense of belonging manifests itself in drug or alcohol abuse and despair, perpetuating the stereotype of the drunken, down-and-out Indian visible in so many of the continents' city centres. To survive, many have turned to crime or prostitution (Plate 52), and suicide levels have soared. 'There's two worlds. Sometimes you feel kind of in the middle,' confesses Alice, an Inuit prostitute in the white world of Montreal, an indigenous mother back in her own isolated northern community.

Women First: The Vanguard of the Resistance

Women have been at the forefront of both the move to the cities and the social organization that has sprung up in the urban slums. Initially they came as young domestic servants or travelled into towns and cities as market traders. More recently, they have moved with their families or migrated as displaced widows in countries such as Peru and Guatemala, the victims of civil wars and military

146

52. *Bolivia: Teresa, an Ayoreo Indian, works as a prostitute at the side of the railway track in the boom town of Santa Cruz.*
© LUKE HOLLAND

repression. Today many have jobs in light manufacturing plants on industrial estates that ring the big cities, part of the revolution in jobs in the Americas; others have become mobile hawkers, stallholders or shopkeepers, a minority of them relatively prosperous; some have secured further education and jobs in government, health services, schools or private business; still others are beggars.

In the villages, forests or on the reservations women have always upheld traditional indigenous culture more vigorously than men. They are more likely to be monolingual in their native language, to wear traditional indigenous dress, to remain loyal to traditional spiritual and health care practices. As mothers they play a crucial role in passing on their stories, customs and dress to succeeding generations.

Given the nature of most indigenous resistance, cultural rather than physical, subtle rather than confrontational, women have often been better suited to the frontline, becoming the 'keepers of the culture', as Mary Ellen Tempel, a Canadian activist puts it. As a Cheyenne proverb explains:

> A nation is not conquered
> Until the hearts of its women
> Are on the ground.
>
> Then it is done, no matter
> How brave its warriors
> Or how strong its weapons.

Before the mass urban migration of the twentieth century, women's pre-eminent role as 'keepers of the culture' could have been explained by the fact that they were less affected by some of the most potent assimilating forces, such as work in the cities, labour on the plantations or compulsory service in the military. However, a trip to the main square of Guatemala City on a Sunday afternoon or a glance around the street markets of Quito or La Paz today confirms that urban indigenous women are still much more likely to wear their traditional dress and speak their own language than their male counterparts (Plate 53). Indigenous women living in the cities have used their culture as an important defence mechanism against a doubly hostile world in which racism and sexism are the norm.

Indigenous dress can be used as protective clothing, a statement proclaiming that the wearer is not available to *mestizos* or white men. 'When a Maya woman wears her indigenous dress she is stating where and to whom she belongs,' says Angela Pérez, a K'iche' grassroots organizer based in Guatemala City. Many attribute an almost mystical power of collective identity to their indigenous dress that they find difficult to express in words, especially the words of a second language that does not relate to their culture.

Women have emerged at the forefront of the urban grassroots organizations for a variety of reasons. Migration from the cities has broken down the traditional division of labour between the genders, whereby the male tended the staple crops or sought paid work and the woman tended a vegetable garden and the smaller livestock, such as chickens.

Social relations have been further transformed by the informal economy of the city, which provides money-making opportunities to women. These often make them an equal, or even main, breadwinner within a family. Above all, necessity means that women often lead co-operative organizations as part of their quest for better food, housing, sanitation, health care and education.

Many women arrive in the cities without their husbands or menfolk, obliging them to take up new roles and opportunities. In Peru, Chile and Guatemala, in particular, women have been radicalized by systematic rape, the murder or disappearance of husbands, sons or brothers and the destruction of their villages at the hands of the military. Victims have gradually become protagonists.

'Women reflected on their individual stories and connected them as part of

148

53. *Guatemala: Couple wearing combination of traditional and western clothes. Women usually take the lead in retaining indigenous customs, language and dress.*
© ROBERT FRANCIS/HUTCHISON

recognizing their potential to struggle for change,' according to Carmen Beatriz Ruiz, an Aymara woman working in the Gregoria Apaza Centre for the Advancement of Women in La Paz. The political consciousness born of shared experience saw social organization go hand in hand with political campaigns for information on the whereabouts of relatives.

It is not just the absence of their menfolk that thrusts women into such leadership roles. In testifying to the indigenous experience, women have a unique appeal, particularly as the world has become more sensitive to indigenous issues. 'The public is willing to listen to people who speak the truth. Women speak from the heart, not the head,' observes Katie Rich, an Innu and the first female mayor of Utshimassits (Davis Inlet).

Strong links with indigenous villages have spurred the development of grass-roots groups in the countryside with resources, experience and political expertise provided by activists blooded, often literally, in the cities. By 1994 CONAVIGUA, the National Co-ordinating Committee of Guatemalan Widows, a totally female organization, boasted 14,000 members, organizing and voting within a democratic structure operating at village/neighbourhood, departmental and national level. 'We widows are beginning to learn a little,' Doña Flora, a

149

K'iche' Maya, told one anthropologist. 'Before, as wives, when we went to the town we would not even think of ascending the steps of the town hall. Now we not only ascend the steps but talk to the mayor!' Such comments illustrate the liberation many indigenous women have experienced in recovering their birthright, the equality that formed the basis of male–female relations in so many indigenous societies before the conquest. Some groups, such as the Micaela Bastidas Women's Organization in Bolivia, emphasize the fact by naming their groups after role models like Micaela Bastidas, Tupaq Amaru's wife and principal political adviser.

In getting organized, many women speak of achieving 'internal healing' or 'spiritual recovery' as well as political consciousness. 'We are curing ourselves of prejudices, feelings of inferiority, of self-marginalization,' says Tarcila Rivera Zea. 'We must regain our identity. Without it we cannot help ourselves, let alone others.'

The Development Battle: 'We Don't Want Your Dam!'

At the root of urban migration and indigenous women's struggle is a fundamental battle over indigenous people's right to decide their own development path. The issue remains inseparable from the struggle for self-determination – economic, political, social and judicial. The right to set their own course for economic development is a litmus test of a community or ethnic group's right to self-determination while an agreed economic development strategy within such a community or ethnic group is the most important means of underwriting such self-determination. 'An organization that revolves around productive concerns and puts money in the family purse will survive and thrive,' argues Patricio Camacho, an economist with Maquita Cushunchij, a grassroots organization in Ecuador. 'By increasing our economic power, our organizations will be better able to make their voices heard politically,' says CONAIE official Ampam Karakras.

The battle over economic development was at the heart of the culture clash which followed the conquest: community needs versus individual greed, sustainable evolution versus winner-take-all destruction, subsistence survival versus capitalist profit. 'Indians chase the vision, white men chase the dollar,' as John Lame Deer, a Rosebud Lakota, said in 1972. The battles have been played out most ferociously on indigenous lands, in the burning and logging of rain forests in Brazil, in oil exploration and drilling in Ecuador, Colombia, Peru and Mexico, in the cultivation of export crops in Canada and the United States, and in the construction of some of the world's largest hydroelectric dams from Quebec in the north to Paraguay in the south. Such 'development' lies at the

150

heart of today's continuing conquest. Almost all the projects referred to above have been imposed on indigenous societies without consultation. Indigenous peoples were lucky if their very presence was even recognized in the regions in which such developments took place, a continuation of the *terra nullus* (empty land) concept of the original invaders.

Yet in many cases indigenous resistance has given governments, state companies and multinationals a rude awakening, often becoming the focus of international attention and galvanizing moves to cultural revival in the process. One of the most dramatic examples took place in February 1989, at Altamira, Brazil, in the heart of Kayapó territory. After a year's intense campaigning against the construction of the Barbaquara and Kararao dams on the Xingu River, a campaign that had taken them to Washington and Brasilia, the Kayapó called an international meeting at Altamira. Officials from Eletronorte, the Brazilian power supply company, shared the platform with feather-head-dressed, war-painted Kayapó chiefs to address about 650 indigenous representatives from 40 different nations, along with 400 foreign journalists.

Two moments encapsulated a stormy meeting: the first, when an old Indian woman marched to the podium and slapped an Eletronorte engineer on the cheeks with the flat blade of her machete; the second, when a Kayapó woman rose to speak. 'We don't need your electricity. It won't give us food ... we need our forests to hunt and gather in. We don't want your dam,' she exclaimed. Her words echoed an old Amuit Indian saying to the white man in North America, 'Only when you have felled the last tree, caught the last fish and polluted the last river will you realize that you can't eat money.' In those few moments, televised around the world, the Kayapó spoke for indigenous people worldwide and addressed the non-indigenous world everywhere. The following month the World Bank announced that it would no longer fund the dams.

It was but one victory. The scale of the threat could be seen in Brazil's planned electricity expansion programme of the time: 136 dams, 68 of them on indigenous land flooding up to 100,000 square miles and displacing 500,000 people. The Kayapó's battle is being re-fought today in dozens of locations in the Americas from the land of the Cree in Canada to that of the Mapuche in Chile.

Indigenous people are not against economic development, modernity or even what is still often termed 'progress'. 'We do not oppose development as such,' says Ailton Krenak, co-ordinator of Brazil's Union of Indigenous Nations. 'We oppose the development model pursed to date – it has been destructive, nefarious, stupid and disastrous. We oppose monoculture, the grass and the bull. What native peoples want is to adapt new technologies to the traditional practices of Indians.'

The indigenous cameramen filming the proceedings in Altamira (Plate 54) for colleagues to watch back home in their remote forest communities were doing

151

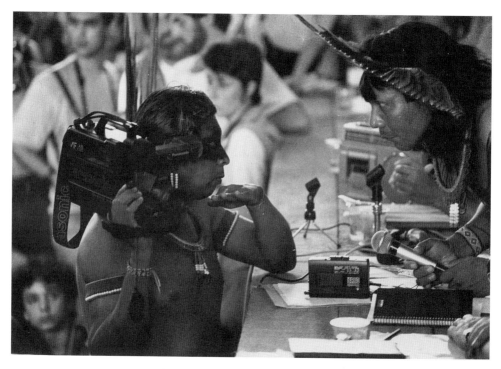

54. *Brazil: high-profile protest against a new dam in Altamira in 1989. Kayapó leaders have proved adept at using Western technology to defend lands and livelihoods. The following month the World Bank announced that it would no longer fund the dams.*
© SUE CUNNINGHAM/SURVIVAL INTERNATIONAL

just that. The adaptation of modern technology to reinforce and protect indigenous culture is evident everywhere in the Americas, where faxes, two-way radios and satellite telephones are becoming basic tools for hundreds of Indian organizations. Within hours of the Zapatista National Liberation Army's takeover of four towns in Chiapas, Mexico, on 1 January 1994, computer screens around the world were full of news of the uprising as the rebels went on-line with e-mailed communiqués.

The choice is often between 'inward-looking' modernization, where people make changes by choice and consensus without causing a breakdown in the system, and 'outward-looking' modernization, which involves involuntary changes imposed by another culture and people. The first preserves and reinforces indigenous culture; the second often submerges it.

Nowhere has the issue of destructive development and cultural annihilation been more obvious than in the Amazonian areas of Ecuador, where an oil boom since the early 1970s has left a trail of devastation. During the course of its 20-year contract with the government, Texaco, which dominated the industry in Ecuador, allowed an estimated 16.8 million gallons of oil to spill from pipelines, abandoned 1,000 uncovered oil-waste ponds and discarded 20 billion gallons of toxic waste into the environment.

The construction of a network of 300 miles of roads opened the region to a wave of colonization and led directly to the clearing of more than 2 million acres of rain forest. The Huaroni, Siona and Secoya peoples have been devastated. Displaced by the oil company infrastructure and settlers, poisoned by the pollution and 'saved' by the evangelical missionaries who followed, their numbers have declined from about 20,000 in each group in the late 1960s to between 700 and 1,200 today.

Others have fared even worse. The Cofanes, in whose territory the main Texaco refinery was built, slumped in number from 3,000 to 300. Lago Agrio, the site of the first well, was a village of Tetete people. They are now extinct. Texaco may be forced by legal action to clean up the mess but it will of course be too late for the Indians. They cannot possibly benefit from Texaco vice-president Yorick Foncesca's commitment to 'remediate whatever damage is identified'.

Moreover, what has happened in the north of the Ecuadorean Amazon now threatens the southern provinces of Sucumbillos, Napo and Pastaza. The Ecuadorean government is bent on doubling oil production by 1996, having issued tenders for drilling on 2 million acres of land in these 'undeveloped regions' in 1993, much of it on indigenous land. The government will not get things all its own way. The devastation in Ecuador has been partially responsible for producing one of the most effective indigenous movements in the world (Plate 55). The local Organization of Indigenous Peoples of Pastaza (OPIP) has already won important concessions from the government on the terms of oil development. Others are aiming higher. The national Indian confederation, CONAIE, is demanding a 15-year moratorium on new oil development. 'Assaults on the rights of our people are declared acts of war. We will resist ecological terrorism and know how to defend ourselves,' pledges Luis Macas, CONAIE's president.

The assault by the oil industry in Ecuador is being repeated throughout the western and northern Amazon basin in Colombia, Peru and Venezuela. In Peru, 23 Amazon oil concessions have been awarded in indigenous territories. In Colombia the industry is already exacting its toll with little regard for the local inhabitants. 'Each year, 5 billion pesos are taken from Putumayo while the people live in physical misery,' Colombian senator Gabriel Muyuy points out, referring to just one Amazon region. 'Only 20 per cent of the oil royalties are reinvested in the region.'

55. *Ecuador: Luis Vargas, Achuar Indian and a leading figure in indigenous
protests against environmental damage by multinational oil and gas companies
in the Ecuadorean Amazon.*
© LUKE HOLLAND

Ethno-development: Consider the Seventh Generation

Such conflicts spring from the arrogance of the first Europeans to arrive in the
Americas, who saw all the indigenous societies around them as primitive versions of their own. 'Development' meant the wholesale adoption of European
ways despite the differences in climate, environment and social organization,
let alone culture. For hundreds of years, the governments and non-indigenous
peoples of the Americas measured success by an 'index of modernity', showing
how close their economic, political and social institutions were to those of
Europe. There were two inevitable results. First, anything indigenous was marginalized and stigmatized. Second, the new societies in the Americas were
condemned to poverty because they depended on European (later North
American) resources and markets.

At issue is who defines and decides on 'development'. To date, large-scale
'economic development' has invariably been imposed on indigenous communities by outsiders, legitimizing the appropriation or theft of indigenous resources

154

such as minerals, oil, lumber, water, fish or land, while centralizing and increasing the political power of the state over indigenous people and their territory. Now, without exception, indigenous peoples are demanding ethno-development, or self-development, in essence the power to decide things for themselves. They are also demanding sustainable development, something that to them has always been second nature and which is now being praised, though rarely practised, by Western nations.

Nothing illustrates such thinking better than the North American Indian Seventh Generation Fund (SGF). With a budget of several million US dollars and offices throughout the United States, SGF funds projects based on self-reliance, indigenous ways of life, the protection or reclaiming of land, resources and sovereignty, and projects dedicated to indigenous women. SGF was created in 1977 on the premise that Indians needed to move beyond the rhetoric of sovereignty towards concrete efforts to rebuild the infrastructure of indigenous communities. Its name is taken from the old Iroquois custom of considering the impact of any major decisions on the seventh future generation before acting.

As foreign aid agencies have learned, economic development projects which emerge from within communities or ethnic groups are more likely to succeed, not just in their own economic terms. Many such projects reinforce local cultures and reinvigorate communities by reducing the pressures to migrate. They also encourage the struggle for self-determination by making communities more aware of the possibilities of planned collective effort.

Recovering or discovering technologies and methods from the past has played a vital part in the growth of ethno-development in the Americas. In northern Bolivia, Aymara villagers have begun to record what agronomists believe are world record yields for potatoes, producing 28 tons per acre compared with yields of just one ton in the mid-1980s. The difference is due not to artificial fertilizer, tractors or Western seed strains, but to the revival of the the *suka kollus* or raised platform fields used in Inka times (Plate 56).

Where indigenous peoples have secured the rights to their land and thus to exploit their resources, there have been some surprising developments. In northern Canada, the Inuvialuit obtained control of 35,000 square miles of mineral-rich territory from the Canadian government in 1984 and set up their own oil-producing company, the Inuvialuit Petroleum Corporation (IPC). The company pumps out 6,000 barrels of oil a day, along with 28 million cubic feet of natural gas. 'They are pro-development because they are confident it will be done on the right terms and conditions, protecting their environment and traditional activities,' says IPC chairman Russel Newmark.

In Brazil, however, the experience of the Kayapó demonstrates the pitfalls of what some see as indigenized Western development. In 1991, the Kayapó won

56. *Peru: Quechua Indians harvesting barley. The revival of the* suka kollus *or raised platform fields used in Inka times has enabled Aymara villagers to record what agronomists believe are world record yields for potatoes.*
© TONY MORRISON/SOUTH AMERICAN PICTURES

control of 17,000 square miles of rain forest. They were soon accused of exploiting their gold and timber reserves as readily and in as environmentally harmful a manner as the loggers and miners whom they had once campaigned to expel, but with whom they now struck business deals. The Kayapó say their hands have been forced by the sickness and environmental problems introduced by outsiders before they won control of their own territory. 'Why do we need planes? To bring the sick from the villages. Why do we need roads and cars? To take doctors to the villages. Why do we need to sell mahogany? To pay for medicine, fuel and hospitals,' says Kube-I, a young Kayapó leader.

In the past, the Kayapó have been an outstanding example of an elementary form of ethno-development. Between 1981 and 1985, unable to remove *garimpeiros* (wildcat gold miners) from their land by force, they decided to regulate them. The Kayapó started charging a tax of between 1 and 10 per cent of production while policing the mining areas themselves. In 1985, they closed down the María Bonita mine when a contract providing them with only 1 per cent of production expired. With the help of the Brazilian military, they managed to expel more than 5,000 miners from the site. The Kayapó then agreed to reopen the mine on condition FUNAI, the Brazilian Indian agency, agreed to demarcate their land. In May of that year, they signed an agreement establishing a 7.4 million acre reserve. The mine reopened with a 5 per cent tax in place.

Despite the problems, the Kayapó's success in bargaining access to their resources in return for state recognition of their lands shows that ethno-development can be achieved. Few others have had as much success as the Kayapó, but some other peoples have managed to limit the damage and even take advantage of Western-style development. The anthropologist Andrew Gray cites the Amarakaeri (Arakmbut) of the Madre de Dios region of Peru, who have themselves worked as miners on and off since the 1970s. For them, he says, the gold economy is 'a change but not a threat'.

Many indigenous groups have asserted their right to self-development by taking control of the tourist trade, for which indigenous people, their villages, reservations and lifestyles are a growing attraction. Some merely sell crafts or cultural goods to passing visitors, but others, such as the Kuna of Panama and the Miccosukee of Florida, have set up companies specializing in cultural education or eco-tourism (Plate 57). Both groups have sought to take control of outside developments on their land, trying to harness these forces for their own ends to educate white visitors, limit the numbers coming on to their land and meet the growing economic imperative of raising cash.

Steve Tiger, a Miccosukee who runs the the American Indian Experience for tourists in the Everglades of Florida, has been at the forefront of such efforts. 'You can call it a sell-out or a buy-in,' he says, responding to criticism that 'professional Indians', as they are sometimes scathingly known by colleagues, are cheapening Indian culture. 'Adaptation avoids assimiliation,' he believes.

Gene Genie: 'The Last Great Resource Rush'

In recent years, ethno-development has assumed a new importance as indigenous territories are besieged by what has been termed 'the last great resource rush', the scramble for genetic and biological material and the indigenous knowledge that makes it worth tens of billions of dollars.

Ever since Indian medical expertise gave the world quinine to treat malaria in the seventeenth century, pharmaceutical and agricultural companies have been exploiting indigenous knowledge of local germplasm. A single wild tomato variety taken from Peru in 1962 has contributed US$8 million a year to the American tomato-processing industry. An extract from the tiki-uba plant developed by the Uru-Eu-Uau-Uau Indians in Brazil is expected to make many

157

57. *USA: Steve Tiger, a Miccosukee who runs the American Indian Experience for tourists in the Everglades of Florida. 'You can call it a sell-out or a buy-in' he says, but 'adaptation avoids assimilation.'*
© BRIAN MOSER/HUTCHISON

millions more in the hands of the US chemical company Merck, Sharp & Dohme, who plan to market it as a new anticoagulant. D-Tubocurarine, a muscle relaxant from the Amazonian liana; the steroid diosgenin, originally from a Mexican yam and now used to make birth control pills – the list is endless.

What is new are the stakes, which have grown enormously. More than 9,000 natural compounds accounted for nearly half the estimated US$100 billion world pharmaceutical trade in 1992. The development of genetic engineering, biotechnology, the growth in consumption and the savings in research costs that plant-based drugs can bring are creating a further surge in demand.

The 121 plant-derived prescription drugs now in use were discovered through the testing of about 35,000 species, only about 5,000 of which were exhaustively analysed, according to Jack Kloppenburg, a rural sociologist and the author of *First the Seed: The Political Economy of Plant Biotechnology*. There are an estimated 300,000–750,000 plant species in the world, most of them in the most biodiverse areas, especially rain forests.

158

The issues for indigenous peoples are the same as in other fields: consultation, rights and benefits. Intellectual property rights are notoriously difficult to enforce, but it is accepted in industrialized societies that if a private company accumulates commercially useful knowledge through research and development, it is entitled to a percentage of the profits by means of a patent. Indigenous people are increasingly demanding the same rights.

The Indigenous Peoples' Biodiversity Network (IPBN), a global coalition of indigenous peoples formed to protect biocultural resources and prevent what has been labelled bio-imperialism, lobbies for indigenous peoples' rights within the Biodiversity Convention agreed at the 'Earth Summit' in Rio de Janeiro in 1992. 'For the first time the provisions of the Biodiversity Convention may offer opportunities to effectively protect rights to biocultural resources,' says Alejandro Argumedo, a Quechua from Peru who heads Cultural Survival in Canada.

In 1988 the Kuna of Panama showed the way when they produced a set of rules for researchers and scientists entering their lands, a 26-page booklet entitled *Research Program: Scientific Monitoring and Cooperation*. These rules have largely been adhered to simply because the Kuna have been able to establish effective control over their territory and thus those who enter it. The Kuna have also been innovative in demanding that visiting scientists file reports on their research and employ Kuna assistants, guides and informants to transfer 'knowledge and technologies with the objective of training Kuna scientists'. 'We have established control of our territories. Establishing control of our scientific resources is the obvious next step,' says Léonidas Valdez, a Kuna leader.

In 1988 another potential scientific threat came to light. The Human Genome Diversity Project aims to map each of the 100,000 genes found in mankind by the year 2005. The project is particularly keen to collect samples of blood and hair from 'endangered' indigenous populations or 'isolates of historic interest', as scientists call them (Plate 58). By exploring the genetic composition of different ethnic groups, scientists hope to gain a better understanding of why diseases vary so much in their geographic distribution. This, they believe, could provide vital clues in efforts to combat fatal disease.

The issue came to a head in 1993 when the United States Department of Commerce tried to take out a patent claim on the DNA in white blood cells taken from a 26-year-old Guaymí woman from the forests of eastern Panama. The DNA was believed to confer the possibility of immunity to the HTLV virus that causes leukaemia, making the cells a potential goldmine. The Guaymí woman's cells, stored at the American Type Culture Collection (ATCC), had been collected in disputed circumstances. Calls for their return were refused, but after worldwide protests from indigenous peoples and their supporters the US Department of Commerce abandoned its attempts to register the patent.

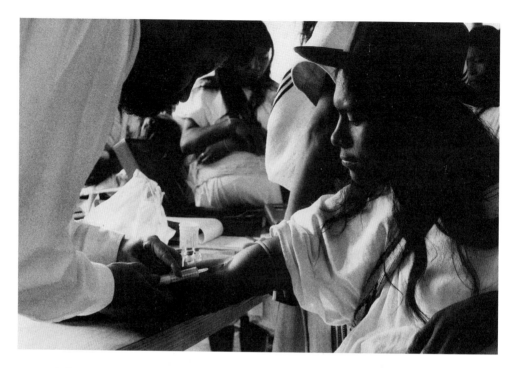

58. *Colombia: a geneticist takes a blood sample from an Arhuaco Indian for DNA analysis. The Human Genome Diversity Project, a major international effort to collect genetic material from native peoples worldwide, has provoked controversy and Indian protests.*
© LUKE HOLLAND

The quest, however, went on. In November 1995 the US Department of Health and Human Services awarded itself a patent on the DNA of a member of the Hagahai people of Papua New Guinea. The DNA had a similar profile to that of the Guaymí woman.

To many indigenous peoples in the Americas, the plunder of their biodiversity is the ultimate irony. What they always said was true wealth – the natural world – is proving to be so even on the white man's terms. Their nature, their environment, has become increasingly attractive simply because, against all the odds, they have managed to defend it against the encroachment of generations of settlers who would have destroyed it. 'Today the white world talks about ecology but it is really only interested in saving what serves its own purposes,' complains Adrián Esquina Lisco, of the National Association of Indigenous Peoples of El Salvador. 'Today the white world wants to understand native cultures and extract those fragments of wisdom that extend its own dominion.'

160

Neo-liberalism: The Invisible Fist of the Market

The economic needs addressed by ethno-development are largely the result of the scale of the assault on indigenous resources and land in the twentieth century. Mining, agriculture, forestry, dam and road construction have all taken their toll, but since the onset of the debt crisis in the early 1980s neo-liberalism, a virulent form of free-market economics, has greatly magnified their impact.

Neo-liberalism's prescription has been foisted on the continent by the international banks and multilateral lending agencies such as the International Monetary Fund (IMF) and World Bank. It involves what have become known as recession-inducing 'stabilization' programmes, followed by 'structural adjustment' of the economy. In practice, this has meant cutbacks in state spending, deregulation of the workforce, liberalization of trade and investment, and the privatization of state industries.

Duncan Green, author of *Silent Revolution: The Rise of Market Economics in Latin America* (London: Cassell, 1995), believes that:

> With its focus on individualism and the market, the [neo-liberal] revolution stands diametrically opposed to the indigenous traditions of community, subsistence agriculture and reciprocal aid. Indians have been sacked from the factories and mines, paid less on agricultural plantations, and have faced massively increased costs for transport, education and health care. They have seen the markets for their basic crops undercut by cheap imports and suffered further pressure on their land in the drive to export more minerals, oil, timber or cash crops.

Indigenous peoples, invariably the poorest by orthodox economic criteria, have suffered most. The governments of Bolivia, Peru and Mexico, all countries with large indigenous populations, have been some of the most avid exponents of economic adjustment. Study after study has confirmed that inequality and poverty rose markedly throughout the Americas during the 1980s, now widely known as 'the lost decade'. It was a decade whose effects a whole generation of Indian children in particular will go on feeling for the rest of their lives. 'We want them to study but they are so malnourished … they don't do their homework and then they fail the year … we have nothing, nothing,' one Quechua mother forced to scour the tin slag-heaps of Potosí told Duncan Green.

The statistics encapsulate such human tragedies. By 1991, 80 per cent of Bolivian households lived below the poverty line, unable to satisfy basic needs including food, clothing, education and health care. Fifty per cent were even worse off, unable even to feed themselves. Throughout Latin America in the 1980s, 60 million people joined the ranks of the poor, taking the overall figure to nearly 200 million, 46 per cent of the population. Almost half of them were unable to afford enough basic food.

161

In the United States, Reaganomics had a similar impact. In 1983 alone, the Indian aid budget was cut by more than a third from US$3.5 billion to US$2 billion. Programmes on every reservation were hit: the Poncas in Oklahoma lost 200 jobs overnight; the indigenous Alcohol Treatment Center in Montana lost half its counsellors and most of its beds; large slumps in per capita income became the norm.

Even before such cuts, the 1980 census revealed that 28 per cent of the country's 1.75 million Indians, Inuits and Aleuts were living below the poverty line. 'Trickle-down economics feels a lot like being pissed on,' complained one indigenous official. The lack of understanding behind such actions stung many indigenous people. In 1988 President Reagan outraged Indian leaders when he told a student in Moscow, 'Maybe we made a mistake in trying to maintain Indian cultures. Maybe we should not have humoured them in wanting to stay in that kind of primitive lifestyle.'

In Bolivia one Agrarian Reform Commission official was equally blunt: 'Certain *campesino* sectors will lose their lands. This is an inevitable if painful consequence of development.' Antonio Aramayo, director of Qhana, a rural development centre in Bolivia, put it another way: 'They plan to take the land once and for all and complete the denial of indigenous land rights that began with the conquest.'

Neo-liberalism makes white economics even more of a mystery than they already are to many Indians. 'How come the white man got the country for nothing and now owes everyone for it?', asked one North American Indian leader. 'It mystifies me,' said a South American counterpart on hearing of the debt-for-nature swaps that became fashionable palliatives for the foreign debt crisis. 'It's our nature, but it's not our debt.'

Many see it as another stage in their impoverishment: first land, then resources, now welfare and minimal social services – all taken away. 'Sometimes I wish white people hadn't taught us about cash. We had everything with nature. Now they say we're lazy and give us welfare, but I say, "Who taught us about cash?" It was the white people,' says Margaret Siwallace, a Nuxalk.

Others try to couch their arguments in white terms. 'Look upon the natural resources of this world as capital, not income,' urges Russell Means, a Lakota Sioux. 'Our oil, our uranium, our coal, our timber, all of these natural resources are capital. If you look at them as capital, then maybe you will think of the future.'

Neo-liberalism has certainly forced indigenous activists to concentrate on practicalities. 'We used to work much more on organizational issues,' says Antonio Aramayo of Qhana in La Paz. 'Now it's the realities. Economic enterprises can provide communities with greater security and the capacity to negotiate with the neo-liberal model.'

Many observers agree that growing economic independence and the application of indigenous value systems could form the basis of resistance to the neo-liberal economic model. 'Indigenous people insist that wealth must be socially redistributed, a logic which opposes the dominant system of accumulation,' says Zulema Lehm of Beni Department's Regional Development Centre in Bolivia. 'What they basically stand for is a reordering of society. It might yet represent a political challenge to the model.'

By the 1990s it was clear that Indian conceptions of economic development could be one of the most potent forces in the battle against assimilation and cultural absorption. Economic regeneration, whether through the development of tourist trips through the Florida Everglades or the rediscovery of traditional potato-raising techniques in the Andes, gives indigenous peoples the opportunity to deal with the outside world on more equal terms. As a result, the prospects for the Indians of today are infinitely more encouraging than those of their ancestors seven generations ago.

Bibliography

Arguedas, José María, *Katatay* (Lima: Editorial Horizonte, 1984).

Beauclark, John, and Narby, Jeremy, with Townsend, Janet, *Indigenous Peoples: A Fieldguide for Development* (Oxford: Oxfam, 1988).

Carlessi, Carolina, 'The reconquest'. *NACLA Report on the Americas* (New York: North American Congress on Latin America), vol. 23, no. 4 (Nov./Dec. 1989).

Condori, Ana María, *Nayan Uñatatawi – Mi Despertar* (La Paz: Hisbol, 1988).

Carneiro da Cunha, Manuela, 'Native *Realpolitik*'. *NACLA Report on the Americas* (New York: North American Congress on Latin America), vol. 23, no. 1 (May 1989).

'Intellectual property rights: the politics of ownership'. *Cultural Survival Quarterly*, vol. 15, no. 3 (Summer 1991).

International Work Group for Indigenous Affairs, *Indigenous Self-Development in the Americas*, Document no. 63 (Copenhagen: IWGIA, 1983).

International Work Group for Indigenous Affairs, *And After the Gold Rush? Human Rights and Self-Development among the Amarakaeri of Southeastern Peru*, Document no. 55 (Copenhagen: IWGIA, 1986).

Mallon, Florencia, E., 'Indian communities, political cultures, and the state in Latin America, 1780–1990'. *Journal of Latin American Studies*, vol. 24 (Quincentenary Supplement, 1992).

Shiva, Vandina, 'Biodiversity, biotechnology and profit: the need for a peoples' plan to protect biological diversity'. *The Ecologist*, vol. 20, no. 2 (March/April 1990).

Spiwak, Daniela, 'Gene genie and science's thirst for information with indigenous blood'. *Abya Yala News* (Oakland, CA.), vol. 7, no. 3/4 (Fall/Winter 1993).

Switkes, Glenn, 'The people vs. Texaco'. *NACLA Report on the Americas* (New York: North American Congress on Latin America), vol. 28, no. 2 (Sept./Oct. 1994).

6
Organization and Revival

A ripple ran through the national stadium. All eyes were trained on two figures who stood before a roaring fire tended by three *amautas* (priests) wearing the trademark woollen caps and rubber-tyre sandals of Bolivia's highland peoples. The couple were an incongruous sight; she in the latest European fashion and high heels, his Western suit shrouded by the flowing robes and feather head-dress in which the leader of a lowland nation had just draped him. Both seemed to be hesitating to join another couple to their right who were already kneeling as the *amautas* began the chanting that would accompany the sacred burning of offerings to the Pacha Mama, the Earth Goddess. Finally, hoisting the unfamiliar robe to his knees, Gonzalo Sánchez de Lozada, the American-educated mining magnate shortly to be inaugurated as Bolivia's new president, fell to his knees. He raised a hand to his wife who joined him and cast a nervous smile at Víctor Hugo Cárdenas, the Aymara next to him who would soon be his vice-president. The audience, studded with the *bombín* bowlers hats and *pollera* dresses of Bolivia's indigenous women, and the *ponchos* and *pututus* (cere-monial horns) of their men, erupted in approval, waving the *wiphala*, the rainbow-coloured Inka flag, and homemade placards bearing the names of their communities.

The ceremony in the National Stadium in August 1993 was billed as the bestowing of authority by the country's indigenous people on the incoming executive. Watched by indigenous delegates from as far afield as Chile and Canada and flanked by Rigoberta Menchú, wearing her gold Nobel Peace Prize medal, Cárdenas and Sánchez de Lozada had received armfuls of symbols of authority from indigenous leaders.

Two days later, still wearing one such gift, a vicuña scarf, Víctor Hugo Cárdenas became the first Indian to assume major executive office in the Americas since Benito Juárez in Mexico more than 130 years earlier. Overlooked by the august Victorian grandees of Bolivian politics, who stared down from their oil portraits in apparent disapproval, Cárdenas made a point of becoming the first indigenous leader to make a speech in Congress in Quechua, Aymara and

Guaraní, Bolivia's three main indigenous languages. He echoed the themes of his campaign, of Bolivia as 'a nation of many nations' in which he promised to build 'a multicultural, multiethnic and pluricultural country', ideas that would have been unthinkable just four years earlier. But he went further, stating:

> After 500 years of colonial silence and 168 years of republican exclusion, we have come forward to tell our truth. Ours has been a history of permanent struggle for freedom and justice, for multicultural and multiethnic democracy. Today we are entering the age of a new *pachakut'i*, a fundamental change. We Bolivians, united, are beginning to transform those 500 years of exclusion and marginality.

The life and times of Víctor Hugo Cárdenas mirror those of thousands of indigenous people at the forefront of the current renaissance. Born in 1952, the year of the Bolivian revolution which abolished the *haciendas* and introduced land reform, he was a product of the ensuing indigenous push for education. After completing his primary education in the Aymara area around Lake Titicaca, he had to migrate to La Paz for his secondary education, where he subsequently worked his way through university as a mini-bus driver.

Cárdenas has never forgotten his roots. His father changed his Aymara surname from Choquehuanca to Cárdenas in a desperate effort to spare his children the discrimination he had suffered. His wife, Lidia Katari, had had to give up her job as a teacher because she refused to change her *manta* (shawl), *pollera* (skirt) and *chollos* (braids) for what Aymaras call *vestido* (Western dress). Víctor Hugo Cárdenas knows members of a generation for whom literacy was an offence. 'I have within my family relatives whose fingers were cut off by landlords when they found out that they could sign their names,' he told one newspaper editor in September 1993.

The indigenous organization from which Cárdenas emerged sprang up in the universities and high schools of Bolivia in the late 1960s. The Kataristas took their name from Tupaq Katari, the Aymara leader executed for leading a rebellion against the Spanish in 1780. They shared the new ways of organizing which were evolving simultaneously throughout the Americas.

One of the first signs of the new consciousness the Kataristas represented was the seminal Manifesto of Tiawanaku, drawn up by four indigenous organizations in La Paz in July 1973. The manifesto began by quoting Inka Yupanki, who had told the Spaniards, 'A nation that oppresses another nation cannot be free.' It went on to reassert Indian identity, saying that peasants were Indians and the economic powerhouse of the 'nation'; to acknowledge a debt to left-wing political parties, tempered by scepticism that the leadership had the interests of the Indians at heart; to recognize the role of modern technology, medicine and education in indigenous communities; and to demand control over their own cultural institutions. It concluded: 'Virtually everything remains to be done. We do not want anybody to do it for us; we only want to be allowed to do it ourselves.'

The Manifesto of Tiawanaku was followed by a spate of other declarations from indigenous nations throughout the Americas, most notably the Dene Declaration of 1974, which began, 'The government of Canada is not the government of the Dene.' The Declaration of the Haudenosaunee, or the Six Nations Iroquois Confederacy, followed in 1979 announcing itself as 'among the most ancient continuously operating governments in the world'.

Such moves were reciprocated at the international level. In 1971 the World Council of Churches sponsored a conference in Barbados on the 'Liberation of the Indian'. Although attended mostly by anthropologists and advocates, it stimulated efforts to place indigenous people themselves at the forefront in the struggle for indigenous rights. The ensuing Declaration of Barbados explained that: 'It is necessary to keep in mind that the liberation of the indigenous populations must be accomplished by themselves or it is not liberation.'

Return of the Indian: Major Organizations Emerge

The new organizations that began to spring up in the 1970s had a number of common characteristics. They worked on a wide range of different fronts – cultural, economic, political and intellectual – in a network of organizations and programmes which overlapped but whose connection was often not immediately obvious. Many activists worked, at least initially, through existing organizations, seeking to get their agenda adopted by trade unions, political parties, churches and grassroots groups. These activists became steadily more 'Indianist' in their demands, co-opting the groups they worked in or, as they became more confident, setting up separate organizations with specifically indigenous agendas. Their philosophy, which became known as '*Indianismo*' (Indianism), was ethnic nationalism, a radical force in which Indians led their own movement and decided on their own demands. It was the antithesis of *indigenismo*, the paternalistic assimiliationism that emerged in the 1920s.

The new groups built from the bottom upwards, with village, *barrio* or college organizations, becoming members of regional, then national, and by the 1980s international groups. The result was the steady emergence of a pan-Indian nationalism in which highland and lowland, traditional and modern, educated and illiterate, urban and rural Indians came together and, however cautiously, began to work and lobby jointly.

All such organization was a response to local factors such as racism, discrimination, land seizures, mining or agricultural development, or just a general deterioration of people's economic conditions at a time of rising expectations.

166

In many instances all these causes merged, especially in the case of lowland peoples who began to suffer the multiple effects of mass colonization by land-less *mestizos* or mineral prospectors in the 1960s and 1970s.

However, the most successful organizations all had one thing in common: initially, they were not overtly political. They dealt with immediate needs, building a bedrock of support that gradually allowed them to make more polit-ical demands or to point out to a wider audience the links between culture and politics.

Among the first to draw attention to their plight were the Shuar and Achuar nations on the western edge of the Amazon forest in southeastern Ecuador. In 1964 they formed a federation and thirty years on they are still in the vanguard of the Indian movement in the Americas. From their headquarters in Sucúa, a huge concrete building that replaced the community centre burned down by colonists in 1969, the Shuar–Achuar run marketing organizations, a revolu-tionary radio school (see Chapter 5), legal services, a fleet of vehicles and two light aircraft to transport people and produce.

Their federation is composed of 60,000 people grouped into 30 associations made up of 400 local centres or communities. The sense of belonging is reflected in a motto prominently displayed inside the community headquarters, '*Shuar iruntramuka AMEKETME, tuma asamtai YAIMKIATNIUITME*' – 'The Shuar–Achuar Federation is you, no one else. Support it.'

Such organizations swiftly attracted repression. Violence was particularly acute in southwestern Colombia, where another seminal indigenous organization, CRIC, the Indigenous Regional Council of the Cauca, was formed by 2,000 Páez, Coconucos and Guambianos in 1971. CRIC's main aim was to recover the rights to their lands, in particular the reservations (*resguardos*) granted by the Spaniards and nominally confirmed by law in 1890. The organi-zation aimed to strengthen the indigenous councils (*cabildos*) which theoretically exercised political and administrative authority over the reserva-tions but had either collapsed or come under the control of landowners or politicians as the reservations had been broken up. CRIC also had broader cultural aims, such as promoting indigenous history, culture and language and training bilingual teachers.

CRIC has been phenomenally successful. By the end of 1993, it had re-established 102 *cabildos* as genuinely indigenous organizations, recovered an estimated 100,000 acres of land, re-establishing the concept of community land in the process, and set up 120 community agriculture enterprises, 90 co-operative shops and 50 bilingual schools. With health schemes, credit programmes and its own newspaper, CRIC has, like the Shuar–Achuar Federation, become a parallel and certainly more effective and accountable government. It has paid the price. 'In 22 years we have lost 382 activists to the military, police, *pájaros* (hired killers)

59. *Colombia: reading the newspaper while waiting for a demonstration to start in the Cauca region.*
© JOE FISH

and the guerrillas,' notes Marco Aníbal Anivama, CRIC's president, nonchalantly thrusting a recent newspaper cutting about another murder across his desk at the organization's headquarters in Popayán.

CRIC was among the first of the new indigenous organizations to experience what were to become common problems. The first were problems with the political left. The leadership struggled hard in the 1970s against revolutionary groups intent on trying to take over the organization, and today CRIC members continue to be victims of guerrillas from the Revolutionary Armed Forces of Colombia (FARC).

Second, CRIC fell out with the National Association of Peasants, a government-sponsored organization, when the latter refused to push the indigenous issue high enough up its agenda. 'It's a very simple problem. They want us to follow their agenda; we have to follow our own,' says Marco Aníbal Anivama. Though the problems were common, some of the solutions were unique. In 1984 the Comando Quintín Lame, an armed defence force, was set up to protect indigenous land and development projects. Quintín Lame has been the only specifically indigenous armed force in the Americas in recent history. When it was disbanded in 1989 it had 200 armed fighters.

CRIC and the Shuar–Achuar Federation were just two of dozens of organizations for which tactics quickly became an issue. In the United States, the American Indian Movement (AIM) emerged out of the prisons and indigenous ghetto in Minneapolis in 1969, the product of a general sense of alienation among the children of indigenous people who had been relocated to the cities in the 1950s. AIM's tactics reflected the militancy brought on by relocation, disaffection over government inaction on indigenous grievances and the growing violence of US cities. 'Members wanted to redefine what they were. One of the first questions they asked was "What is an Indian?"', AIM founder Vernon Bellecourt recalled of a visit to a South Dakota medicine man, Leonard Crow Dog. 'We put out a bumper sticker "AIM for Sovereignty". Most of our people didn't even know what the word "sovereignty" meant. Now they know.'

AIM launched itself with a series of high-profile protests. In November 1969, 14 'Indians of all Tribes' took possession of the island of Alcatraz, whose notorious prison had closed five years earlier. They claimed their 'right of discovery', invoking an 1868 Sioux treaty which turned over all abandoned federal properties to indigenous people.

In August 1970, AIM leader Dennis Banks hauled a large cross on to a Lutheran Church conference podium to illustrate the current crucifixion of indigenous peoples. Representatives quickly pledged him $250,000. Two years later, AIM and other groups converged on Washington in a caravan of cars calling itself the 'Trail of Broken Treaties'. They presented a 20-point position paper to the Bureau of Indian Affairs (BIA), demanding a return of indigenous sovereignty. When no senior BIA official would speak to them, they occupied the building.

Three months later in February 1973, members of AIM occupied the village of Wounded Knee (Plate 60), the scene of the infamous 1890 massacre. AIM riflemen posed defiantly as the international media swooped to cover what became a 71-day siege. Two AIM activists died in gun battles before a truce was negotiated, but by the time it was over, indigenous people had reminded many North Americans that they still existed.

The FBI promptly added AIM to the list of civil rights, black power and anti-Vietnam war organizations that it now infiltrated. Many AIM members died in mysterious circumstances before a gun battle on the Pine Ridge reservation ended with the death of two FBI agents and one Indian in June 1975. The trial and conviction, widely considered unsafe, of AIM member Leonard Peltier in 1977 proved another catalyst for renewed Indian protest throughout the 1980s.

Building Pyramids: Local, Regional, National, International

In the 1970s and 1980s, the 'pyramid' building of indigenous organizational structures took off. CRIC, an organization composed of dozens of local *cabildos*, became a member of ONIC, the National Indigenous Organization of Colombia, which in turn affiliated to what from 1984 became the largest indigenous organization in the Americas, COICA, the Coordination of Indigenous Organizations of the Amazon Basin. The Shuar–Achuar Federation became a founding member of CONFENAIE, the Confederation of Indigenous Nationalities of Ecuadorean Amazonia, which in turn became a component of CONAIE, the Confederation of Indian Nationalities of Ecuador, and another key affiliate of COICA.

Each new level of organization marked a corresponding improvement in negotiating clout and the emergence of an increasingly confident leadership, according to a member of AIDESEP, the Inter-Ethnic Association for the Development of the Peruvian Forest:

> As a community group based in one village or river valley we may have been able to negotiate with a mayor or minor local official. As a regional organization we might get to see the governor. As a national organization we soon got to see ministers and even Presidents and as an international organization we've been to see the President of the World Bank and top United Nations people.

Lowland peoples took the lead in much of this organizing. Vociferous young leaders such as Valerio Grefa in Ecuador, Evaristo Nugkuag in Peru and Ernesto

60. *USA: a member of the American Indian Movement (AIM) keeping watch from the bell tower after seizing the trading post at Wounded Knee. Two AIM activists died in gun battles during the ensuing 71-day siege.*
© AP

Noé in Bolivia emerged from missionary schools in the Amazon basin relatively untouched by the structures that had at least partially incorporated their high-land colleagues into their respective states. But although less affected by the land reform and peasant organizing which had imposed new 'national' identi-ties on highland peoples, lowland peoples faced more immediate threats.

From the 1960s onwards, colonists, loggers, ranchers and miners began what can only be termed a second conquest in the Amazon basin, Central American rain forest and Canadian Arctic, pushing roads, airstrips, snowmobiles and motor launches into regions which had rarely, if ever, seen outsiders. When the Yanomami, led by Davi Yanomami, became news in the 1980s they even referred to incoming settlers as *os Portugueses*, the Portuguese. 'Even the Spanish conquest was not as direct as this,' complained Rafael Pandam, leader of Ecuador's CONAIE.

Nowhere was this campaign more active or urgent than Brazil. In the eight years to 1990, no fewer than 48 indigenous organizations sprang up, 31 of them in the most vulnerable states of Amazonas, Roraima and Acre. Increasingly, Indians themselves led the way, taking over from anthropologists, human rights activists and lawyers, some of whom had little or no contact with the people they were campaigning for.

As the gold rush and the Calha Norte project to open up the Amazon gathered pace, the scale of the threat intensified. In 1987 alone, some 560 corporate appli-cations for prospecting rights in indigenous areas in Brazil were approved. Meanwhile, tens of thousands of *garimpeiros*, individual gold prospectors and land-hungry settlers made their own way into Indian territory by means of the dirt roads and airstrips that now criss-crossed the Amazon basin.

By 1987, the threat to Indian life and land was a major issue for the Constituent Assembly discussing Brazil's new constitution. The document, finally approved in 1988, included a whole chapter on indigenous peoples and was nominally, at least, a huge step forward. The new constitution called Indians 'Indians' for the first time. It considered the right to Indian lands as original, i.e. prior to Brazilian law, and defined such lands as those deemed necessary not only for habitation but also for production, preservation of the environment and physical and cultural reproduction.

The constitution also recognized the existence of collective rights, Indians' social organizations and their practices, religions, languages and beliefs. It gave communities the right to express opinions about the exploitation of natural resources and allowed them to plead in the courts. The exploitation of miner-als would now require approval from Congress; the removal of Indian populations was now forbidden.

Above all, the Constitution included a five-year deadline, expiring in October 1993, for the demarcation of officially recognized indigenous territory. By late

172

1993, less than half of more than 500 territories had been demarcated. Despite a brief respite in 1991–2, when international pressure forced Brazilian President Collor de Mello to delimit 36 million acres and take real action to expel invaders from Yanomami territory, invasions continued and by 1994 a general backlash had set in.

Although the constitution is often more honoured in the breach, it has given indigenous people in Brazil and international supporters beyond something with which to campaign. At its first general assembly in Luziana, Goias state, in April 1995, the Joint Council of Indigenous Peoples and Organizations of Brazil (CAPOIB) made clear it would be doing just that, demanding a timetable for demarcations and sufficient funds to enable such a programme to be carried out.

Meanwhile highland peoples in the Americas were far from inactive during this period. From the 1960s onwards, a similar quiet revolution gathered force in the mountains of Mexico, Guatemala, Peru, Bolivia and Ecuador. Highland peoples' primary aim has been practical: developing agricultural or craft co-operatives and providing basic healthcare and education. Such grassroots 'self-help' development, ranging from pig-breeding co-ops to open-air literacy classes, has enabled a rapidly growing population to offer some resistance to the socio-economic forces ranged against it: a growing population, a shrinking land base and, in the 1980s at least, hyper-inflation, savage government budget cuts and a precipitous slump in crop prices.

Indianism: 'The Past Is a Tool to Analyse the Present'

Despite the distinctions between the way highland and lowland cultures have tried to combat the new threats of recent years, the similarities far outweigh the differences. Nowhere is this more true than in countries such as Colombia and Ecuador, where indigenous organizations have come together in a single body, co-ordinating the efforts of both highland and lowland nations. What unites both groups is what has become known as 'Indianism' (or *Indianismo*), a philosophy which emphasizes that indigenous peoples should lead the struggle for recognition of their own culture, needs and rights. 'Indianism' has gone through different phases in different countries at different times. Broadly speaking, there are three different schools of thought.

The first, widespread in the 1970s and early 1980s, sees indigenous values as compatible with left-wing ideology and objectives. Proponents tend to work within left-wing parties, unions and armed guerrilla groups.

The second trend dissociates itself from both the left and the right, arguing that only indigenous people can really comprehend the complete powerlessness and cultural abuse they have suffered over the past five centuries. Many indigenous leaders have supported it as a direct result of the discrimination and racism they experienced working within leftist organizations. They push an agenda of cultural purity based on a return to traditional organization or thinking such as the *Tawantinsuyu*, the socio-cosmological structure on which the Inka state was based.

The third current of thought within Indianism is that which dominates today, namely a centrist position which argues that indigenous people should organize, lobby and campaign in structures of their own but in alliance with other, non-indigenous organizations when and where appropriate. In other words, action and organization should reflect the multicultural, plural nature of the societies in which indigenous people live.

Indigenous attitudes to forging alliances with the left are worth examining in some detail because such alliances have proved to be a crucial influence on many of today's most prominent indigenous leaders. In the early days of the upsurge in indigenous consciousness, alliance or incorporation into left-wing trade unions, parties, grassroots groups or even guerrilla armies seemed logical and sensible. Indigenous experience of organizing to make demands on governments was minimal; the practical demands of both groups, such as access to land, health care, education, minimum wages, housing and sanitation, were broadly the same. Furthermore, in areas where repression was fierce, particularly the repression fuelled by racist fears of an indigenous rebellion, it made sense to seek the additional security of greater numbers and even to arm in self-defence.

Many unions, left-wing parties and guerrilla groups set out to mobilize indigenous people in the 1970s and 1980s. Like Che Guevara, who set off to launch the revolution in Bolivia in 1966, they argued that, as the poorest, most marginalized and most repressed sector of the population, indigenous peoples should logically make the most willing recruits to the revolutionary cause.

To the Latin American left, indigenous peoples were an exploited class first and 'Indians' second, whereas most Indians sufficiently conscious to become involved politically believed that they were indigenous first and exploited second. Most of the *mestizo*, often urban, leadership of the left in Latin America thought that cultural differences would melt away as Indians were recruited *en masse* and class consciousness replaced ethnic consciousness.

In practice, struggling alongside *mestizo* colleagues to bring piped water to a shanty town in Lima or to repel army attacks in rural Guatemala served to heighten the ethnic consciousness of many indigenous peoples. Many of their natural ideological allies turned out to be as culturally insensitive and as 'assimilationist' in their aims as their enemies on the right. An intense new version of the class–ethnicity debate broke out in many areas as indigenous activists increasingly 'ethnicized' unions, parties and popular organizations.

174

The demise of the left in the wake of electoral defeats, the eclipse of guerrilla movements and the collapse of the Soviet Union have created a political vacuum in Latin America which in some cases is being filled by ethnic nationalism. The left's collapse has been most severe where the unions, parties or armed movements have not taken the ethnic dimension of their struggle seriously enough. What some leftist leaders took to describing as the ethnic–national contradiction was no contradiction at all for indigenous peoples; their ethnicity has always been national, but ethnically so, in terms of their own nations.

The class–ethnicity debate has informed the strategy and tactics of many of the new organizations. Alliances make sense on particular issues that concern both non-indigenous and indigenous people, such as wages, social provision and human rights issues. They may even help in the struggle for land rights in ethnically mixed communities. However, where cultural rights are at stake or begin to emerge from such practical struggles, indigenous activists soon seek to develop their own organizations.

The very process of political *concientización*, consciousness-raising, or making essentially political demands, serves to heighten cultural awareness. In reality, practical and cultural demands often overlap. 'It's not one first, the other second. They are the same,' one activist explains. 'You can't eat culture but you certainly can eat potatoes grown as a result of the cultural revival of old farming techniques.'

For many indigenous organizations, rediscovering a traditional strain of potato or maize, Inka irrigation techniques, or the herbal medicines used by their grandparents is as much part of survival as a deliberate quest for cultural revival. The practical and cultural go hand in hand, giving the organizational upsurge a double vigour.

Spirituality is a particularly noticeable facet of the revival. An all-pervading sense of the religious, magical and supernatural has been rediscovered by younger generations as they redefine themselves. Stories, myths and customs in which animals talk, plants have emotions, ghosts are everywhere, hoes work alone or souls leave bodies for days at a time have once again become mainstream fare.

There has been a correspondingly dramatic rise in interest in oral tradition, indigenous medicine, traditional calendars and religion. Workshops have begun to publish the oral histories and folklore still found among the older members of ethnic groups; thousands of young men and women have started to demand training as shamans; printing presses have sprung up to satisfy a growing hunger for manuals, texts and folklore, often in indigenous languages. Those who cannot read are read to by their children or provide the material for others to 'formalize' the semi-secret spiritual world that has been at the

175

61. Guatemala: a protest against the civil patrols imposed in many indigenous villages. Villagers are forced to patrol, and often become either victims or reluctant accomplices of the army in human rights violations.
© PAUL SMITH

heart of the almost invisible indigenous resistance for centuries.

For some the new emphasis on culture and the spiritual is in itself an act of political resistance; it is apparently less political, and thus attracts less repression, yet can be just as potent. 'Now we talk about the times of our ancestors and let people make their own connections,' explains Herminio Pérez, a Mam radio broadcaster in highland Guatemala, where the repression has been particularly fierce. 'For us the past is a tool to analyse the present in order to plan the future.'

In some instances this spiritual cultural revival has even been encouraged by governments. 'Some governments seem to consider minimal concessions to ethnic pressure a useful vent for general social protest. Ethnicity seems a much less potent force than left-wing ideology so they encourage it as the lesser of two evils,' observes one anthropologist.

176

The Political Route: Using and Changing the System

The shift towards democracy in Latin America in the 1980s opened another front for indigenous pressure in national and local politics. In 1980, Julio Tumiri and Constantino Lima of the (Katarista) MITKA party won seats in the Bolivian parliament. Three years later Mario Juruna, a Xavánte, became the first indigenous member of the Brazilian Congress. Since then, indigenous people have been elected throughout the Americas. Colombia, where four separate indigenous parties currently have three senators, several congressional representatives and scores of mayors and councillors, has taken the lead. 'The political route has given us a completely new level of influence and that shows in what we've achieved in a very short time,' claims Páez Indian leader Jesús Pinakul, a candidate for the Colombian Congress in 1994.

To date, the greatest achievement has been Colombia's 1991 constitution, which sets out the most comprehensive set of rights enjoyed by indigenous peoples anywhere in the Americas. The constitution recognizes Colombia as a plural and multiethnic country, accords all indigenous lands legal status as 'territorial entities' and makes indigenous languages official within indigenous territories. It also grants dual nationality to members of ethnic groups living on the country's borders, acknowledges the existence of indigenous law and judicial systems, and recognizes indigenous reservations and *cabildos*. Exploitation of natural resources in indigenous territories must be 'without the impairment of cultural, social and economic integrity' and must involve the 'participation of the indigenous communities'.

As elsewhere, the provisions left plenty of loopholes, and the real test remains the degree of successful implementation. Constitutional provisions require laws to give them effect and some of the laws since proposed in the wake of a backlash in the Colombian Congress have directly contradicted constitutional articles. The law needed to implement demarcation provisions has been particularly contentious, and indigenous organizations claim that the government has violated constitutional guidelines by ignoring its own proposals.

The problems illustrate the extent to which such constitutional or legislative successes are a response to pressure rather than representing any real change of heart on the issue of indigenous territories in the Amazon basin. Declarations of intent on territorial recognition have only become official demarcations, which in turn lead to formal titling, after tough battles every inch of the way. 'Policies continue to be carried out as if no constitutional modifications have been agreed,' complains Jesús Avirama, a former CRIC president.

Indigenous people have been most potent in exercising their political muscle at the local level, where they have been reclaiming the town halls occupied by *mestizo* government officials since the first half of the century. Some have been

177

62. *USA 1991: Members of the Apache Survival Coalition file a lawsuit against the*
construction of an observatory on Mount Graham,
a sacred Apache site, southwest Arizona.
© SURVIVAL INTERNATIONAL

elected mayor on party tickets, but many successful candidates have run as independents or as local civic committee representatives.

Guatemala is just one country where the results from the predominantly Maya highlands make fascinating reading. In the 1985 municipal elections, 59 Maya and 111 *mestizo* mayors were elected. In 1988, electors returned 68 Maya mayors and 80 *mestizos*. By 1993, 92 Maya mayors had won office as against just 56 *mestizos*.

More crucially still, some national governments have begun to recognize traditional indigenous authorities as legitimate representatives of their community, effectively turning them into the local government (Plate 63). Such recognition, already the norm in the United States and Canada under the system of tribal governance, has recently been extended to Colombia, Nicaragua and, in 1993, to Mexico, through an amendment to Article 4 of the

178

63. *USA: Judge Minnie Bert; the Miccosukee reservation is self-governing.*
© JACQUIE SPECTOR/SURVIVAL INTERNATIONAL

Constitution. In addition, Mexico, Venezuela and Colombia have all adopted indigenous demands for a guaranteed portion of the seats in Congress.

In some cases, such recognition is part of a broader decentralization process. In April 1994, the Bolivian government promulgated a law of popular participation, granting local communities the power to administer public services, local schools and health provision. In Guatemala, 8 per cent of income from value-added tax now has to be directed to local communities – a dramatic shift of power away from the *mestizo*-dominated capital city to the indigenous provinces. Such devolution is largely responsible for generating interest in getting indigenous mayors into the country's town halls.

Occasionally, the individual votes of indigenous representatives in local or national assemblies have had dramatic impacts. In Canada in June 1990, Elijah Harper, a Cree-Ojibwa, killed off the new constitutional deal designed to keep Quebec within Canada (the Meech Lake Accord) with an emphatic shake of his head and the wave of an eagle feather. The Manitoba legislature's rules required a unanimous vote to approve the accord before the deadline. Harper's historic vote (he was the first Indian to sit in the assembly) made him a hero to Canada's indigenous people, outraged by their exclusion from an accord which portrayed the country as the product of 'two founding peoples'.

His refusal proved a major watershed in Canadian politics. Within two years the country's white politicians had accepted that a revised constitution would have to recognize indigenous people's 'inherent right to self-government'. What that means still has to be worked out, following the rejection of a new Canadian constitutional deal worked out at Charlottetown and put to the electorate in a referendum in October 1992. Many indigenous people in Canada rejected the Charlottetown proposals because they thought they would block the way to full nationhood. The proposals did, however, acknowledge the indigenous right to self-government.

Elsewhere in Canada, indigenous people have been at the forefront of the increasingly pan-American *pachakut'i*. In May 1992, 27,390 people, 85 per cent of them Inuit, voted in favour of carving a 770,000-square-mile self-governing territory (about one-fifth of the Canadian landmass) out of the eastern half of what had been known as the Northwest Territories. Stretching from the northern tip of Ellesmere Island to the Beaufort Sea in the west and south down the Hudson Bay to the border with Manitoba, the land has been renamed Nunavut, Inuit for 'Our Land'.

The following November, 8,000 Inuit in 27 far-flung settlements voted to accept outright ownership of 136,000 square miles. Nunavut will come into existence in 1999 with a Can$1.17 billion payment from the Canadian government in compensation for giving up claims to even more land. 'In creating this homeland we have become the world's largest private landlords,' claimed Jack

64. *Canada: Innu women play a leading role in the campaign to halt the military use of native lands in northern Canada.*
© BOB BARTEL/SURVIVAL INTERNATIONAL

Kupeuna, vice-president of the Tungavik Federation of Nunavut from his Baffin Island community of Iqaluit. 'It's a historic day for Inuit people.'

Nicaragua is the only other country in the Americas to have made advances similar to those of Colombia and Canada towards legal recognition of the multicultural, multiethnic nature of its society and the need for the self-determination of its indigenous peoples. In 1987, in the middle of the US-backed Contra war against the Sandinista government, the country became the first nation in the Americas to recognize its multiethnic nature when its Autonomy Law was passed unanimously by the National Assembly. The Autonomy Law guaranteed the cultural, linguistic and religious rights demanded by the Sumos, Ramas and Miskitos of the Atlantic Coast. Moreover, it went one vital step further in recognizing that such rights could not be fully exercised unless those minorities enjoyed sufficient economic resources to guarantee not just survival, but also growth and development. Although considered by many to be weak on land provisions, the Law set up special development funds and established two democratically elected Regional Councils to represent the new North and South Atlantic Autonomous Regions. However, the experience has demonstrated the difficulty of overcoming centuries of mistrust even with the best of intentions. A change of government in 1990 and the fact that autonomy was always identified with the Sandinistas, who had pursued an integrationist, repressive policy towards the coastal population until their change of heart in the mid-1980s, have proved major obstacles to progress.

The Nicaraguan experience has made it clear that genuine multiculturalism requires more than laws and goodwill. An attitude of mind that recognizes indigenous peoples' ability to be multi-cultural individuals, to hold more than one identity simultaneously, is essential. 'We didn't allow people to be both Miskito and Sandinista; we made them choose between the two,' admits one Miskito official, in regret.

Five Hundred Years and Counting: Rediscovering Resistance

Organization, revival and political involvement were galvanized in the late 1980s by the impending 500th anniversary of Columbus' arrival in the Americas. International plans to celebrate the event provoked a reaction to 500 years of history that had canonized Columbus as a hero and indigenous people as savages. The real achievement of what was to become a pan-American campaign was to deflect international attention away from Columbus himself towards current issues. 'We're not upset with Columbus – he's dead,' remarked Gitksan leader Wii Seeks. 'We're upset with governments for perpetuating the colonial policies started by Columbus.'

Scores of community, regional and national indigenous organizations came together in the Continental Campaign of 500 Years of Indigenous, Popular and Black Resistance, which met in Quito, Ecuador, for the first time in 1990. Throughout Europe, affiliated solidarity organizations worked to further raise awareness of indigenous issues.

In the run-up to 1992, a number of countries witnessed seminal protests which served to illustrate the depth of organization and feeling among the continents' indigenous nations. In May 1990, 160 members of the Confederation of Indigenous Nationalities of Ecuador (CONAIE), the umbrella organization that brings together highland and lowland peoples, occupied the cathedral of Santo Domingo in the heart of the old part of Ecuador's capital, Quito. Demanding the resolution of land disputes in six highland provinces, the protest sparked a national uprising. Roads were blocked with boulders and tree trunks, police and local officials taken hostage and land occupied in provinces whose very names – Chimborazo, Cotopaxi, Tungurahua and Imbabura – testified to their original ownership.

As Ecuador effectively closed down, and with the cities cut off and food shortages pending, senior government ministers were sent to negotiate on CONAIE's 16 demands for cultural rights. 'We are tired of offers and promises ... we are prepared now with our own ideas and our own criteria,' CONAIE's leader, Cristóbal Tapuy, told them. A conservative Quito daily labelled it the 'sixth Indian insurrection', which CONAIE countered with its own list of 145 indigenous uprisings in Ecuador between 1533 and 1972. However, all agreed that this one was different. National, co-ordinated and with clearly expressed aims, it marked a watershed shift from defence to offence.

In Bolivia, a similarly symbolic event earned front-page news coverage for weeks. In October 1990, 800 Moxeños, Yuracarés, Chimanes and Guaranís set out from the town of Trinidad (altitude 780 feet) in the Amazon basin to walk the 330 miles to the highland capital, La Paz (11,800 feet). They were protesting against government inaction in preventing the extraction of mahogany from a 400,000-acre strip of the Chimane Forest and carried a banner proclaiming their protest 'The March for Land and Dignity' (Plate 65). As they climbed through the mountain passes that link highland and lowland Bolivia, thousands of Quechua and Aymara came out to cheer them on or join the march. Supporters brought food, woollen clothing and coca tea, the traditional highland remedy for altitude sickness.

The Bolivian President Jaime Paz Zamora and most of his cabinet took the sensible precaution of going out to meet the marchers *en route* before holding six days of intense negotiation with them on their arrival in the capital, La Paz. The government agreed to demand the withdrawal of the loggers by the end of the year, while granting the protesters title to 4 million acres in three separate

65. *Bolivia, 1990: 'March for Land and Dignity'. 800 Moxeños, Yuracarés, Chimanes and Guaraníes set out from the Amazon Basin to walk to La Paz, protesting about government inaction on mahogany extraction. Thousands of Aymara and Quechua join the march as it passes through the highlands.*
© PHILIP EDWARDS/SURVIVAL INTERNATIONAL

areas of Amazon forest. Agriculture Minister Mauro Bertero promised a new law on indigenous people, noting that the current law gave the forest people the same civil and legal status as the forest's plants and animals.

The 33-day march showed how an essentially local indigenous issue could, in the volatile atmosphere leading up to the 1992 anniversary, become a national cause almost overnight. Catching the new public mood, scores of such protests broke out throughout the Americas. Governments ignored them at their peril.

Many people beyond the villages, forests and slums where indigenous people predominated now saw indigenous demands for environmental protection, land rights and better social services as part of their own agenda. 'We have walked so that everyone in Bolivia and throughout the world will know that we exist and that we have rights,' as Marcial Fabricano, one of the march leaders, put it.

Elsewhere, protests were equally direct and often less peaceably resolved. Less than three weeks after the death of the Meech Lake Accord in Canada, Quebec provincial police stormed a barricade in the town of Oka (Plate 66).

184

66. *Canada, 1990: Quebec provincial police stormed a barricade in the town of Oka, 1990, after Kanesatake Mohawks had put up the symbolic barrier to mark their opposition to the town council's plans to expand a golf course into a small copse of pines surrounding a sacred Mohawk cemetery. A gun battle ensued in which a police officer was shot dead.*
© AP

Kanesatake Mohawks had put up the symbolic barrier to mark their opposition
to the town council's plans to expand a golf course into a small copse of pines
surrounding a sacred Mohawk cemetery. A gun battle ensued, and when the
smoke bombs and tear-gas cleared one Sûreté du Québec officer lay dead.

The attack prompted a series of uprisings across Canada, a sort of
mini-*intifada* of empathy by those struggling to protect dwindling indigenous
lands from the developers. Alerted by short-wave radio, hundreds of Mohawks
blocked the Mercier Bridge, a major thoroughfare in greater Montreal running
through a Mohawk community. Suddenly, the issue of rights of access through
indigenous territory was brought home to thousands of Quebecois commuters,
who mounted noisy protests. 'They complain they have been inconvenienced
for a few weeks; we have been inconvenienced for centuries,' noted one
Mohawk statement.

In British Columbia, indigenous groups barricaded several key roads. In
southern Ontario they felled power lines. In southern Alberta, members of the
Peigan Lonefighters Society dug a mile-long ditch on their reserve around an
irrigation weir, part of a dam project on the Oldman River going ahead without
federal environmental assessment.

Barricades sprang up on roads in downtown Vancouver and Calgary; indigenous peace camps were set up in several provincial legislatures. As in Latin
America, significant numbers of non-indigenous people were now identifying
with issues on which indigenous people were leading the way, issues such as
sustainable development, environmental protection, civil liberties, education
and health care.

By the time the 500th anniversary of Columbus's arrival dawned on 12
October 1992, the day had been well and truly hijacked by the descendants of
the victims of conquest (Plate 67). In the years running up to the anniversary,
indigenous people had begun to present their version of history, to recover their
memory in a tangible way. Increasingly sensitive to the issue as a result of
indigenous pressure, governments had tried to present plans to mark the day as
'an encounter' between two worlds and two cultures. In the end, official celebrations were abandoned throughout the continents. Bob Hope was forced to
ditch a live Columbus television special in the United States.

No Latin American head of state considered it worth the risk of attending the
most ambitious event of them all, the inauguration of a huge crucifix-shaped
monument to the Discovery and Evangelization of the Americas in the
Dominican Republic, a country where not a single indigenous person had survived the impact of the Europeans' arrival. The structure, a pet project of
President Joaquín Balaguer, sported huge spotlights designed to make the shape
of a cross in the night sky. In the run-up to the anniversary, the lighthouse's
estimated US$400 million cost and the power cuts its lights caused had become

67. *Peru 1992: march in the Inka capital of Qosqo on the 500th anniversary of*
Christopher Columbus's arrival in the Americas. The march commemorates
500 years of indigenous resistance, with a sign reading
'Long Live Our Dark-Skinned America!'
© ANNIE BUNGAROTH

the focus of large demonstrations in the surrounding shanty towns. The day itself was no different. Pope John Paul II, one of the few dignitaries present in Santo Domingo, received a protesting delegation of indigenous leaders and admitted to the Church's partial responsibility for the slaughter of their ancestors.

Elsewhere, more than 2,000 Quechua and Aymara climbed the Cerro Rico in Potosí to symbolically reclaim it. Statues of Columbus and Spanish monarchs were daubed with red paint and mock trials of Christopher Columbus took place.

Indigenous Internationalism: 'No Longer Prepared to Be Silent'

The Columbus anniversary reinforced and stimulated indigenous organization, and the momentum of protest has since been maintained. Days after the quincentenary, what was now increasingly a transcontinental indigenous movement received another boost. Just before dawn on 16 October 1992, Rigoberta

Menchú Tum received a telephone call at the San Marcos office of the National Widows' Organization (CONAVIGUA) in Guatemala. The Norwegian ambassador to Mexico briefly congratulated her on being awarded the 1992 Nobel Peace Prize. 'The prize is a tribute to the indigenous women of Guatemala, indeed the whole world, and it carries a huge responsibility,' she told the press outside the office. 'I only wish my parents could have been present.' Her mother, father and younger brother had all been killed in separate acts of army brutality in the 1980s, just three of the tens of thousands of Maya victims killed in one of the most brutal episodes of the continuing conquest.

The Nobel Committee could scarcely have chosen a more representative indigenous spokesperson. Rigoberta Menchú's life, movingly recorded in her autobiography, *I, Rigoberta Menchú* (London: Verso, 1984), was the experience of millions of others. As she explained in the book's opening lines, 'My personal experience is the reality of a whole people.' As a tireless campaigner and internationally renowned lobbyist for indigenous peoples, she represents the present, a new generation 'no longer prepared to be silent'. As a refugee living in exile in Mexico, whose home village and family have been destroyed, she is timeless, standing for all indigenous people who have suffered the same fate over the past five hundred years. As someone who has come from being an illiterate peasant, from virtual slavery as a coffee-picker and domestic servant to become the youngest-ever Nobel Peace Prize laureate, Rigoberta Menchú inspires hope for the future throughout the Americas. 'It is a recognition of the European debt to the indigenous peoples of the Americas; it is an appeal to the conscience of humanity; it is a cry for life, peace, justice, equality and fraternity between human beings,' she stated in accepting the Nobel Prize in Oslo's City Hall on 10 December 1992 (Plate 68).

Rigoberta Menchú won the Nobel Peace Prize from exile, epitomizing the prophet without honour in her own land. Only in exile could she have survived to speak for her people, a point lost on none who listened to her demands for the reversal of five hundred years of dispossession and desperation. This internationalization of the struggle for justice, recognized by the Nobel Peace Prize committee, has been one of the most crucial factors in the indigenous revival of the past 25 years.

Like indigenous organization itself, 'indigenous internationalism', as one refugee dubbed it, has evolved simultaneously on several fronts, most notably through the cross-border migration of indigenous peoples in the Americas for both economic and political reasons. In recent times the most obvious examples have been the migration of Mixtecs or Zapotecs from Oaxaca, Mexico, to California's Central Valley to work as migrant farmhands; the flight of more than 100,000 Guatemalan Maya to Mexico's border states and beyond in their desperate efforts to escape the massacres perpetrated by the Guatemalan army;

68. *Oslo: Rigoberta Menchú receives the Nobel Peace Prize, December 1992.*
© AP

and the migration of Quechua shepherds from Peru to Argentina and western US states such as Utah and Nevada in a search for work.

On a more formal level, there has been the growing interchange between indigenous representatives and international bodies, whether non-governmental organizations such as development or environmental agencies, multilateral lending agencies like the World Bank or the International Monetary Fund, or inter-governmental bodies like the Organization of American States (OAS) or the United Nations.

Relations with the last of these have been formalized by the creation of a Working Group on Indigenous Populations, a subsidiary body of the United Nations Sub-Commission on the Prevention of Discrimination and Protection of Minorities. The Working Group has met every year since 1982, its growing importance as a forum reflected in the steadily increasing numbers of indigenous representatives who have gone to Geneva to contribute oral testimony and ideas as part of its open format. The Working Group has generated critical studies, expert meetings and various forms of practical actions, and in 1993 completed its main task by presenting a draft of a Universal Declaration on Indigenous Rights to the Sub-Commission. It was the first step towards the proposed adoption of a UN Declaration or even Convention by the United Nations General Assembly sometime during the UN-sponsored Decade of Indigenous Peoples (1995–2004).

Such moves are part of general efforts to improve on the only existing international statute on the issue, the International Labour Organization's Convention on Indigenous and Tribal Peoples (Convention 169). International legal efforts are an extension of indigenous organizations' domestic strategy to force legal or constitutional changes, then to use them as a stick with which to beat governments by demanding their effective implementation.

The effect of all such forms of internationalization has been to bring indigenous people in the Americas together in various fora in an unprecedented fashion. Shared problems, they have quickly realized, spring from a shared history, a shared experience and a shared world-view. International meetings provide solidarity, and sometimes safety, for those engaged in often lonely and dangerous struggles. 'Meeting others engaged in the same struggle is very inspiring, very encouraging. We have a lot in common and a lot to learn from each other,' observed Rigoberta Menchú on one visit to North America in 1990.

The experience has been a two-way process: indigenous people have begun to go out into the world just as the outside world has started to come to them in unprecedented numbers. Radio, foreign development workers, missionaries and even returning native sons and daughters have supplemented indigenous people's own travel in communities throughout the Americas. A parochial world-view has rapidly broadened. Many have begun to see themselves as part of something bigger, part of a continental 'pan-Indian movement', a development which has both sharpened the sense of self and identity and helped to redefine it.

Nayrapacha: A Past That Is a Future

It is impossible to say where the cultural revival now in train will lead. Autonomy and the right to self-determination mean different things to different indigenous nations. Collective ethnic choice and the prevailing political, economic and social conditions are the key determinants; the struggle in which indigenous nations are now engaged is about creating the conditions to be able to make such a choice.

One thing is clear: it is not about culture *per se*. Culture is a means to an end. 'We are not fighting for our culture, we already have it. We want only our rights: the right to peace, the right to define our own path to development, the right to educate our children, the right to represent ourselves,' one Maya observes.

For some in North America, such rights could be guaranteed simply by ensuring that existing treaties are honoured; for others, in countries such as Bolivia, Peru, Ecuador and Guatemala, it is as much about opting in as opting out, securing the democratic rights and full participation in national life that have been denied them for so long. For still others, particularly those with little previous contact with the European societies now encroaching on their lands, it is about finding some *modus vivendi* with the invading forces before it is too late. 'We are being asked to travel thousands of years in just a decade,' notes one Inuit elder. 'Just give us the time to come to terms with these changes on our own terms.'

Indigenous peoples all over the Americas are coming to terms with such changes by using any means at their disposal. Usually that involves resisting such changes so that they can accommodate or adapt to them in their own time, for their own interests. Such resistance ranges from international lobbying to dissimulation and foot-dragging. In resisting, in protesting, they remind us that they are still very much present, that their history is unfinished. In doing so they create (we might say buy) their own time – the oscillating, renewable sense of time implied by the traditional Andean concept of *nayrapacha*. '*Nayrapacha* means a past that can also be a future. It implies that this world can be changed,' say Carlos Mamani, an Aymara activist. 'It means ancient times, but not in the sense of a past that is dead, incapable of renovation.'

Perhaps 'back to the future' should be an indigenous slogan, for the idea of the past becoming and redeeming the future encapsulates the current ethnic revival in the Americas. By recapturing their own time and living in it, indigenous people are recapturing their own history. That in turn vindicates the millions of ancestors whose insistence on keeping alive ancient customs and traditions must, at times, have seemed like a death wish.

The two continents of the Americas are littered with places named after or named by peoples who no longer exist. That holocaust continues today. At least one indigenous ethnic group in the Americas is wiped out every year, land and mineral deposits go on being seized, and where these have already gone, newly recognized resources such as indigenous biotechnology and even genes are being exploited. 'If you kill us all you must get rid of all your photos of us, because future generations will demand to know why you allowed this to happen,' says one forest Indian.

But it would be wrong to underestimate the scale of the current reaction to such processes. It is international, sustained and public in a way previous indigenous revivals have never been. Many indigenous peoples in the Americas see this as a fulfilment of prophecy, a messianic return to something like the old days heralded by a belief in a balance between opposites, of action breeding reaction, cause producing an equal and opposite effect. Such beliefs have been

191

vindicated by the way in which ethnocide has in turn bred ethnogenesis, the most forceful cultural fightback often coming from those most threatened. It is hard not to see today's revival in indigenous terms, as the beginning of the Inka's *pachakut'i*, the overturning of worlds, when the eras change place in a cosmic upheaval and disruption of the universe.

Today the word *pachakut'i* has moved in from the realm of myth and aspiration to become an everyday concept in the two main Andean languages, Quechua and Aymara. But it is clear that the indigenous revolution will not, as some legends maintain, come down from the mountains or in from the forest or tundra in the same violent, sudden way in which the European conquest moved in from the coast. This is an evolutionary process that is perhaps most likely to show itself in the next two decades in the same way as indigenous organization has in the past two decades. It will show itself in the indigenization of existing structures, perhaps even state structures, and society itself.

Indigenous peoples in the Americas now have a historic opportunity. Rarely has the world been more receptive to their vision of a multicultural, democratic, environmentally-conscious society. As the militaristic nation-state changes form or is even eclipsed in the post-Cold War age, indigenous organizations can count on a wide range of allies both at home and abroad.

An 'indigenization' of the *mestizo* or European state, reversing the acculturation or assimilation that is so often the fate of indigenous peoples in the Americas, may sound improbable. But then four hundred years, one hundred years ago, even fifty years ago, so did the very survival of the continents' native peoples.

Real democracy, where everyone's opinions are heard and valued, is the basis of indigenous kinship or village decision-making; real environmentalism is the basis of indigenous survival; real multiethnicity, where mutual respect underpins treatment of others, is the basis of indigenous belief. In the words of one Maya community organizer, Manuel Colop, 'We do things the way our governments should; we have all the skills and qualities they urgently need.'

The past cannot be changed but it can be understood and blame acknowledged. The greatest challenge facing governments in the Americas is still overcoming their own myths about the indigenous peoples of the continents, their own myths about discovery and conquest, their own myths about what indigenous people want today. It is these myths and the attitudes they engender that more than anything else ensure the whites remain settlers and their indigenous counterparts remain natives in the land both must now share.

> The white man does not understand the Indian for the reason he does not understand America. He is too far removed from its formative processes. The roots of the tree of his life have not yet grasped the rock and soil ... The man from Europe is still a foreigner and an alien.

192

So observed Luther Standing Bear, a Lakota Sioux, in 1933. Those who were there before the whites came could not be more rooted in the soil, forest, snow and mountains of the Americas. Robbie Niquanicappo, a Cree whose land remains threatened by Hydro-Quebec's dams, speaks for all the indigenous peoples of the Americas as he listens to the cries of his infant son and stares out of the window at the snow-laden evergreens: 'I want my son to see and enjoy the land his grandfathers walked on and now sleep in. That's my life out there. That's our whole history out there.'

Bibliography

Albó, Javier, 'El retorno del Indio'. *Revista Andina* (Cuzco: Centro de Estudios Rurales Andinos Bartolomé de las Casas), year 9, no. 2 (Dec. 1991).

Brazil: A Mask Called Progress. An Oxfam Report (Oxford: Oxfam, 1991).

Durston, John, 'Indigenous peoples and modernity'. *CEPAL Review* (Santiago), no. 51 (Dec. 1993).

The first nations, 1492–1992. NACLA Report on the Americas (New York: North American Congress on Latin America), vol. 25, no. 3 (Dec. 1991).

Materne, Yves (ed.), *The Indian Awakening in Latin America* (New York: Friendship Press, 1980).

Stern, Steve, 'Paradigms of conquest: history, historiography and politics'. *Journal of Latin American Studies* (Cambridge: Cambridge University Press), vol. 24 (Quincentenary Supplement, 1992).

Ströbele-Gregor, Juliana, 'From *indio* to *mestizo* to *indio*: new Indianist movements in Bolivia'. *Latin American Perspectives* (Thousand Oaks, CA: Sage Publications), issue 81, vol. 21, no. 2 (Spring 1994).

Van Cott, Donna Lee (ed.), *Indigenous Peoples and Democracy in Latin America* (Basingstoke: Macmillan, 1994).

Wright, Ronald, *Stolen Continents: The Indian Story* (London: Pimlico Books, 1992).

Indigenous Chronology

Compiled by Emma Pearce

7000–2000 BC	Pre-Ceramic period. Beginnings of agriculture with techniques used by small semi-nomadic groups, such as the digging-stick. Crop cultivation, pottery and metalworking are developing. Intensive agriculture, particularly in Mexico and the Central Andes, leads to the emergence of urban civilizations.
c. 5000 BC	Hieroglyphic writing in use at Monte Albán, Mexico.
2,000 BC–AD 1	Pre-Classic period. Evolution of a settled agrarian economy based on kinship groups living in villages.
c. 200 BC–AD 200	The Hopewell culture in the Illinois and Ohio valleys emerges. Trading contacts stretch as far as the Gulf of Mexico.
AD 1–900	Classic period. Emergence of cities, ceremonial centres built of stone, and the evolution of a powerful state ruled by a king and priestly caste. Examples include the Maya in Mesoamerica, the Huari and Tiahuanaco cultures in the Andes and the Moche and Nazca on the coast of Peru.
AD 900–1500	Post-Classic period.
c. AD 990	The Inka Empire in the Andes begins to expand. By the fifteenth century it includes modern Peru, Ecuador, Bolivia and parts of Argentina and Chile.
c. AD 1000–1200	Toltecs establish a large empire in central and southern Mexico.
1006	A Norse saga relates how Leif Eriksson's brother, Thorwald, exploring the coast of North America, seizes and kills eight Indians, referred to as 'Skrellings'. Oldest known account of contact between peoples of Americas and Europe.
1325	The Aztecs found Tenochtitlán, the site of modern Mexico, which becomes the capital of an aggressive military empire.
Oct. 1492	Columbus lands in what is now the Bahamas.

1494	The Treaty of Tordesillas divides the Indies between Spain and Portugal.
1495	The Spanish begin enslaving the Arawak people of Hispaniola during the administration of Columbus and his brothers Bartolomé and Diego. Thousands die. By 1502, so few survive that the Spanish begin to import black slaves from Africa.
1497	John Cabot, Genoese explorer, lands in Newfoundland.
1519–40	The main period of Spanish conquest of the Aztec, Maya and Inka civilizations, aided by smallpox, which kills up to half the Aztec and Inka populations.
1533	The Spaniard Francisco Pizarro executes the Inka, Atawallpa.
1536	Manku Inka, originally backed by Pizarro as a puppet for the royal throne, besieges Qosqo (Cusco) for four months. Retreats to Vilcabamba from where he continues to harass the Spaniards.
1542	Spain tries to end the worst excesses of cruelty against the Indians with the New Laws of the Indies, but these are widely ignored.
1560	Bartolomé de las Casas estimates that up to 40 million Indians may have died from contact with the Spanish.
1562	*Auto-da-fé* in Yucatán. Thousands of Maya artefacts and books are burned, while 4,500 Maya are tortured and a further 158 killed during interrogation.
1569–81	Viceroy Toledo's reforms reorganize the colonial state and establish the system for the next two hundred years, including tribute (a poll tax paid by all able-bodied men), *mit'a* (forced labour in the mines), and forced resettlement of Andean peasants into *reducciones*.
1560s	*Takiy onkoy* (dancing sickness) – Indian religious movement in the southern Andes. Preaches withdrawal from Spanish customs and goods and calls for a return to the pre-Inka cult of *wak'as*, or ancestor worship.
1500s–1670s	*Extirpación de Idolatrías*. Official campaign against native beliefs waged in the Andes. 1540s: beginnings of the elimination of rites and ceremonies. 1551: 1st Conciliar Council of Lima declares that all pre-Christian Indians are considered to be in hell. By the beginning of the seventeenth century, the campaign has had limited success in replacing Andean with Christian beliefs. Early seventeenth century: archbishop of Lima campaigns to expose and eliminate all vestiges of Andean religious beliefs and practices. Eventually campaign eases off, in part owing to changing views in Europe.
1600	At least 15 major epidemics have by now reduced the native

	population of the Americas to as little as one-tenth of its pre-1492 size.
1607	First permanent English settlement established in North America at Jamestown, Virginia, in a region ruled by the Powhatan. Sporadic clashes. At one point governor Thomas Dale staved off war with the Indians by kidnapping Pocahontas, the daughter of the Powhatan chief.
1609	Dutch settlers found the colony of New Amsterdam. Some time later one of the members of the Wappinger Indian confederacy, the Manhattes, trades Manhattan island for goods reportedly worth $24.
1620	Pilgrim Fathers come ashore at Cape Cod, moving on to establish a settlement they name Plymouth in an area previously depopulated of Indians by an epidemic introduced by European traders.
1637	British colonists kill almost the entire Pequot tribe in Connecticut.
1645	The Dutch become probably the first European power to enter into a formal treaty with Indians, the Mohawk.
1675–6	Metacom, an Algonquin chief, leads the bloodiest Indian war against non-Indian settlers in New England's history.
1695	Gold is discovered in Minas Gerais, Brazil, attracting tens of thousands of prospectors and devastating tribal life.
1697	The Spanish finally overrun a Maya free state, Tayasal, in the Petén jungle.
1744	The Iroquois recommend their own federal structure as a model for the emerging states of what will eventually become the USA.
1740s–50s	Juan Santos Atawallpa, a *mestizo* claiming Inka descent, launches a military campaign which drives the colonial authorities out of an area of the central highlands of the Andes. There is no decisive defeat; instead, the authorities establish a military fort system to prevent the spread of insurrection.
1751	Kayapó Indians attack the city of Goias, Brazil.
1761	The Maya rebel against the Spanish at Cisteil, near Chichén Itzá, Mexico.
1763	Indian resistance to British settlement in New England forces the English Crown to declare a British royal proclamation, banning colonial settlements in 'lands reserved for Indians'. This remains the legal foundation of reserves, land claims and aboriginal rights in Canada and the USA.
1776	US Independence.
1780	Civil war breaks out in the southern Andean highlands. In Chayanta (now in Bolivia) an apparently spontaneous revolt breaks out to free

an Indian *cacique* (leader), Tomás Katari, jailed after a dispute with local authorities.

Nov. 1780	Tupaq Amaru II leads a well-organized rebellion near Qosqo (Cuzco).
1781	Tupaq Katari, an Indian commoner from Sikasika (Bolivia), lays siege to La Paz from March to October, during which a quarter of the city's population dies. Tupaq Katari is later executed by the colonial authorities.
1780s	Bourbon reforms, involving efforts by the Spanish Crown and Lima's ruling élite to increase the efficiency of mercantile exploitation in response to growing pressures of debt and commercial stagnation. The reforms create *corregidores* – provincial administrators who in practice become ruthless exploiters of Indian land and labour in the *repartimiento de mercancías* (distribution of goods which Indians are forced to buy).
1801	Indian rebellion in Nayarit, Mexico.
1808–28	Creoles (American-born people of Spanish descent) lead independence movements throughout Latin America. The new republics generally see Indians as obstacles to modernization and seek control of their lands.
1820s	Independence for majority of Latin American countries from the Spanish Crown.
1821	After 12 years' labour, Sequoyah, an untrained Cherokee craftsman with the English name of George Guess, devises a Cherokee alphabet of 86 characters which is quickly adopted for newspapers, books and letters.
1830	The Indian Removal Act in the USA leads to the removal of 100,000 Indians, mainly Cherokee and Seminole, from their land over the next decade.
1838	'Trail of Tears'. Some 16,000 Cherokee are marched on foot from Georgia to Oklahoma. Nearly a quarter of the nation die from cold and starvation.
1847–8	Caste War. Maya Indians rebel against plantation owners in Yucatán, Mexico.
1850	Communal land ownership abolished in Colombia.
1851	The first step towards a reservation system in North America. The Northern Plains tribes are offered $50,000 a year, plus guns, if they keep away from the migrant trails and confine themselves to designated areas.
1854	Thirty-five years of bitter warfare between the US army and the Lakota Sioux begin.

1861	Benito Juárez, a Zapotec lawyer who spoke no Spanish until the age of 12, becomes the first civilian to be elected president in Mexico.
1862	Great Sioux Uprising in Minnesota, United States. Santee warriors kill hundreds of white settlers.
1864	Sand Creek Massacre. Twenty-eight men and 105 Cheyenne and Arapaho women are killed by US soldiers.
1868	Sioux treaty turns over all abandoned US federal properties to indigenous people.
1871	US Indian Appropriation Act explains, 'No Indian nation or tribe within the territory of the United States shall be acknowledged and recognized as an independent nation, tribe or power with whom the United States may contract by treaty.'
1874	Law of Expropriation, Bolivia, decrees the abolition of the *ayllu*, the basic unit of Andean society, involving communal land ownership. It is replaced by a system of individual private property. Great resistance to the reforms leads to the law being repealed in 1902.
1876	The Battle of the Little Big Horn, in which General Custer's punitive expedition is wiped out by Lakota and Cheyenne Indians, led by Sitting Bull and Crazy Horse.
1880	Canadian Indian Act deprives the Indians of most of their lands and isolates them from white society. The Act subdivides Indians into Inuit, 'status Indians' and 'non-status Indians'.
1884	Mapuche Indians, defeated by the Chilean army, are rounded up and settled on land equivalent to 5 per cent of their original tribal homeland.
1887	Dawes Act or General Allotment Act in USA destroys the system of communal property vital to Indian social survival. Indian land is divided into private plots of approximately 160 acres; the 'surplus' is sold off by the federal government to whites.
1889	Ghost Dance religion spreads rapidly on Indian reservations throughout the USA. Indians believe the sacred dance will hasten the coming of the new world, when all the whites will disappear, all the dead ancestors will come back to life and the buffalo will return to the prairies.
1890	Massacre at Wounded Knee, South Dakota. Over 200 Sioux are surrounded and massacred by a US cavalry contingent.
1894	The South American rubber boom begins, wreaking havoc among the jungle tribes of Brazil, Bolivia, Colombia, Peru and Venezuela. Some 40,000 Indians die gathering rubber in Colombia alone in the next 25 years.

From late 1800s	Great wave of land seizures in Peru and Bolivia. By the late 1920s the *haciendas* – estates – have taken over most of the lands controlled by indigenous communities during the nineteenth century.
1910	Indians fight in the Mexican Revolution to regain lands originally lost to the Spanish. However, after the Revolution Indian rights are largely ignored.
1919	Emiliano Zapata, Nahuatl-speaking peasant revolutionary leader, champion of agrarian reform, and radical voice of the Mexican Revolution, assassinated.
1920s	Emergence of *indigenismo* as a political movement in Mexico and Peru. Powerful intellectual and political movement, with radical mentors such as José Carlos Mariátegui and Víctor Raúl Haya de la Torre, founder of the APRA party in Peru.
1932	Indigenous people in El Salvador are the main targets when a peasant uprising is put down at the cost of 30,000 lives.
1934	The Reorganization Act in the USA re-establishes the sovereignty of Indian tribes and gives tribal governments the authority to draw up constitutions and to assume judicial and fiscal control over the reservations. Allotment (division into individual farms) of tribal lands is halted.
1934	US Dawes Act of 1887 repealed. Over the intervening years, indigenous people in the USA have lost two-thirds of their lands.
1940	First Inter-American Indigenist Congress held in Pátzcuaro, Mexico, discusses the co-ordination of state integrationist policies.
1952	Bolivian Revolution, led by the National Revolutionary Movement (MNR), a populist coalition subsequently pushed to the left in 1952–3 by armed mineworkers and Indian peasants. The MNR agrees to the nationalization of the tin mines and the expropriation of highland *haciendas*. However, the Agrarian Reform of 1953 divides up the land into thousands of individual allotments, resulting in the disintegration of many communities.
1964	Shuar and Achuar tribes of Ecuador form an indigenous federation.
1968	Reformist military officers seize power in Peru and launch 'military socialism'. An agrarian reform challenges the highland oligarchy, while the military junta eventually makes Quechua an official language. The reforms emphasize communality, but problems with lack of credit, a weak infrastructure and the machinations of landlords limit their effect.
1969	Brazilian government agencies accused of waging biological warfare against Indians.

1969	American Indian Movement (AIM) emerges out of an indigenous ghetto community in Minneapolis.
1971	The CRIC (Indigenous Regional Council of the Cauca) is formed by 2,000 Páez, Coconucos and Guambianos in Colombia.
1973	Two members of the American Indian Movement die in gun battles during a 71-day siege at Wounded Knee, the site of the 1890 massacre.
1973	The Katarista movement in Bolivia issues the Manifesto of Tiawanaku, drawn up by four indigenous organizations in La Paz. The manifesto begins by quoting Inka Yupanqui, who had told the Spaniards, 'A nation that oppresses another nation cannot be free.' The movement is self-consciously ethnic in language and its use of symbols, stressing the combined struggles against ethnic and class exploitation. Its name links the contemporary quest for indigenous rights with that of Tupaq Katari.
1974	Dene Declaration is issued, which begins, 'The government of Canada is not the government of the Dene.'
1977	The trial and conviction, widely considered unsafe, of AIM member Leonard Peltier. Protests at his conviction become a catalyst for renewed Indian protest throughout the 1980s.
1979	The Declaration of the Haudenosaunee, or the Six Nations Iroquois Confederacy, announces itself as 'among the most ancient continously operating governments in the world'.
1979	The military dictatorship of General Pinochet in Chile passes a law forcing the division of lands belonging to the Mapuche Indians.
1980	US census reveals that 28 per cent of the country's 1.75 million Indians, Inuits and Aleuts are living below the poverty line.
1980–4	Counter-insurgency operations by the Guatemalan army destroy 440 mainly Maya villages, kill some 40,000 people and drive a million more from their homes.
1983	Mario Juruna, a Xavánte, becomes the first indigenous member of the Brazilian Congress.
1984	The Guambiano and Páez Indians of Colombia establish the Comando Quintín Lame guerrilla organization to resist seizures of their land. Quintín Lame becomes the only specifically indigenous armed force in the Americas in recent history.
1984	Founding of COICA, the indigenous peoples' organization of the Amazon and the largest indigenous organization in the Americas.
1984	In northern Canada, the Inuvialuit obtain control of 35,000 square miles of mineral-rich territory from the Canadian government and set

up their own oil-producing company, the Inuvialuit Petroleum Corporation (IPC).

1985   In Accomarca, Ayacucho, Peru about 70 Quechua, including women and children, are slaughtered by the army. It is just one of countless massacres in the Peruvian highlands in the counter-insurgency war against Shining Path guerrillas.

1985   Kayapó warriors in Brazil close down the María Bonita mine when a contract providing them with only 1 per cent of production expires. With the help of the Brazilian military, they expel more than 5,000 miners from the site. The Kayapó then agree to reopen the mine on condition FUNAI, the Brazilian Indian agency, agrees to demarcate their land. In May they sign an agreement establishing a 3 million hectare reserve. The mine reopens with a 5 per cent tax in place.

1987   In the middle of the US-backed Contra war against the Sandinista government, Nicaragua becomes the first nation in the Americas to recognize its multiethnic nature when its Autonomy Law is passed unanimously by the National Assembly. The new law guarantees the cultural, linguistic and religious rights demanded by the Sumos, Ramas and Miskitos of the Atlantic coast, and goes further in recognizing that such rights cannot be fully exercised unless those minorities enjoy sufficient economic resources to guarantee not just survival, but also growth and development.

1987   Kayapó Indian leaders join with the leaders of 28 other Brazilian Indian tribes to oppose hydroelectric development of the Amazon basin. The Union of Indigenous Nations in Brazil demands constitutional protection for indigenous peoples.

1988   The Kuna of Panama produce a set of rules for researchers and scientists entering their lands, in a 26-page booklet entitled *Research Program: Scientific Monitoring and Cooperation*. The Kuna also demand that visiting scientists file reports on their research and employ Kuna assistants, guides and informants to transfer 'knowledge and technologies with the objective of training Kuna scientists'.

1988   Brazil's new constitution approved, including a whole chapter on indigenous peoples. The constitution recognizes the existence of collective rights, Indians' social organizations, and their practices, religions, languages and beliefs. It gives communities the right to express opinions about the exploitation of natural resources and allows them to plead in the courts. Above all, the constitution includes a five-year deadline, expiring in October 1993, for the demarcation of officially recognized indigenous territory. By late 1993, fewer than half of more than 500 territories have been demarcated.

1988–95	Malaria and influenza are among the diseases introduced by non-Indians which kill 21 per cent of the Yanomami in the Amazon.
1989	Approval of the International Labour Organization's Indigenous and Tribal People's Convention no. 169. This is the only current international convention on the rights of indigenous people. From September 1991, when it comes into force, until 1996, only six governments in the Americas sign it.
1990	In Canada, Elijah Harper, a Cree-Ojibwa politician, blocks a constitutional agreement with Quebec, opening the way for a new deal for the country's indigenous people, including a constitution recognizing native peoples' 'inherent right to self-rule'.
1990	The Kayapó call an international meeting to protest against the dam-building programme on their lands at Altamira. Officials from Eletronorte, the Brazilian power supply company, share the platform with Kayapó chiefs to address about 650 indigenous representatives from 40 different nations, along with 400 foreign journalists. The following month the World Bank announces that it will no longer fund the dams.
1990	Protesting Mohawk Indians take part in an 11-week siege at Oka, Quebec.
1990	'March for Land and Dignity' in Bolivia. Eight hundred Moxeños, Yuracarés, Chimanes and Guaranís set out from the town of Trinidad (altitude 780 ft) in the Amazon basin to walk the 330 miles to the highland capital, La Paz (11,900 ft). They are protesting against government inaction in preventing the extraction of mahogany from a 400,000-acre strip of the Chimane Forest and carry a banner proclaiming their protest 'The March for Land and Dignity'. As they climb through the mountain passes that link highland and lowland Bolivia, thousands of Quechua and Aymara come out to cheer them on or join the march.
1990	One hundred and sixty members of the Confederation of Indigenous Nationalities of Ecuador (CONAIE) occupy the cathedral of Santo Domingo in the heart of Ecuador's capital, Quito, demanding the resolution of land disputes in six highland provinces. The protest sparks a national uprising as roads are blocked, police and local officials taken hostage and land occupied. As the country effectively closes down, senior government ministers are sent to negotiate on CONAIE's 16 demands for cultural rights.
1990	The inhabitants of Santiago Atitlán, an indigenous town in Guatemala, secure the removal of the army garrison after a massacre by the troops leaves 13 residents dead. In the 10 years the army has been in occupation, 268 Atitecos have been murdered and scores more have 'disappeared'.

1991	Over 500 delegates from indigenous groups from 27 American countries meet in Guatemala in the run-up to the Columbus quincentenary.
1991	Colombia's new constitution sets out the most comprehensive set of rights enjoyed by indigenous peoples anywhere in the Americas.
1992	Five hundredth anniversary of Columbus's arrival in the Americas. Protests across the continents. Rigoberta Menchú Tum, a Maya human rights activist, is awarded the Nobel Peace Prize.
1992	About 90 of the 230 indigenous tribes that lived in the Amazon at the turn of the century have by now disappeared.
1993	UN Year of Indigenous Peoples. UN Working Group on Indigenous Populations presents a draft for a Universal Declaration on Indigenous Rights to the Sub–Commission on the Prevention of Discrimination and Protection of Minorities.
1993	When President Gonzalo Sánchez de Lozada leaves the country on an official trip, Víctor Hugo Cárdenas, vice-president of Bolivia, becomes the first indigenous person to assume major executive office in the Americas since Benito Juárez.
1993	On the Ene River in Peru's Amazon, Shining Path guerrillas kill about 60 Ashaninka Indians in reprisals for the Ashaninkas' agreement to co-operate with the authorities by organizing civil patrols in their area.
1993	Bent on doubling oil production by 1996, the Ecuadorean government issues tenders for drilling on 2 million acres of land in 'undeveloped regions' in 1993, much of it on indigenous land.
1993	The Canadian Commission on Human Rights issues an unequivocal report concluding that 'It is clear that the Mushuau Innu are the victims of ethnocide or cultural genocide.' The report blames the Canadian and Newfoundland governments.
1993	Acting on behalf of 30,000 Ecuadorean Indian plaintiffs, a team of US lawyers brings a $1.5 billion lawsuit against the Texaco oil company in a New York federal court, demanding that it 'make good on the damage it caused to the people and environment' of the Ecuadorean Oriente during 20 years of drilling. The pressure forces Texaco to agree to fund a clean-up campaign in the Ecuadorean rain forest.
Jan. 1994	The largely-Indian Zapatista National Liberation Army (EZLN) occupies four towns in Chiapas, Mexico.
1995	Start of the UN Decade of Indigenous Peoples.

Appendix 1:
Indigenous Population Figures

Compiled by Emma Pearce

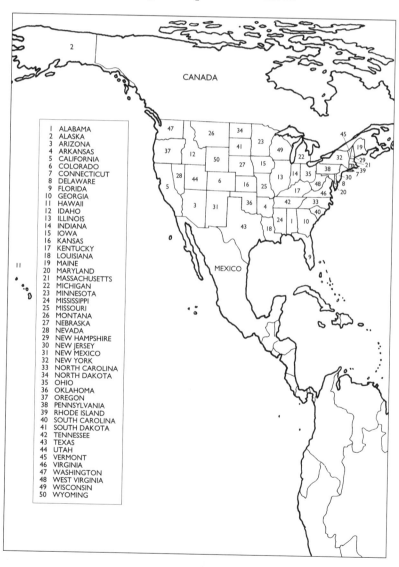

1 ALABAMA
2 ALASKA
3 ARIZONA
4 ARKANSAS
5 CALIFORNIA
6 COLORADO
7 CONNECTICUT
8 DELAWARE
9 FLORIDA
10 GEORGIA
11 HAWAII
12 IDAHO
13 ILLINOIS
14 INDIANA
15 IOWA
16 KANSAS
17 KENTUCKY
18 LOUISIANA
19 MAINE
20 MARYLAND
21 MASSACHUSETTS
22 MICHIGAN
23 MINNESOTA
24 MISSISSIPPI
25 MISSOURI
26 MONTANA
27 NEBRASKA
28 NEVADA
29 NEW HAMPSHIRE
30 NEW JERSEY
31 NEW MEXICO
32 NEW YORK
33 NORTH CAROLINA
34 NORTH DAKOTA
35 OHIO
36 OKLAHOMA
37 OREGON
38 PENNSYLVANIA
39 RHODE ISLAND
40 SOUTH CAROLINA
41 SOUTH DAKOTA
42 TENNESSEE
43 TEXAS
44 UTAH
45 VERMONT
46 VIRGINIA
47 WASHINGTON
48 WEST VIRGINIA
49 WISCONSIN
50 WYOMING

Political Map of the Americas
ANDY DARK

For reasons of space, only those indigenous groups with a population of 1,000 or over are listed. Figures in brackets are the number of speakers of the group's language, where known.

Argentina

Chiriguano	15,000
Chorote	2,300
Mapudungun	40,000
Mocoví	3,000–4,000
Pilagá	2,000
Quechua	855,000
Quichua	75,000
Toba	15,000–20,000
Wichí Lhamtés Vejoz	25,000

Belize

Kekchí	10,000–20,000
Mopán Maya	6,000
Yucateco	5,800

Bolivia

Aymara	1,785,000
Ayoreo	1,000–1,500
Cavineña	1,000
Chipaya	1,000
Chiquitano	20,000
Chiriguano	15,000
Guaraní	1,000–3,000
Guaruyu	5,000
Ignaciano	4,000
Movima	1,000
Quechua	2,899,000
Reyesano	1,000
Tacana	3,500
Trinitario	5,000
Tsimané	5,500
Wichí Lhamtés Nocten	1,427
Yuracare	2,500

Brazil

Apurinã	1,500
Baniwa	5,460
Bora	1,500–2,000
Canela	2,500

Chiripá	2,500
Curripaco	340–1,500
Desano	1,586
Fulniô	1,526–3,500
Gavião do Jiparaná	1,070–1,615
Guajajára	10,000
Guaraní	26,000 (942,500–943,000)
Hupdë	1,580
Kaingang	18,000
Kaiwá	12,000–14,000
Karajá	2,700
Katukína, panoan	1,000
Kayapó	2,208
Krahô	1,200
Makuxí	3,800
Mundurukú	1,700
Nhengatu	3,000
Pakaásnovos	990–1,147
Potiguára	4,000
Sateré-Mawé	5,000
Terêna	15,000
Ticuna	12,000
Tucano	2,631
Waiwai	886–1,058
Wapishana	1,500
Xavánte	7,500
Yanomami	16,000

Canada

Abnaki-Penobscot	1,800 inc. USA (20)
Algonquin	5,000 (3,000)
Assiniboine	3,500 inc. USA (150–200)
Atikamekw	3,255 (3,255)
Babine	2,200 (1,600)
Blackfoot	15,000 inc. USA (9,000)
Carrier	2,600 (2,000)
Cayuga	3,000 inc. USA (380)
Chilcotin	1,800 (1,200)
Chipewyan	5,000 (4,000)
Cree	64,000 inc. USA (46,700)
Dakota	23,000 inc. USA (19,000)
Dogrib	2,300 (2,300)
Gwich'in	2,600 inc. USA (1,500)
Haida	2,000 inc. USA (295)

Haisla	1,000 (250)
Halkomelem	6,700 (500)
Heiltsuk	1,200 (450)
Inuit	33,000 (18,840)
Kutenai	1,500 inc. USA (100)
Kwakiutl	3,300 (1,000)
Lakota	20,000 inc. USA (6,000)
Lilooet	2,800 (300–400)
Malecite-Passamaquoddy	3,000 inc. USA (1,500)
Micmac	11,000 (6,000)
Mohawk	10,000 inc. USA (3,000)
Montagnais	9,000 (7,000)
Nass-Gitskian	5,000 (2,500)
Nootka	3,500 (500)
Ojibwa	93,000 inc. USA (51,000)
Okanagan	3,000 inc. USA (500)
Onandaga	1,500 inc. USA (100)
Oneida	7,000 inc. USA (250)
Potawatomi	7,500 inc. USA (500)
Salish	3,000 (30)
Seneca	8,000 inc. USA (200)
Shuswap	6,500 (500)
Slavey	5,000 (4,000)
Squamish	2,300 (20)
Stoney	3,200 (1,000–1,500)
Thompson	3,000 (500)
Tlingit	9,500 inc. USA (2,000)
Tshimshian	4,000 inc. USA (1,435)
Tuscarora	1,000 inc. USA (30)
Tutchone	1,500 (450)
Wyandot	2,500 inc. USA (0)

Chile

Aymara	20,000 ('few')
Huilliche	156,000 ('several thousand')
Mapudungun (Mapuche)	400,000 (200,000)
Rapanui	2,200 on Easter Island, 200–300 on mainland Chile

Colombia

Camsá	4,000
Catío	15,000–20,000
Chamí	9,000
Cogui	3,000–5,000
Cuaiquer	20,000

208

Cubeo	5,000
Cuiba	2,000
Curripaco	2,000–2,500
Embera	2,000
Epena Saija	3,500
Guahibo	15,000
Guajiro	82,000
Guambiano	9,000
Huitoto	3,000–4,000
Ica	5,272
Inga	11,000–16,000
Koreguaje	1,750
Motilón	1,500–2,000
Nhengatu	3,000
Páez	40,000
Palenquero	2,500
Piapoco	3,000
Puinave	2,000
Sáliba	2,000
Tadó	1,000
Ticuna	4,000
Tucano	2,000
Tunebo	1,800
Waumeo	3,000
Yucuna	800–1,000
Yukpa	2,500

Costa Rica

Boruca	1,000 (5)
Bribri	5,000
Cabécar	3,000

Ecuador

Achuar-Shiwiar	2,000
Chachi	5,000
Colorado	1,800
Quichua	1,456,000–1,479,000
Shuar	30,000–32,000

El Salvador

Kekchí	12,300
Lenca	36,858
Pipil	196,600 (20)

French Guiana

Aukaans	6,000–8,000
Kahlina	1,200

Greenland

Inuit	40,000

Guatemala

Achí	55,000
Aguacateco	16,700
Cakchiquel	442,600
Chortí	31,500
Chuj	41,600
Ixil	52,900
Jacalteco	37,300
K'iche'	886,900
Kekchí	335,800
Mam	430,800–445,800
Mopán Maya	2,600
Pokomam	40,400
Pokomchí	54,100
Q'anjob'al	49,000
Sacapulteco	36,800
Sipacapense	6,000
Tacaneco	20,000
Tectiteco	2,600
Tzutujil	81,900
Uspanteco	2,000

Guyana

Akawaio	3,000–4,000
Arawak	5,000 (1,500)
Makuxí	1,300
Patamona	3,000–4,000
Waiwai	886–1,058
Wapishana	9,000

Honduras

Lenca	50,000 ('few')
Miskito	10,000

Mexico

Amuzgo	31,800–34,500
Chatino	37,500–39,000
Chichimeca	2,200–3,200
Chicomuceltec	1,500
Chinanteco	61,300–65,900
Chocho	2,500
Chol	85,000–90,000
Chontal	39,000–50,000
Chuj	2,000–3,000
Cora	15,000
Cuicateco	21,000–27,000
Huarijío	3,000–5,000
Huasteco	73,300
Huave	21,000–23,000
Huichol	12,500
Jacalteco, Western	1,000
Mam	11,000
Matlatzinca	2,000–2,200
Mayo	50,000
Mazahua	250,000–400,000
Mazateco	160,200–215,200
Mixe	89,500–92,500
Mixteco	256,000–276,000
Nahuatl	1,743,500–1,759,100
Otomí	184,500–221,500
Pame, Central	4,350
Pima bajo	2,000
Popoloca	27,500–28,500
Popoluca	38,100–38,200
Tarahumara	35,600–50,600
Tarasco	57,000–60,000
Tectiteco	1,000
Tepehua	8,000–14,500
Tepehuan	14,000–19,000
Tlapaneco	40,000
Tojolab'al	12,000–14,000
Totonaco	256,500–268,800
Trique	16,000
Tzeltal	45,000
Tzotzil	135,000
Yaqui	12,000
Yucatec	914,200–934,200

Zapotec	506,700
Zoque	17,200–18,200

Nicaragua

Miskito	150,000
Monimbo	10,000 (0)
Subtiaba	5,000 (0)
Sumo	6,700

Panama

Buglere	2,500
Embera	7,000–8,000
Guaymí	70,000
Kuna	45,000–50,000
Teribe	1,500–2,000
Waumeo	3,000

Paraguay

Angaite	4,000
Ayoreo	3,000
Chamococo	1,800
Chiriguano	2,000
Chiripá	7,000
Chulupí	18,000
Guaraní	35,000 (3,068,000)
Lengua	10,000
Maca	1,000
Pai Tavytera	10,000–12,000
Sanapaná	2,900
Tapieté	1,800
Toba-Maskoy	2,500

Peru

Achuar-shiwiar	3,000–3,500
Aguaruna	25,000–30,000
Amahuaca	500–1,500
Amuesha	4,000–8,000
Aymara	300,000–500,000
Bora	1,000–1,500
Campa	29,000–37,000
Candoshi-Shapra	3,000
Cashibo-Cacataibo	1,000–1,500
Cashinahua	850–1,200

Chayahuita	6,000
Cocama-Cocamilla	15,000–18,000
Huambisa	6,000–10,000
Huitoto	1,200–1,500
Jaqaru	2,000
Jebero	2,300–3,000
Machiguenga	6,000–8,000
Nomatsiguenga	2,500–4,000
Piro	1,700–2,500
Quechua	3,318,900–3,350,900
Quichua	8,000–10,000
Shipibo-Conibo	11,300–15,000
Ticuna	6,000
Urarina	2,000–3,500
Yagua	3,000–4,000
Yaminahua	700–1,100

Surinam

Arawak	2,000 (700)
Aukaans	25,000
Kalihna	2,500

USA

Abnaki-Penobscot	1,800 inc. Canada (20)
Aleut	2,000 (500)
Apache	17,000 (14,300)
Arapaho	5,000 (1,500)
Arikara	1,000 (200)
Assiniboine	3,500 inc. Canada (150–200)
Blackfoot	15,000 inc. Canada (9,000)
Caddo	1,800 (300)
Cayuga	3,000 inc. Canada (380)
Cherokee	78,500 (22,500)
Cheyenne	5,000 (2,000)
Choctaw-Chickasaw	25,000 (12,000)
Comanche	6,000 (500)
Cree	64,000 inc. Canada (46,700)
Crow	7,000 (5,500)
Dakota	23,000 (19,000)
Flathead-Kalispel	3,000 (800)
Gros Ventre	1,200 (10)
Gwich'in	2,600 inc. Canada (1,500)
Havasupai-Walapai-Yavapai	1,500 (1,200)
Hidatsa	1,200 (100)

213

Hopi	6,500 (5,000)
Inuit	16,000 (7,500)
Iowa	1,000 (5)
Jemez	1,488 (1,263)
Karok	3,781 (100)
Keres	11,500 (8,000)
Kikapoo	1,500 (1,200)
Kiowa	6,000 (800)
Klamath-Modoc	2,000 (150)
Koyukon	2,200 (700)
Kutenai	1,500 inc. Canada (100)
Lakota	20,000 inc. Canada (6,000)
Luiseño	1,500 (100)
Lumbee	30,000 (0)
Lushootseed	2,000 (60)
Malecite-Passamaquoddy	3,000 inc. Canada (1,500)
Menomini	3,500 (50)
Mesquakie	2,500 (800)
Miami	2,000 (0)
Micmac	2,100
Miccosukee	1,200 (1,000)
Mohave	1,500 (700)
Mohawk	10,000 inc. Canada (3,000)
Mohegan-Montauk-Narragansett	1,400 (0)
Muskogee	20,000 (10,000)
Navaho	200,000 (130,000)
Nez Percé	1,500 (500)
Ojibwa	85,000 (42,000)
Okanagan	3,000 inc. Canada (500)
Omaha	2,500 (1,500)
Onandaga	1,500 inc. Canada (100)
Oneida	7,000 inc. Canada (250)
Osage	2,500 (5)
Oto	1,400 (50)
Paiute	4,000 (2,000)
Papago-Pima	20,000 (15,000)
Pawnee	2,000 (200)
Pomo	1,000 (100)
Ponca	2,000 (25)
Potawatomi	7,500 inc. Canada (500)
Powhatan	3,000 (0)
Quapaw	2,000 (0)
Quechan	1,500 (500)
Quinault	1,500 (6)

Salish	5,000 (80)
Seneca	8,000 inc. Canada (200)
Shawnee	2,000 (200)
Shoshone	7,000 (3,000)
Spokane	1,000 (50)
Tenino	1,000 (200)
Tewa	2,383 (1,298)
Tiwa	3,635 (2,659)
Tlingit	9,500 inc. Canada (2,000)
Tshimshian	4,000 inc. Canada (1,435)
Tuscarora	1,000 inc. Canada
Unami	2,000 (10)
Ute	5,000 (2,500)
Washo	1,000 (100)
Winnebago	3,500 (1,500)
Wintu	1,000 (20)
Wyandot	2,500 inc. Canada (0)
Yakima	8,000 (3,000)
Yaqui	5,000
Yuchi	1,500 (50)
Yupik	21,000 (16,600)
Yurok	3,000–4,500 (10)
Zuni	5,929 (4,484)

Venezuela

Guahibo	5,000
Guajiro	45,000
Kalihna	4,000–5,000
Mandhuaca	3,000
Maquiritari	4,970
Panare	1,200
Pemon	4,850
Piaroa	12,000
Sanumá	1,000–4,000
Warao	15,000
Yanomamö	12,000–14,000
Yaruro	2,000–3,000

Source: *Ethnologue: Languages of the World*, 12th edition, ed. Barbara F. Grimes (Dallas: Summer Institute of Linguistics, 1992)

Appendix 2:
Contact Organizations
Working on Indigenous Issues

This appendix provides contact details both for research and campaigning organizations, such as Survival International and Cultural Survival, which work on indigenous questions, and for indigenous organizations themselves in both North and South America. Many such organizations change offices and telephone numbers frequently, but the list is correct as of February 1996.

Europe

European Alliance with Indigenous Peoples
Keltenlaan 20
1040 Brussels
Belgium
Contact: Wendel Trio
Tel: 32 2 733 3653
Fax: 32 2 736 8054

International Alliance of the Indigenous
   Peoples of the Tropical Rainforests
23 Bevenden Street
London N1 6BH
United Kingdom
Contact: Maximilian Offt
Tel: 0171 251 5893
Fax: 0171 251 5914

International Working Group on Indigenous
   Affairs (IWGIA)
Fiolstraede 10
DK-1171 Copenhagen K
Denmark
Tel: 45 33 124 724
Fax: 45 33 147 749

Mapuche International Link
6 Lodge Street
Bristol
BS1 5LR
United Kingdom
Tel/fax: 0117 927 9391

Maya International
(Gesellschaft zur Forderung der
   Selbstbestimmung der Maya)
Postfach 200930
5300 Bonn 2
Germany
Tel: 49 228 310 333

NCIV
Dutch Centre for Indigenous Peoples
PB 94098
1090B Amsterdam
The Netherlands
Tel: 31 20 693 8625
Fax: 31 20 665 2818

Steungroep Inheemse Volkeren (KWIA)
Breughelstraat 31–33
B-2018 Antwerpen
Belgium
Tel: 323 218 8488
Fax: 323 230 4540

Survival International, France
45 rue du Faubourg du Temple
75010 Paris
France
Tel: 331 4241 4762

Survival International, Italy
Casella Postale 1194
20101 Milano
Italy
Tel: 392 890 0671
Fax: 392 890 0674

Survival International, Spain
Calle Príncipe 12
Piso 3, Oficina 3
Madrid 28012
Spain
Tel: 341 521 7283
Fax: 341 523 1420

Survival International, UK
11-15 Emerald Street
London WC1N 3QL
United Kingdom
Tel: 0171 242 1441
Fax: 0171 242 1771

Trócaire
169 Booterstown Avenue
Blackrock
Co Dublin
Ireland
Tel: 3531 288 5385
Fax: 3531 288 3577

World Rainforest Movement
Forest Peoples Programme
8 Chapel Row
Chadlington OX7 3NA
United Kingdom
Tel: 01608 676691
Fax: 01608 676743

Canada

Aboriginal Rights Coalition
151 Laurier Avenue East
Ottawa
Ontario
K1N 6N8
Tel: 613 235 9956
Fax: 613 235 1302

Assembly of First Nations
1 Nicholas Street
Ottawa
Ontario
K1N 7B7
Tel: 613 241 6789
Fax: 613 241 5808

Association of Iroquois and Allied Indians
387 Princess Avenue
London
N Ontario
N6B 2A7
Tel: 519 434 2761
Fax: 519 679 1653

Canadian Alliance in Solidarity with Native
  Peoples
39 Spadina Road
Toronto
Ontario
M5R 2S9
Tel: 416 972 1573
Fax: 416 972 6232

Canadian Indigenous Women's
  Resource Institute
226, 3715–51 Street SW
Calgary
T3E 6V2
Alberta
Tel: 403 242 7082
Fax: 403 242 7083

Confederacy of Treaty Six First Nations
Suite 601, 10025–106 Street
Calgary
Alberta T5J 1G4
Tel: 403 944 0334
Fax: 403 944 0346

Council of Yukon First Nations
11 Nisutlin Drive
Whitehorse
Yukon
Y1A 3S4
Tel: 403 667 7631
Fax: 403 668 6577

Cree Nation Youth Council of Quebec
Cree Nation Building
2 Lakeshore Road
Nemaska
James Bay
Quebec
J0Y 3B0
Tel: 819 673 2600
Fax: 819 673 2606

Federation of Saskatchewan Indian Nations
107 Hodsman Road
Regina
Saskatchewan
S4N 5W5
Tel: 306 721 2822
Fax: 306 721 2707

Four Nations Administrative Office
PO Box 279
Hobbema
Alberta
T0C 1N0
Tel: 403 585 3790
Fax: 403 585 2282

Grand Council of the Crees of Quebec
2 Lakeshore Road
Nemaska
James Bay
Quebec
J0Y 3B0
Tel: 819 673 2600
Fax: 819 673 2606

Inuit Circumpolar Conference
Suite 504
170 Laurier Avenue West
Ottawa
Ontario
K1P 5V5
Tel: 613 563 2642
Fax: 613 565 3089

Inuit Taparisat of Canada
Suite 510
170 Laurier Avenue West
Ottawa
Ontario
K1P 5V5
Tel: 613 238 8181
Fax: 613 234 1991

Native Council of Canada
65 Bank Street, 4th floor
Ottawa
Ontario
K1P 5N2
Tel: 613 238 3511
Fax: 613 230 6273

Native News Network
University of Western Ontario
Social Science Centre
3rd floor #3254
London
Ontario
N6A 5C2
Tel: 519 661 2111

Native Women's Association of Canada
9 Melrose Avenue
Ottawa
Ontario
K1Y 1T8
Tel: 613 722 3033
Fax: 613 722 7687

Plains Indians Cultural Survival School
1723–33 Street SW
Calgary
Alberta
T3C 1P4
Tel: 403 777 7860
Fax: 403 686 1055

The Eastern Door
PO Box 1170
Kahnawake
Quebec
J0L 1B0
Tel: 514 635 3050
Fax: 514 635 8479

Union of BC Indian Chiefs
5th floor
342 Water Street
Vancouver
British Columbia
V6B 1B6
Tel: 604 684 0231
Fax: 604 684 5726

Union of New Brunswick Indians
385 Wilsey Road, Compartment 44
Fredericton
New Brunswick
E3B 5N6
Tel: 506 458 9444
Fax: 506 458 2850

Union of Nova Scotia Indians
PO Box 400
Shubenacadie
Nova Scotia
B02 2H0
Tel: 902 758 2346

Union of Ontario Indians
Box 711
North Bay
Ontario
P1B 8J8
Tel: 705 497 9127
Fax: 705 497 9135

United States of America

Alaska Federation of Natives Inc.
1577 C Street, Suite 100
Anchorage
AK 99501
Tel: 907 274 3611

American Indian Law Alliance
404 Lafayette Street
New York
NY 10003
Tel: 212 598 0100 Ext 257
Fax: 212 598 4909

American Indian Movement
2300 Cedar Avenue South
Minneapolis
MN 55404
Tel: 612 724 3129
Fax: 612 724 8090

American Indian Program
Cornell University
300 Caldwell Hall
Ithaca
NY 14853
Tel: 607 255 4308
Fax: 607 255 0185

Apache Survival Coalition
PO Box 249
San Carlos
AZ 85550
Tel: 520 475 2545

Centre for Indigenous Rights and
    Development
PO Box 95560
Seattle
WA 98145
Tel: 206 368 0981
Fax: 206 367 3533

Colorado River Indian Nations
Rt. 1
Box 23-B
Parker
AZ 85344
Tel: 602 669 9211

Cultural Survival
46 Brattle Street
Cambridge
MA 02138
Tel: 617 441 5400
Fax: 617 441 5417

Duckwater Shoshone Tribe
PO Box 140068
Duckwater
NV 89314-0068
Tel: 702 863 0227
Fax: 702 863 0301

219

Indian Law Resource Center
508 Stuart Street
Helena
MT 59601
Tel: 406 449 2006
Fax: 406 449 2031

Indigenous World Association
1663 18th Street
San Francisco 94107
CA
Tel: 415 647 1966
Fax: 510 854 786

International Indian Treaty Council
54 Mint Street, Suite 400
San Francisco 94103
CA
Tel: 415 512 1501
Fax: 415 512 1507

Mohawk Nation
PO Box 196
Via Roosevelttown
NY 13683-0196
Tel: 518 358 9531
Fax: 613 575 2935

National Congress of American Indians
2010 Massachusetts Avenue NW
Second floor
Washington DC 20036
Tel: 202 466 7767
Fax: 202 466 7797

National Indian Youth Council
318 Elm Street, SE
Albuquerque
NM 87102
Tel: 505 247 2251
Fax: 505 247 4251

Native American Public
  Telecommunications Inc.
PO Box 83111
Lincoln
NB 68501
Tel: 402 472 3522
Fax: 402 472 1785

Native American Rights Fund
1506 Broadway
Boulder
CO 80302
Tel: 303 447 8760
Fax: 303 443 7776

Native Lands Research and Policy Institute
809 Copper NW #200
Albuquerque
NM 87102
Tel: 505 242 4020
Fax: 505 842 6124

Navaho Nation
PO Drawer 308
Window Rock
Navaho Nation
AZ 86515
Tel: 602 871 6352

Oglala Sioux Tribe of the Pine Ridge
  Reservation
Oglala Sioux Tribal Council
Pine Ridge
SD 57548

Pawnee Tribe
PO Box 470
Pawnee
OK 74058
Tel: 918 762 3621

Sioux Tribe of the Cheyenne River
  Reservation
Sioux Tribal Council
PO Box 590
Eagle Butte
SD 57625
Tel: 605 964 4155

United National Indian Tribal Youth
4010 Lincoln Blvd #202
Oklahoma City
OK 73125
Tel: 405 424 3010
Fax: 405 424 3018

Regional Organizations in the Americas

Coordinadora de las Organizaciones
Indígenas de la Cuenca Amazónica (COICA)
Casilla Postal 17-21-753
Quito
Ecuador
Tel/fax: 5932 553 297

Fundación Rigoberta Menchú
Heriberto Frias 339
Colonia Navarte 03020
Mexico DF
Tel: 525 639 1492 / 639 3091
Fax: 525 638 0439

Instituto Indigenista Interamericano
Nubes 232
Pedregal de San Angel
Delegación Alvaro Obregón
Mexico DF 01900
Tel: 525 652 1133
Fax: 525 652 1274

South and Meso-American Indian
Information Center
PO Box 28703
Oakland
CA 94604
USA
Tel: 510 834 4263
Fax: 510 834 4264

World Council of Indigenous Peoples
100 Argyle
Ottawa
Ontario
K2P 1B6
Canada
Tel: 613 230 9030
Fax: 613 230 9340

Argentina

Asociación Indígena de la República de
Argentina
Balbastro 1790
1406 Buenos Aires
Tel: 541 977 308
Fax: 541 827 1113

Bolivia

Central de Pueblos Indígenas del Beni
(CPIB)
Casilla 58
Trinidad
Beni
Tel: 5914 621 575

Centro de Difusión Ideológica de la Mujer
Aymara
Nicasio Cardoso #450
Zona Central
La Paz
Tel/fax: 5912 354 874

Comisión Internacional de Derechos de
Pueblos Indígenas de Sudamérica
Calle Isaac Arias #1055
Villa Dolores
El Alto
Tel/fax: 5912 824 124

Confederación Indígena del Oriente
Boliviano (CIDOB)
Casilla 4213
Santa Cruz de la Sierra
Tel/fax: 5913 346 714

Organización de Mujeres Aymaras del
Kollasuyo (OMAK)
Casilla 13195
Correo Central
La Paz
Tel: 5912 813 529/97

Brazil

Associação Nacional de Apoio ao Indio da
Bahia (ANAI-BA)
Rua Borges dos Reis, N. 46 – sala 5H – Rio
Vermelho
40223-000 Salvador – BA
Tel/fax: 5571 247 0464

CAPOIB
SDS Ed. Venancio III, 1o andar, sala 107
Brasília DF 70393-900
Tel/fax: 5561 322 4133

Return of the Indian

Centro Ecumênico de Documentaçao e
  Informaçao (CEDI)
Av. Higienópolis 983
01238-001 Sao Paulo SP
Tel: 5511 825 5544
Fax: 5511 825 7861

Conselho Indígena de Roraima (CIR)
Caiza Postal 323
Av. Sebastiao Diniz 1672 W
Bairro de Sao Vicente
69.303-120 Boa Vista RR
Tel/fax: 5595 224 5761

COIAB
CP 1081
Agencia Monsenhor Coutinho
69-025-290 Manaus AM
Tel: 5592 233 0548
Fax: 5592 233 0209

Conselho Indigenista Missionarário (CIMI)
SDS – ED. Venancio III – salas 309–314
70393–900 Brasíli DF
Tel: 5561 225 9457
Fax: 5561 225 9401

Grupo de Trabalho Missionário Evangélico
  Em Solidariedade aos Povos Indígenas
  (GTME)
Av. dos Trabalhadores 3.419
78005-970 Cuiabá MT
Tel: 5565 322 7476

Projeto Estudo sobre Terras Indígenas no
  Brasil
Museu Nacional / UFRJ
Quinta da Boa Vista s/n
São Cristovao
20942-040 Rio de Janeiro RJ
Tel: 5521 248 9642
Fax: 5521 254 6695

Chile

Coordinadora de Instituciones Mapuches
General Carrera 165
Temuco
Tel/fax: 5645 234 790

Colombia

Consejo Regional Indígena del Cauca
  (CRIC)
Calle 1a No 4-50
AA 516
Popayan
Cauca
Tel: 57 928 242 153
Fax: 57 928 240 343
  or
AA 12611
Bogotá
Tel: 571 286 6559

Organización Nacional Indígena de
  Colombia (ONIC)
Apartado Aereo 32395
Santa Fé de Bogotá
Tel: 571 342 3054
Fax: 571 284 3465

Costa Rica

Asociación Sejekto-Sejto
Apartado 906-2150
Moravia
San José
Tel: 5062 402 275

Ecuador

Confederación de Nacionalidades Indígenas
  del Ecuador (CONAIE)
Casilla 17-171235
Quito
Tel: 5932 248 930
Fax: 5932 442 271

Confederación de Naciones Indígenas de la
  Amazonia Ecuatoriana (CONFENAIE)
Av. 6 de Diciembre y 159 Pazmino
Edificio Parlamento, 4 piso, Of. 408
Quito
Tel: 5932 543 973
Fax: 5932 220 325

222

Coordinadora de las Organizaciones
  Indígenas de la Cuenca Amazónica
  (COICA)
Casilla Postal 17-21-753
Quito
Tel/fax: 5932 553 297

ECUARUNARI
Eduador Runacunapac Riccharimui
Apt. 96-C
Sucursal 15
Quito
Tel: 5932 520 873

Federación de Centros Shuar-Achuar
Domingo Comín 17-38
Morona Santiago
Sucúa
Región Amazónica
Tel/fax: 5937 740 108
Tel: (Quito office) 5932 504 264

El Salvador

Asociación Nacional Indígena Salvadoreña
  (ANIS)
Calle Obispo Marroquín
Oficina Antigua Aduana 5-1
Sonsonate
Tel: 503 451 1721/0742

Guatemala

Consejo de Comunidades Etnicas 'Runujel
  Junam' (CERJ)
5a Avenida 3-26
Zona 5
Santa Cruz de Quiche
Tel/fax: 502 9 551 853

Consejo de Mujeres Mayas de Guatemala
2a Calle 3-40
Zona 3
Chimaltenango
Tel/fax: 502 9 392 709

Consejo de Organizaciones Mayas de
  Guatemala
2a Calle 3-40
Zona 3
Chimaltenango
Tel/fax: 502 9 392 709

Consejo de Pueblos Mayas de Guatemala
2a Calle 1-55
Zona 2
Chimaltenango
Tel/fax: 502 9 391 563

Coordinadora Cakchiquel de Desarrollo
  Integral
Aptdo 16
Chimaltenango
Tel: 502 9 391 563
Fax: 502 9 391 473

Coordinadora Nacional de Viudas de
  Guatemala (CONAVIGUA)
8z Avenida 2-19
Zona 1
01001
Guatemala City
Tel: 502 2 537 914
Fax: 502 2 25642

Guyana

Amerindian Peoples' Association
71 Quamina Street
Georgetown
Tel: 5922 61789/70275

Honduras

Confederación de Pueblos Autóctonos de
  Honduras
Aptdo 20-585
Comayagüela
Tel/fax: 504 344 925

Mexico

Consejo Nacional de la Cultura Náhuatl
Sinaloa 54-4
Mexico 06700
Tel: 525 511 1776
Fax: 525 665 8645

Coordinadora Nacional de Pueblos Indios
Mesones #45
Interior-4
Centro Historico de la Ciudad de Mexico
   06080
Tel: 525 709 4333

Frente Independiente de Pueblos Indios
Apartado Postal 28-145
Col. Centro
Mexico DF
CP 06080
Tel/fax: 525 783 8002

Grupo de Apoyo a Pueblos Indios
Teran #16
Coatepec
Veracruz 91501
Tel/fax: 522 816 2919

Panama

Asociación Kunas Unidos por Napguana
Apartado 536
Via España, Edificio Dominó
Piso 2, Oficina 31
Panama 1
Tel: 507 269 6525/6
Fax: 507 269 3514

Consultorio Jurídico de los Pueblos
   Indígenas de Panamá
Apartado Postal 536
Panama 1
Tel/fax: 507 263 8879

Coordinadora Nacional de los Pueblos
   Indígenas de Panamá
Apartado 44-73
Zona 5
Avenida Balboa Calle 26
Tel: 507 262 8448

Paraguay

Tierra Viva
Casilla de Correo 789
Asunción
Tel/fax: 595 21 85209

Peru

Asociación Interétnica para el Desarrollo de
   la Selva Peruana
Avenida San Eugenio 981
Urb. Santa Catalina
La Victoria
Lima 13
Tel/fax: 5114 724 605

Comisión Jurídica de los Pueblos de
   Integración Tawantinsuyana
Casilla 230
Arequipa
Tel/fax: 5154 421 652

Federación de Comunidades Nativas del
   Ucayali (FECONAU)
Apartado 194
Pucallpa
Ucayali

Organización Kichwaruna Wangurina
Apartado 216
Iquitos
Amazonas

Venezuela

MOIIN
Apartado Postal 15366
Maracaibo
4005 Zulia
Tel: 5861 416 305

Further Reading

Books in English

Wright, Ronald, *Stolen Continents: The Indian Story* (London: Pimlico Books, 1992).

If you read only one book on this list, make sure it's this one. Enormously readable, rigorously researched, dramatically portrayed, it covers the Americas by telling the stories of five indigenous peoples – the Aztecs, Mayas, Inkas, Cherokee and Iroquois – through three periods of their history: invasion, resistance and rebirth. In more of a travel-writing mode, but with the same sense of alternative history, informed discovery and deep sensitivity are Ronald Wright's *Cut Stones and Crossroads: A Journey in Peru* (Viking-Penguin, New York, 1984) and *Time Among the Maya* (New York: Weidenfeld & Nicolson, 1989).

Some other suggestions are:

The Gaia Atlas of First Peoples, ed. Julian Burger, with campaigning groups and native peoples worldwide (London: Gaia Books, 1990).

A lavishly illustrated book about indigenous peoples' way of life, alternative visions and the threats opposing them, using thumbnail sketches of key aspects of individual peoples' lives and beliefs. The text comes in bite-sized illustrative chunks punctuated by incisive quotes from the peoples themselves. Global but with more than its fair share of contributions from the Americas. A great campaigning tool for teenagers but it will teach most adults just as much.

Burger, Julian, *Report from the Frontier: The State of the World's Indigenous Peoples* (London: Zed Press, 1987).

Deals with definitions, philosophy, marginalization and the colonial experience in general sections before detailing the situation in Mesoamerica, South America and North America in geographic sections that cover the globe. When published, the book was well ahead of its time in focusing on the major sources of conflict between governments, multinationals and indigenous communities and the growing levels of indigenous resistance. Sadly, it is not as out of date as it should be; a decade on, the issues remain largely the same, and Burger's profound understanding of how they interrelate shines through.

Brotherston, Gordon, *Book of the Fourth World: Reading the Native Americas through Their Literature* (Cambridge: Cambridge University Press, 1993).

Just what it says: an attempt to interpret the indigenous peoples of the Americas through their texts and testimonies. The book rehabilitates the original inhabitants of the continent at an intellectual level, posing and answering the question of who entered whose history, originally asked by the authors of the *Chilam Balam* Books. With numerous quotes and illustrations, it's a scholarly work that anyone but the serious academic may prefer to dip into, rather than read cover to cover.

Cultural Survival, *State of the Peoples: A Global Human Rights Report on Societies in Danger*. Project Director Mare S. Miller (Boston: Beacon Press, 1993).

A campaigning tool which includes a number of short essays on the state of a range of indigenous peoples from the Americas and around the world. The book includes thematic contributions from a broad spectrum of experts and concerned parties, a 'Resources for Action' section and more than 90 photographs, charts and maps. Ultimately, the choice of peoples profiled is somewhat arbitrary and there is little historical perspective. However, it remains an attractive book for the campaigner, although only a quarter of it covers the Americas.

Debo, Angie, *A History of the Indians of the United States* (London: Pimlico Books, 1995).

Seen by many as the best one-volume history of the Indians of the United States. Its major weakness is its time-span: despite being in its seventh edition, it effectively stops in the 1960s. Its major strengths are its scholarship and the way its weaves common themes together through the individual experiences and histories of scores of separate nations.

Deloria, Vine, Jr., *Red Earth, White Lies: Native Americans and the Myth of Scientific Fact* (New York: Scribner, 1995).

The latest of more than a dozen books from the man who, more than any other author, initiated the modern Indian renaissance in the United States with his first offering, *Custer Died for Your Sins* (1970). In *Red Earth, White Lies* Deloria turns his fire on modern science as it relates to traditional Indian knowledge, defending the latter as a more accurate account of the history of the earth. Ethnocentric Western learning from anthropological fieldwork to archaeological carbon dating comes in for scrutiny and often scathing criticism. Deloria at his best, but don't ignore some of his other works, including *We Talk, You Listen, God Is Red; Behind the Trail of Broken Treaties* and *The Nations Within* (with Clifford Lytle).

Dunbar Ortiz, Roxanne, *Indians of the Americas: Human Rights and Self-Determination* (London: Zed Books, 1984).

A book that assumes a certain knowledge – a study in theory and methodology, rather than a comprehensive survey as the title suggests. The book's debate revolves around the Indian 'national' question in the Americas, with the first half dealing with self-determination and human rights, the second half studying the issues through two case studies, Indians in the United States (in particular the Navaho and the Sioux) and the Miskito nation in Sandinista Nicaragua. The book reflects the intensity of the ethnicity–class debate taking place on the left of the political spectrum at the time of its publication.

Galeano, Eduardo, *Memory of Fire* (three volumes): *Genesis, Faces and Masks* and *Century of the Wind* (New York: Pantheon Books, 1985, 1987, 1989).

An alternative history of the Americas from pre-Columbian times to the present in the

226

form of an anthology drawn from documents, diaries, speeches and literature that the official version of events has buried, forgotten or destroyed. Much of the three-volume chronicle draws on indigenous sources or concerns observations about indigenous peoples. *Memory of Fire* supplements Galeano's earlier work, the seminal *Open Veins of Latin America*, the subtitle of which, *Five Centuries of the Pillage of a Continent*, conveys the gist of both that earlier work and this trilogy.

Hill, Norbert S., Jr (ed.), *Words of Power: Voices from Indian America* (Golden, CO: Fulcrum Publishing, 1994).

'Enduring bits of wisdom that transcend culture and race,' as editor Norbert S. Hill, an Oneida, says in his introduction. This is an anthology of Indian quotations, almost all of them drawn from North America, divided by themes ranging from 'Spirituality, Religion' to 'Land, Environment'. All the selections speak of 'a time and a cultural context in which consistency and integrity were the struts and buttresses of human society,' in the words of the foreword by Vine Deloria Jr.

Jennings, Francis, *The Founders of America: From the Earliest Migrations to the Present* (New York: W. W. Norton, 1994).

The whole sweep of Indian history, concentrating on North America but making the occasional foray south of the border into Mexico and Peru. A comprehensive account of how Indians discovered the land, adapted to it, were, in the author's words, plunged into a Dark Age by conquest, then readapted over the centuries to eventually fight back. Slaughters several common US, if not general American, myths – benevolent discovery, peaceful expansion and the primacy of race – in the most readable and convincing manner. In the words of the author's introduction, 'The organising themes are culture as the product of human ingenuity and tradition, and caste as the product of conquest.'

Josephy, Alvin M., Jr (ed.), *America in 1492: The World of the Indian Peoples before the Arrival of Columbus* (New York: Vintage Books, 1993).

'A teeming panorama of North and South American life from prehistoric times through the fifteenth century,' says the back-page blurb, for once no exaggeration. Alvin Josephy – a leading authority and author of *Red Power* and *The Indian Heritage of America* – has assembled an impressive collection, which includes contributions from indigenous authors Vine Deloria, Jr, and N. Scott Momaday. The book is divided into two parts. The first, 'We the People', covers indigenous societies in the whole of the Americas in seven regions; the second, 'American Civilization 1492', covers the region by theme: religion, language, system of knowledge, community organization. Highlights are Joel Sherzer's 'A richness of voices' and Sam Gill's 'Religious forms and themes'. Overall the best comparative study of life in the Americas before Europe intruded; scholarly but riveting.

Josephy, Alvin M., Jr, *The Indian Heritage of America* (New York: Houghton Mifflin, 1991).

A complete history with a complete vision. This volume covers all the indigenous peoples of the Americas from prehistoric times to the twentieth century in 28 chapters and more than 400 pages. Setting out the stereotypical view of the Indian and 'Indianness' in the early chapters, Josephy revises that perspective in the remainder of the book in one of the most thorough reviews of Indian ethnology, history and culture available today.

Kicza, John E. (ed.), *The Indian in Latin American History: Resistance, Resilience and Acculturation* (Wilmington DE: Scholarly Resources Inc. Jaguar Books on Latin America, 1993).

A collection of essays and articles from some of the leading lights of anthropology and history in Latin America. All 10 contributions explore Indian–white relations and the complex interplay of cultures from initial contact to contemporary struggle. The articles range from Steve J. Stern on 'Early Spanish accommodation in the Andes' to Robert Charles Padden's 'Cultural adaptation and militant autonomy among the Araucanians of Chile' and Evon Z. Vogt's 'The maintenance of Mayan distinctiveness'.

Koning, Hans, *The Conquest of America: How the Indian Nations Lost Their Continent* (New York: Monthly Review Press, 1993).

A short (150-page), passionate book that covers all the historical ground to the present but in which the author's desire to provoke can at times be counter-productive. However, the book keeps well to its themes of exploitation, elimination and betrayal, and remains one of the few volumes with a genuinely alternative continental perspective, drawing its history and illustrations from North, South and Central America in a very satisfactory balance.

McLuhan, T. C. (ed.), *Touch the Earth: A Self-Portrait of Indian Existence* (London: Abacus, 1993).

Another anthology of statements and writings from North America, most of which run to no more than a page, some little more than a sentence. All concentrate on relations with the white man – the tone of concern and interest gradually giving way to frustration, anger and desperation.

Materne, Yves (ed.), *The Indian Awakening in Latin America* (New York: Friendship Press, 1980).

A compelling insight into the beginning of the most recent phase of the growth in indigenous organization and consciousness. The book consists of Indian manifestos, declarations and speeches from meetings or congresses in seven countries in Latin America during the 1970s. Indian demands and thinking are laid bare, along with the emerging emphases on organization and self-determination. The themes are drawn together in an admirable postscript by the French anthropologist Michel de Certeau.

'I, Rigoberta Menchú': An Indian Woman in Guatemala, ed. Elisabeth Burgos-Debray (London: Verso, 1984).

The startling early-life story of an individual who has come to represent a nation, a continent and now a worldwide movement. Nobel Peace Prize laureate Rigoberta Menchú recounts the story of her highland Maya childhood in Guatemala, the growing political crisis of the 1970s, the brutal deaths of her mother, father and brother, and her escape into exile in Mexico. Depicting the exceptional that has been the norm for so many, the book speaks across frontiers and generations, illustrating how the conquest continues today and why resistance to it is now claiming international attention.

228

Moody, Roger (ed.), *The Indigenous Voice: Visions and Realities* (Utrecht: International Books, 1993).

A massive 750-page anthology of indigenous testimony, speeches, writing and literature from around the world. Organized by themes, it covers historic and current issues ranging from racism to dams. Each section is introduced by a few pages of penetrating analysis from the author, who demonstrates the fruits of half a lifetime's experience of monitoring indigenous issues and opinions.

Nabokov, Peter (ed.), *Native American Testimony: A Chronicle of Indian–White Relations from Prophecy to the Present, 1492–1992* (New York: Viking Penguin, 1992).

An anthology of indigenous writing, speeches and testimony from the United States with a foreword by Vine Deloria Jr. Organized by theme in chronological order with good analytical overviews from the author preceding each introduction. Invaluable to dip into; the genuine indigenous voice with all its diversity and insight.

The South and Meso-American Indian Information Center (SAIIC), *Daughters of Abya Yala: Indigenous Women Regaining Control*, by indigenous women from North, South and Central America (Oakland, CA: SAIIC, 1992).

A compilation of testimonies from more than 20 women ranging from Cecilia Fire Thunder of the Lakota to Ana Llao of the Mapuche, interspersed with statements and policy pronouncements by women's groups from throughout the Americas. The book is a compelling blend of the individual and general, confirming the place of women in the vanguard of the current indigenous revival.

Sioui, Georges E., *For an American Autohistory* (Montreal: Queen's University Press, 1992).

'A literate and well-argued plea for a reassessment of Canadian history from the Amerindian point of view,' in the words of one reviewer. This is a philosophical polemic, part of the worldwide effort by a growing number of indigenous historians and anthropologists to reassess their own history and set guidelines for its study and interpretation. Drawing heavily on the beliefs and oral testimony of his own Huron people, Sioui argues that the greatness of indigenous culture in the past will return, providing the ideas and thinking that will be essential for a viable way of life in North America and worldwide.

Turner, Frederick (ed.), *The Portable North American Indian Reader* (New York: Viking Penguin, 1977).

An excellent anthology divided into four parts. The first and second are collections of myths, oral history, poetry and oratory from nations ranging from the Penobscot to the Blackfoot. The third part, 'Cultural Contact', is a selection of explorers' accounts, captives' narratives and Indian autobiographies. The fourth part, entitled 'Image and Anti-image', contrasts popular images of Indians in white literature with indigenous assessments by writers such as Luther Standing Bear, N. Scott Momaday and Vine Deloria Jr. The only possible improvement would be an updated edition.

Urban, Greg, and Sherzer, Noel (eds.), *Nation States and Indians in Latin America*

(Austin: University of Texas Press, 1991).

A collection of articles on the theme of cultural adaptation by both nation-states and indigenous peoples when they contact, collide or collude. Part of a growing challenge to classical anthropological theory in which Indian cultures have been analysed in isolation rather than in the context of state interventions. The volume covers different aspects of this theme in Nicaragua, Brazil, Bolivia, Peru, Paraguay, Chile, Central America and Ecuador with some of the best-known names in Latin American anthropology.

Van Cott, Donna Lee (ed.), *Indigenous Peoples and Democracy in Latin America* (Basingstoke: Macmillan, 1994).

The best up-to-date 'academic' book on indigenous peoples from Mexico southwards. A collect of essays with a mind-expanding variety of different emphases, with such leading lights as Xavier Albó writing on Bolivia and Richard Adams on Guatemala. Bound together with overall perspectives from editor Donna Lee Van Cott and Alison Brysk. A must for anyone seeking a general but country-by-country up-to-date view of indigenous affairs in Latin America.

Weatherford, Jack, *Indian Givers: How the Indians of the Americas Transformed the World* (New York: Crown, 1988).

As the title suggests, this book is about what the Indian nations of the Americas have given European society: the foodstuffs (60 per cent of the food eaten in the world today is of American origin); the medicines (quinine, aspirin-related tree-bark extracts, antibacterial medicines) and the minerals (gold, silver and base metals). Weatherford's skill is taking the argument further into lesser-known realms to show how, for example, long-strand cotton and the indigo and cochineal dyes of the New World underpinned industrial textile manufacturing, how the humble potato spurred the formation of large armies in Europe from the nineteenth century onwards, and how the Indian caucus with politicians meeting and voters selecting candidates fuelled the move to democracy. The ultimate alternative history, but with too few figures and facts to make fascinating conjecture into conclusive proof. Weatherford is also the author of *Native Roots: How the Indians Enriched America* (New York: Fawcett Columbine, 1991), which explores the home front: the contribution of Indian civilizations to the making of the United States.

Books in Spanish

Chirif, Alberto, García, Pedro, and Chase Smith, Richard, *El indígena y su territorio: estrategias para la defensa de los pueblos y territorios indígenas en la cuenca amazonica* (Lima: Oxfam America and COICA, 1991).

The most complete analysis yet of lowland indigenous peoples' battle to demarcate and protect their territories in the Amazon basin. The book combines the experiences of the authors – two anthropologists and a lawyer – all of whom have been at the forefront of such efforts. In considering the experience of 15 demarcation projects in Ecuador, Peru, Bolivia and Brazil, the authors show the way forward for the many indigenous nations that will follow. A ground-breaking study which gets to the heart of the most crucial issue for indigenous peoples throughout the Americas.

Condori, Ana María, *Nayan uñatatawi – Mi despertar* (La Paz: Hisbol, 1988).

The autobiographical story of the political and social awakening of an Aymara woman from Bolivia. It recounts common indigenous experiences, such as domestic service from the age of nine or migration to a lowland area in search of land, from a personal perspective, with dialogue, anecdotes and experiences. The latter part deals with Ana María Condori's part in the expansion of grassroots development movements in Bolivia in the 1980s. Highly recommended, this is one of a number of Hisbol publications catering for and stimulating the rise of ethnic consciousness in Bolivia.

Stavenhagen, Rodolfo, *Derecho indígena y derechos humanos en América Latina* (Mexico, DF: Instituto Interamericano de Derechos Humanos y El Colegio de México, 1988).

A real *tour de force* from a team of researchers led by one of Latin America's leading anthropologists. A comprehensive survey and discussion of indigenous rights in theory and practice throughout Latin America, it looks at individual countries' constitutions, international legislation and the campaigns indigenous organizations have fought to demand those rights. Detailed case studies of four very different countries – Brazil, Guatemala, Mexico and Peru – lead to the conclusion that indigenous peoples can enjoy full human rights only if their collective rights are recognized as part of multiethnic democratic societies. Despite beginning to show its age, this book remains the most important single volume on indigenous human rights in Latin America today.

Reports

Amnesty International, *The Americas: Human Rights Violations against Indigenous Peoples* (London: Amnesty International, 1992).

Wilson, Richard, *Before Columbus* (Birmingham: External Affairs, Central Television, 1992). A booklet to accompany a three-part television series.

Indigenous Peoples: A Global Quest for Justice, a report for the Independent Commission on International Humanitarian Issues (London: Zed Books, 1987). One-hundred-and-thirty-page report subdivided into three parts: Background, Issues and Action.

Morales, Patricia (ed.), *Indigenous Peoples, Human Rights and Global Interdependence* (Tilburg: International Centre for Human and Public Affairs, 1994).

Minority Rights Group Reports:
Amerindians of South America, Andrew Gray
The Original Americans: US Indians, James Wilson
Canada's Indians, James Wilson
The Inuit (Eskimos) of Canada, Ian Creery
The Maya of Guatemala, Phillip Wearne
The Miskito Indians of Nicaragua, Roxanne Dunbar Ortiz
Land Rights and Minorities, Roger Plant
Education Rights and Minorities, various authors

Reports on the Americas, published five times a year by the North American Congress on Latin America (NACLA) in New York. Of particular interest:
The First Nations 1492–1992, vol. 25, no. 3 (Dec. 1991)
Inventing America 1492–1992, vol. 24, no. 5 (Feb. 1991)
The Conquest of Nature 1492–1992, vol. 25 no. 2 (Sept. 1991)
War in the Amazon, vol. 23, no. 1 (May 1989)

Survival International, *Indians of the Americas: Invaded but Not Conquered* (London: Survival International, 1992). Twenty-two-page basic introduction and campaigning tool. Deals with the issues by means of extensive examples and quotations from indigenous nations throughout the Americas. Illustrated and very readable.

Also from Survival International:
Yanomami
In Bad Faith
Guardians of the Sacred Land

Psacharopoulos, George, and Patrinos, Harry A. (eds.), *Indigenous People and Poverty in Latin America: An Empirical Analysis* (Washington, DC: World Bank Regional and Sectoral Studies Program, 1994).

Thein Durning, Alan, *Guardians of the Land: Indigenous Peoples and the Health of the Earth*, Worldwatch Paper 112 (Washington, DC: Worldwatch Institute, 1992).

Periodicals

Abya Yala News, Quarterly Journal of the South and Meso-American Indian Information Center (SAIIC). Contains features and news updates from a political activist perspective on indigenous peoples in Latin America. Subscriptions/back copies from:
SAIIC,
PO Box 28703
Oakland
CA 94604
USA

Akwe:kon: A Journal of Indigenous Issues. Subscriptions from:
Cornell University
400 Caldwell Hall
Ithaca
NY 14853
USA

Cultural Survival Quarterly, the quarterly publication of Cultural Survival. Carries in-depth articles on indigenous peoples worldwide from an anthropological perspective. Subscriptions from:
Cultural Survival
46 Brattle Street
Cambridge
MA 02138
USA

Indian Rights, Human Rights, quarterly newsletter of the Indian Law Resource Center, concentrating on legal issues, projects and government policies throughout the Americas. Subscriptions from:

> The Indian Law Resource Center
> 508 Stuart Street
> Helena
> MO 59601
> USA

Indigenous Affairs, a quarterly magazine from the International Work Group for Indigenous Affairs (IWGIA) in Copenhagen, which also publishes various thematic reports known as documents and an Annual Report, most recently *The Indigenous World 1994–95* (Copenhagen: IWGIA, 1995). Subscriptions from:

> International Working Group for Indigenous Affairs
> Fiolstaede 10
> DK-1171 Copenhagen K
> Denmark

Indigenous Knowledge and Development Monitor, thrice-yearly publication from the Centre for International Research and Advisory Networks. Subscriptions from:

> Centre for International Research and Advisory Networks
> PO Box 90734
> 2509 LS The Hague
> The Netherlands

Survival, the biannual newsletter of Survival International. Update on Survival International's campaigns with feature articles on indigenous peoples' way of life and beliefs. Free to members of Survival, published in English, Spanish and Italian. Enquiries to:

> Survival International
> 11–15 Emerald Street
> London WC1N 3QL
> UK

Index

Cultural Survival organization 74, 159
Cuz, Andrés 142

dams 186
   Guayanan project 100
   hydro-electric 2, 150–1
   irrigation 120
   Xingu River 82
debt crisis 161–2
debt peonage 62, 88
Declaration of Five County Cherokees 50
Declaration of the Haudenosaunee 166
Deer, John Lame 150
Deer, Kenneth 20
Deloria, Vine Jr. 79, 125
democracy 23, 72, 177, 180, 192
Dene people 13, 83
   Declaration 166
disease, Western 3, 75–6, 84–5, 98, 106, 122, 126
Dominica 75
Dominican Republic 33, 75, 122, 186
Dore, Elizabeth 125
drugs, abuse 146, 158

economic development, impact 100, 113, 161–2
economics, free-market 2, 100, 121, 126, 161–2
Ecuador 1, 5, 8, 11, 22, 29, 33, 38, 46, 48, 64,
   77, 93, 104, 109, 119, 121, 126, 142, 148, 150,
   152–3, 167, 170, 172–3, 183, 191
   1990 uprising 25
Ecumenical Documentation and Information
   Centre (CEDI) 8
education
   bi-lingual 29, 139, 141
   indigenous 143
El Dorado, white myth of 58
El Salvador 21, 38, 78, 160
environmental degradation 121–7, 150–4, 183–4
Eskimoan peoples 37
Esquit, Alberto 14, 73, 139
ethnic consciousness, upsurge in 14–15, 29
ethnicity 134, 176
Evangelical Missionary Society 90

Fabricano, Marcial 184
First Inter-American Indigenist Congress (1940)
   134
First International Congress of EthnoBiology 125
Florida 11, 106
food-for-work schemes 62
forced labour 62, 84–5, 87, 92, 98
Franklin, Benjamin 38
French Guiana 126
fur 76, 107

Galeano, Eduardo 17, 67, 127
Gambill, Jerry 67–8
García, Juan 22
Ge, language 33
George, Chief Dan 67
George, Leonard 50
Gitskan people 182
gold 25, 50, 54, 76–7, 85, 103, 108, 112, 122,
   126–7, 156–7, 172
González, Nicanor 127
Goose Bay NATO base, 83
Gray, Andrew 157
Green, Duncan 161
Grefa, Valerio 20, 29, 170
Gregoria Apaza Centre for the Advancement of
   Women 149
Guajarára people 9
Guajiro people 17, 24, 128
Gualinga, Patricia 93
Guambiano people 17, 167
Guaraní people 1, 8, 33, 128, 165, 183
Guatemala 5, 8, 14, 21, 25, 27, 38–9, 64, 74, 77,
   80, 82–3, 92, 95, 103, 119–20, 135, 137,
   141–2, 146, 148–9, 173, 176, 178, 180, 188,
   191
   'parcellization' 121
   National Indigenist Institute 130
   National Widows Association (CONAVIGUA)
      149, 188
   Nentón massacre 78
   School of Ideological Warfare 79
Guaycuruan
   language group 33
Guaymí people 159
guerrillas 25, 79, 169, 174–5
Guevara, Che 174
Guyana 75, 100, 126

Haiti 33, 75, 122
Handy, Jim 96
Harper, Elijah 1
Haya de la Torre, Víctor Raúl 135
Hayes, Frank 82
health care 84
Hernández, Joel Martínez 16
Honduras 8, 21, 38, 39
Hope, Bob 186
Huanca, Tomás 21
Huancas people 74
Huaroni people 153
Huarpe, language group 33
Human Genome Diversity Project 159–60
human rights 64, 67, 71–2, 74
Hydro-Quebec 2, 15, 193